# VICIOUS CYCLE

# VICIOUS CYCLE

## WHISKEY, WOMEN, AND WATER

Captain Kenton Geer

MOUNTAIN ARBOR PRESS

MOUNTAIN ARBOR
PRESS an imprint of
BookLogix
Alpharetta, GA

Some names and identifying details have been changed to protect the privacy of individuals. The author has tried to recreate events, locations, and conversations from his memories of them. In some instances, in order to maintain their anonymity, the author has changed the names of individuals and places. He may also have changed some identifying characteristics and details such as physical attributes, occupations, and places of residence.

ISBN: 978-1-6653-0065-0 - Paperback
ISBN: 978-1-6653-0066-7 - Hardcover
eISBN: 978-1-6653-0067-4 - ePub
eISBN: 978-1-6653-0068-1 - mobi

This ISBN is the property of Mountain Arbor Press for the express purpose of sales and distribution of this title. The content of this book is the property of the copyright holder only. Mountain Arbor Press does not hold any ownership of the content of this book and is not liable in any way for the materials contained within. The views and opinions expressed in this book are the property of the Author/Copyright holder, and do not necessarily reflect those of Mountain Arbor Press.

Printed in the United States of America                    050321

∞This paper meets the requirements of ANSI/NISO Z39.48-1992 (Permanence of Paper)

*This book is dedicated to those fisherman who can't stop fishing, the drinkers who can't stop drinking and the broken hearted who can't stop loving.*

# ACKNOWLEDGMENTS

I want to thank everyone who made this book a reality.

To the hundreds of people who have sent me messages over the last couple years on social media telling me I should write a book someday. These messages gave me the confidence that I truly had something of value to offer to other people.

To my friends and family who reinforced this idea and encouraged me to pursue the idea of being an author.

Captain Jason "Tiny" Walcott: Perhaps I owe the greatest amount of gratitude. If not for your constant reinsurance and support, I often feel writing this book would be just another hope and aspiration.

A huge thank you is owed as well to my editor, Justin Spizman, who had to deal with the writings of a guy who wrote a 100,000-word book on his iPhone, often with wet hands.

To Kendall Bohn: a taste of my own medicine was inexplicably the cure to my disease.

To my parents: I'm sorry.

To my children: hopefully you can understand someday.

To Captain Jon Lagerstrom: thank you for welcoming me to the sea and teaching me about work ethic.

To Captain Tim Tower: thank you for teaching me that the details truly count.

To Captain Bob Nudd: thank you for teaching me about the reality of being a fisherman and the perseverance required on both land and sea.

To Captain Brad Craft: thank you for reminding me what life is really all about.

To Captain Billy Billson: legends never die.

To Scotty Davidson: Sadly you'll never read this, nor would anyone else if it wasn't for you. Love and respect always my friend. You are truly missed.

# INTRODUCTION

Whiskey often fills my pours. Women often fill my thoughts. But fishing has always filled my heart. For better or worse, a man can drown himself in each of these things. Whiskey, women and water are some of the most powerful influences in life; each with its own unforgettable fragrance of success and failure. Any one of these elements can bring you to your absolute highest of highs, and in the same breath your absolute lowest of lows. They all contain dangerously addictive attributes. Once they begin to speak to you, it's very hard to ignore they're calling. A relationship with any or all of them can be a beautiful yet vicious cycle.

Nothing is more powerful or devastating than the words of a woman. Whiskey can give you the confidence to overcome your deepest fears while at the same time possess the real possibility of causing you to lose everything for which you've ever worked. Yet water might just be the most dangerous of them all. Not just because it can physically kill you, but because there is no turning back once the ocean casts her spell upon you. She will flood into every avenue of your life until there is very little time for anything else.

The ocean calls to us in many forms. Some are destined to surf upon her waves, some submerge their entire lives below her surface, while others are meant to be blown across her, powered merely by her cousin the wind. Then there is us, the fisherman.

We the fisherman are an unlikely family of misfits; drawn together by the bond of the sea and the bounty she possesses. A man can find the ocean at any age and in many forms. It calls to some of us as children, yet for others it takes an entire lifetime to answer the call, only to figure out it was missing all along. No matter the path, the journey begins once you reach your destination. No particular physical characteristics, nor even one particular thought process, defines us. It's something greater than that; it's something primal and very real. It's something that is felt and whole-heartedly understood by another fisherman with a simple reconfirming nod of the head and nothing else. It's not just about being in nature, it's about being an essential part of nature.

Most fisherman don't really fish to catch fish alone. We may appear to only fill our boats with fish, but in reality, we are filling our hearts with purpose. Many of us don't conform to land well, or even at all. We often find ourselves more lost on land than a parakeet in the middle of the ocean. The rogue nature of men who live in a place without roads and traffic signs makes for a bad fit in a society full of rules and regulations.

A life of epic highs and epic lows upon the water might seem tailored fit for those of us facing our own demons upon the land. Sadly, drinking and addiction are synonymous with the term "fisherman." Whereas those of us who truly live the life would never define a fisherman as being either, although we wouldn't deny its presence in our culture. Men who work side by side in an occupation where a misstep or a slight miscalculation could be their final step often find themselves betrayed by the cheap words of land dwellers. However, the truth is that at sea, a man's handshake is still his word. And his word means everything.

Our relationship with the opposite sex is perhaps the most difficult aspect of being a fisherman. We often fight a winless battle between our primordial desire to be accepted and loved verses the unrelenting beckoning of the ocean. A fisherman has two lives— the one where he stares at sea from land and the life where he stares at land from sea. For the fisherman the question is not whether joy or pain are on the horizon, for they've come to learn both live hand in hand as time passes. One learns he cannot appreciate joy without knowing pain, and pain is not fully recognized without first experiencing joy. Loads of fish and welcoming arms are the Ying to the Yang in the darkest nights, both at sea and ashore. Despite being shackled to both like an anchor to a chain, fisherman will forever be hopelessly torn apart so long as the sea has fish, and the land has women.

Although this book is a collection of my own personal tales

from the sea and personal battles on land, I believe they will resonate with every true fisherman out there. I loved the ocean before I even truly knew the definition of love. I have spent my lifetime trying to be nothing more than accepted as a fisherman. I now share those stories and those challenges with you.

This book is for those that understand that beauty can be found in something that seemingly possess no traits of the traditional definition of beautiful.

It is for those that love the waters in spite of the pain and suffering they often offer in return.

This book is for those that often fight the shackles of both land and water, balancing the pain of the sea with the pain of the land.

It cuts both ways, and the saltwater of life burns these open wounds just as much as the saltwater of the sea.

Now, I invite you to navigate a portion of the ocean that is my life. Like all oceans it has its rough days and dark nights. But if father time has taught me anything from my journey, it is through these challenges that we learn the most about ourselves. Fishing isn't always pretty, but it's a beautiful life.

If only life were only as simple as a man and his boat. Read on and enjoy the devastatingly true and harsh realities of a being a fisherman who finds his greatest purpose in the deepest oceans.

# CHAPTER 1

# UNEXPLAINABLY STRANGE LOVE AT KEWALO HARBOR BASIN

I first met her at Kewalo Harbor Basin on a midspring Honolulu morning. She was not the most beautiful thing I ever laid my eyes upon, and I wouldn't call it love at first. She didn't possess the shapely curves and gracious lines of the ladies I had been with in the past. She was short and squatty. Tired and worn. The sun had taken the best out of her exterior and given nothing back in return. Her hair was a shredded, tangled mess of awning from years of an unrelenting Hawaiian trade wind. She had clearly been ridden hard and put away wet.

At first glance, one might not consider giving her a second look. Yet, there was just something about this tired old girl that left you to stare slightly more than just in passing. What she lacked in appearance she made up in her presence. She was not a looker, but she was clearly a goer. You could tell she had been to hell and back and loved every second of the voyage. She had strong, defined shoulders and was stout all around. My grandfather would have said she was "built like a brick shithouse." I might have called her "old-person strong" when I was a kid.

A lifetime of hard work developed a deceptive amount of strength and power in her. She clearly had hidden muscles. Her dock lines creaked and moaned like that of the reins of a horse trying to sprint but forced to trot. She anxiously chomped upon them, growing ever more restless with the change in the tide. She could see the open pasture from the fuel dock and feel the ocean pulsing through her as the south swell churned the harbor.

Like many women, she longed to be out there. The harbor was

not her home. She was a wild stallion, not a show pony. The harbor was a place where men bragged about their accomplishments, giving little if any credit to the vessels that lay there humbly in wait like faithful steeds. She knew as all boats knew that if she wasn't freed of these wooden anchors soon, she, like the others before her, would die a slow, miserable death waiting for a voyage to the scrapyard. Boats preserve in moorage like a man's health bound to the couch, fading into a state of health that becomes too far gone to repair.

When we met, we shared a sense of being forgotten. Confused why after all these years of being loyal to a craft or a captain, we were both left behind. Perhaps she saw in me what I saw in her — a chance to feel important again. To prove to ourselves that the best of us wasn't out of us. To show that we might look down, but we certainly weren't out. We had a lot in common. We weren't good at lying about who we were or were not. What you saw was what you got. Love it or hate it. We weren't going to sell you a bill of goods we couldn't deliver on. Our brutal honesty kept us both restricted like her dock lines.

I had dreamed of owning a boat since I was thirteen years old. However, never once in my dreams did I envision a rig that looked like this one. But, here we were, her eyeballing me and I eyeballing her. We flirted as I ran my hand down her superstructure and aluminum work. Strangely, her unbathed salt accumulated in my hands and brought me comfort in knowing we weren't really that much different. We exchanged looks with each other as I walked up and down the dock, admiring her from every possible angle. It seemed similar to the courtship of a matador and a bull, each one wondering if we were tough enough to handle the other. After thirty minutes of this charade, I wanted her. I wanted her bad. I knew if the current jockey could see how bad I wanted this ride, she would remain out of my league.

So, after some idle chitchat about the boat, I asked about her price. We negotiated hard, but my business partner, Brett, and I departed back to Kona, Hawaii, without her. I can vividly remember staring out the window of the Hawaiian Airlines jet as we took off, peering down to the harbor and trying to catch even a glimpse of her like a junior high school student with a new crush. I could vaguely make her out, more so from knowing the docks and less so from her silhouette distinctly standing out from above the clouds.

I rested my head on the terribly uncomfortable airliner seat that refused to recline. I rubbed my temples and just thought. Over the past two years, I had watched the keys of sportfishing boats I would have considered dream boats go to those who talked a great story but couldn't possibly deliver on their promises. Again and again, I was turned down for these positions because I didn't tell the owners what they wanted to hear. Rather, I told them the truth. A new charter operation would not be profitable if they properly maintained the vessel and staffed it the right way. With the passage of time, all of these operations would go broke, and two of the owners would even come to say that they had wished they had listened to me in the first place; but this realization, coupled with their honeymoon phase, would fade after I had already set my heart on this tired old boat.

I was burnt out on the politics of sportfishing. With a handful of exceptions, high-end sportfishing jobs often had no direct correlation with experience and more often had to do with how hard you were willing to blow a rich owner's ego. I had grown tired of the suckholing, Australian for ass-kissing. I was a fisherman, not a storyteller. I found my happiness in the pursuit and capture of fish. The cost of a vessel or my boat owner's social status and net worth did not matter to me. Although admittedly at times their gold-digging bikini clad girlfriends were kind on the eyes and a pleasure to be around, I'd also grown tired of cleaning drunken broads' red wine off salon carpets and untangling their tampons from macerator pumps.

It seemed that no matter how clearly marked with signage or how many times you told them not to flush anything other than what they digested, you would still find yourself up to your elbows chasing around their tampons in the plumbing. This discovery usually came the following morning on or before another charter. Trust me, it's a great way to start a day. How luxurious the yachting life is all one could think. However, the bathroom is a five-gallon bucket on most commercial fishing boats. Thus, you'd need some type of award or trophy rather than a reprimanding if someone could clog it.

To that end, I was slowly closing the door on the sportfishing business as it was doing the same to me, even though we both knew we could never completely close the door totally shut on each other. But we needed a break. We had a long, wonderful relationship, but somehow our wants and desires began to change. I wanted more—a family and a house. Sportfishing wasn't financially growing with me at the same rate I wanted to acquire these other things. Although sportfishing in Kona can be a very fun job, it's often a very difficult one to make a really good living. And even if you do, Hawaii is an extremely expensive place to live. The high-paying sportfishing jobs of the mainland East Coast and traveling gigs do not readily exist in Hawaii or arguably aren't even there at all.

Sure, at one time I was happy living paycheck to paycheck, drinking away all my tip money and calling the bed of any girl who would let me crawl in it my home. While economically more viable, I wanted more. I was growing tired of just getting by and restless of interacting with unappreciative charter guests. You could have the greatest family on board and unfortunately not get a bite, or you could have the biggest dickwad you've ever met on board and absolutely lay into them or catch him a really big fish for little or no thanks at all. Don't get me wrong—most of the experiences were very positive, and that's why I passionately and happily did the job for so many years. However, the severity of how hard the negative guests treated me began to take a toll on me personally.

It started making the business less and less gratifying. My mood began to reflect this endless beating. I didn't want to be like that; I didn't want to be snappy or put out when someone asked me the same question for the millionth time. I loved fishing, and I wanted to keep it that way. But the problem is that marlin fishing doesn't always necessitate results. No matter how great you are at it, there will always be a luck factor that you cannot control. That's also one of the things that makes marlin fishing so magical. You need look no further than the results of the Kona tournament series, put on every summer to prove this. The people who would be generally considered the best fishermen in the harbor year in and year out don't always win all the tournaments. And sometimes a boat you've never even heard of takes all the prize money home. Like the World Series of Poker, luck can be a true equalizer.

However, the thing I loved most about commercial fishing is that luck and effort can influence the result. The harder you worked and the more you were willing to give, the more you would get paid. Weight on the dock is what matters in commercial fishing, not stories of big ones that got away. You don't get paid for what could have been. Rather, you get paid for what's sitting on the scale, not the inflated sizes of fish encounters or the incredible tales that often ended with boat side heartbreak. Those things didn't matter to me. What mattered was the catching not the fishing. The saying "show me, don't tell me" is perhaps the perfect header to define the economics of commercial fishing versus sportfishing. Whereas sportfishing is "tell me and hopefully show me," a large part of your income in sportfishing comes from gratuities. And many of your best gratuities come from the overall service and not necessarily from bending a rod.

I loved how fair commercial fishing was in this respect. You worked hard, and you got paid. You worked harder, and you got paid more. If you worked even harder, then you got paid even more than that. You worked harder than the guy next to you, you got paid more than him. You worked smarter than the guy next to you, you earned more than him. It was a much more straightforward and simple ladder up than the confusing, sidestepping shuffling of climbing the sportfishing ladder. That ladder often left you wondering, *Who's that guy? How did he get that job? Wasn't he just a bartender at the Four Seasons? What the hell?*

I just wanted to focus on commercial fishing. I just wanted my efforts to be rewarded. I didn't want someone's opinion of me to control my financial future. I didn't want a rich owner who got bored of owning a boat leaving me high and dry one day, which is a common occurrence in the industry. There's a saying in the industry that goes, "Owners are two to five years, captain and crews are forever." There is little to no job security in sportfishing, and a retirement plan is an even far rarer thing than that. I truly loved catching big marlin and the people I worked with. But the actual infrequency at which you caught a truly large one versus the numbers of hours devoted to the pursuit of capturing one in Hawaii was highly disproportionate, especially compared to fishing on the Great Barrier Reef, a place I fished for over a decade and held with the highest regard in my heart.

But this is a story of a man and his boat, not my disdain for marlin fishing. As usual, I had fallen asleep on the plane flight home despite the whole trip taking only twenty-five minutes, tarmac to tarmac. I've often thought, *Well, if my plane crashes, at least I'll die in my sleep.* I awoke to good ole Brett's unshaven sunburnt face and shit-eating grin telling me, "Yo, get up, pussy. We are home."

I am not a good businessman in the traditional sense. I do not like bartering, haggling, or even intense negotiating. I believe in paying people fairly for what they have, and I believe in charging people fairly for what I have. If I say I'm going to do something, I'll do it. My handshake is my word, and it's as solid as a rock. I do not like conflict, and I certainly do not enjoy confrontation. I've been burned several times believing others possess these same qualities.

For these reasons, the following day, after little deliberation between us, Brett and I agreed we wanted the boat. However, we also agreed that the asking price was out of our budget and too high for her current condition and niche nature of her layout. These types of situations were not good for me to deal with because in my logic, if the owner was asking a certain price then he must have felt that was the fair value, as that's how I would try to price something. With that in mind, I wouldn't want to upset the owner by lowballing him with an insulting offer.

However, Brett was as rough as sandpaper when it comes to telling people things they don't want to hear. His delivery is brutally to the point. No massaging it in there or gently tiptoeing around the subject. As Brett himself would say, "Don't worry, I'm only going to put half in," followed by a huge pelvic thrust, a menacing laugh, and the words "the back half!" When necessary, the words "motherfucker" might have been added after "back half" to really emphasize the importance of a particular sentence. The coarseness of his words are legendary. I've watched people look like Mike Tyson just punched them in the face as they digest some of the shit that comes out of Brett's mouth. It's truly his superpower, although not one I personally would want. But I did come to admire its effectiveness. Because he has this skill set, he was chosen to make the call. We would come to call this system, "good cock, bad cock!"

I nervously squirmed in my seat at my driftwood dining table as he dialed away. I reminded him to be nice. He told me to "fuck off" with a loving smile. Matt, the boat owner, was a really cool guy. After a few seconds, he picked up the phone, and Brett quickly started right into his roshambo, a technique referring to immediately kicking the guy in the balls on the asking price.

Brett got up from the table and took the call outside, pacing back and forth past the sliding glass doors that led to a breathtaking panoramic view of the Pacific Ocean just three miles below our home we rented. I couldn't help but wonder what he was saying. I couldn't tell from behind the glass if the conversation was going well or poorly. I looked on with the same excitement and anticipation as when my friend Chris Jackson was sent across the playground courtyard at Main Street School in fourth grade to let

Amanda Drinker know that I liked her. That news certainly wasn't received as well as I had hoped. I prayed for a different result this time.

When he returned indoors, poker faced, he informed me he had some bad news, "bud." Instantly deflated, I said, "That sucks."

"Yeah, it does," he fired back with an ear-to-ear grin.

"We now own the old piece of shit."

I was super excited, but I also thought, *Great. Now how the fuck do I come up with my half of the money to purchase her?* Brett easily had his 50 percent of the money needed to start the business. But I did not. I was not a good candidate for a traditional loan from a bank. My education was unorthodox by a landlubber's perception, with years pursuing the endless summer of fishing viewed as uncommitted and unfocused. I saw going from place to place, boat to boat, as opening my horizons to new and different fishing techniques and methods.

In my opinion, traveling and working with different crews was in actuality the greatest form of education I could have ever possibly received in my chosen field. No matter what boat you work on or where it is located, you could learn something from the experiences. Every person, every attitude, every temperament has a lesson to be taught, even if that lesson is to never, ever treat people the same way a certain asshole did. No education is wasted. I have carried forward tricks and techniques I have learned on different boats from different captains and crews since I was the ripe age of thirteen.

Admittedly, and considering how hard I worked offshore and how successful I had been at fishing, I probably should have had more than enough money for my ownership share. The problem was that since fishing offshore never once felt like work to me, I blew the money with the same disregard that I threw chum over the side of the boat—women, traveling, drinking, and gambling being my main vices and investments. Like many fishermen, I spent it nearly as fast as I made it.

Talk is extremely cheap on sportfishing boats. Every captain and crew have been promised the world at one point or another. Rich people fill the heads of inspiring crews with talk of new boats and projects they will back for them. We know these words hold little value, yet we waste our valuable time talking to people who don't value how precious our time really is at all. Cheap words and promises that will never come to fruition. Checks in the mail that inevitably don't come or bounce when they do. Talk of grandeur with no real intent to fulfill the empty words. We have these talks again and again, with rare follow-through. What is it that excites us about these conversations? Is it the what if? Or the what could be?

Is it the natural human desire for an easier path? A shortcut to success? Hoping to be one of those legendary stories of wealth or fame? A Cinderella story, so to speak? Meaningless words from people who ultimately prove to be meaningless in your life. You yearn for there to be some pinch of truth to it. You want those easily tossed around words they lobbed at you to have some weight. Heartbreakingly and frustratingly, they do not. More pipedreams to bury. You go further and further down the drain, sucked into these spiraling conversations that will almost certainly always result in a dead end.

For you, it's a glimmer of hope, your big shot, you think. It's finally your time to sit high in the saddle and ride. You're going to show the world that, with just a little bit of help, you will hit the promised land. Watch out world, you're coming in hot! However, to the other side, these conversations pass by like the dotted lines in the middle of the highway, one after another after another, no more meaningful than the one before or the one to come. Having had no real impact and being a time filler, they won't be coming back to revisit them. Such was the case when I called upon all my supposed backers and believers.

With the banks and my parents unwilling to bet on me, I soon learned the rich anglers I knew from years of sportfishing were ultimately as cheap as the words and promises they threw around.

That is when I found myself still fifteen grand short of the money I needed to purchase the boat.

However, I would find that fifteen grand in what seemed like the most unlikely of places: my friend Diamond Dave. Knowing what I know about Dave today, this isn't surprising at all. However, at the time, our friendship was young. So, this took me by surprise. For a deckhand or even a captain in Kona, that's a lot of money to bet on someone. I was taken aback, flattered, and honored.

I first met Diamond Dave while he was working the deck of different game boats in Kona. Dave had recently moved to the Big Island from Maui in pursuit of his dreams of capturing large marlin. Although you could catch large marlin off Maui, the frequency of it is few and far between compared to the same effort spent off the Kona coast.

Diamond Dave was seventeen years my elder. He had salt-and-pepper hair and vaguely resembled a slightly overweight Brett Favre. He spoke in a heavy, drawn-out California accent that followed him from being raised in the San Fernando Valley. He called North Hollywood his home. He spoke loudly, yet humbly. He spoke simply, but full heartedly. He inherited his nickname from a skipper named Skillet with whom he had worked in Maui. The name referenced that some days the Diamond shines and some days the Diamond does not.

The Diamond is a simple man with a fifteen-pound heart. He wears his emotions on his sleeve and leaves himself vulnerable to people who take advantage of kindness. He has simple thoughts about what's right and wrong and often gets hurt by people who don't have the same morals he maintains. He is generous to a fault. On the same level, he routinely makes himself his own worst enemy with certain dealings. You will also find how truly beautiful he is in cut and dry simplicity.

When my ex and I were looking for an additional roommate for the house we were living in this time, Diamond Dave was also looking for a place to live. So, it only made sense for us to move in together. At that same house and same table, I painstakingly watched Brett walk back and forth negotiating the boat purchase that Diamond Dave would throw down nearly all the money to his name to back me on.

No contract, no negotiations, just a friend believing in a friend. We shook hands, and I vowed to pay him back as fast as I possibly could. He mumbled something about it being all good and no worries, *mannn*, as he hopped in his truck to make the trek to his favorite restaurant in the world—Panda Express. Billy Squier's "The Stroke" blared from the windows of his gray Toyota Tacoma as I watched him back out of the driveway. I slightly shook my head and remembered saying, "Man, I love that fucking guy," as he rounded the corner and disappeared.

I was excited and anxious. I now had the money to purchase the boat. But that was about it. I would still need to captain the current offshore handline boat called the *Makana* that I was running to cover my monthly bills as well as to build up additional funds for new fishing gear and startup expenses. The Ponzi scheme that was my life kept on trucking. Somehow, I always managed to just pull things off. That was until my employer at the time, Rob, found out Brett and I were purchasing our own boat. Apparently, the idea of us being direct competitors in our small niche market wasn't particularly to his liking. So, as we offloaded our most recent successful catch into the two large flatbed trucks that had been waiting for our arrival, we discovered we had been relieved of our jobs. I had been counting on continuing to run the *Makana* for another month with a different crew as Brett took delivery of our boat and prepped it for our maiden voyage. I was truly hurt. I couldn't believe after all my years of loyally working for Rob that he cut me just like that. This was my first taste of just how cutthroat business really is.

My "replacement," if you will, was a guy by the name of Lazy Boy, a sportfisherman who dabbled in commercial fishing and more so in recreational drugs. Actually, I always really liked Lazy Boy as a person. He was personable and funny, despite his endless stories of cheating on his wife. Having once fished with him offshore, I can attest that his nickname is perfectly fitting seeing I've never met anyone more useless or lazy on an offshore boat in my career. The only thing he excelled at was telling stories and smoking weed.

After getting shit-canned, I took all my personal gear off the boat, still feeling numb as I sat behind the *Makana* just looking at her. All the thousands of miles we had traveled together, all the weather we had faced, and all the metric tons of fish we had caught, and this is how it unceremoniously ended. Brett and I drank two six-packs of Modelo Especial, our lucky beer, behind the boat for good measure. I lovingly said a heartfelt goodbye to this faithful steed. Brett shot a beer bottle top at it like a rocket and said, "See yah, bitch."

In the days that followed, Brett went to Honolulu and took delivery of our boat while I remained back in Kona running sport-fishing charters. The 142-mile steam from Kewalo Harbor Basin in Oahu to Honokohau Harbor on the Big Island went perfectly, especially considering the fact that Brett and the previous owner, Matt, had to hand-steer her since the old girl didn't have a working autopilot. They made good time by our commercial boat standards, crossing in a little less than sixteen hours.

Over the next two weeks, we would work from dusk till dawn and then some installing the new gear we had purchased. We added the autopilot, new hydraulics, safety gear, a new awning, and, of course, brand new fishing gear. Brett and I both, total tackle whores, filled the storage areas to the brim with hooks and more things that glittered. We didn't bother on improving the complexion of the boat, focusing more on the nuts and bolts of the operation. We couldn't afford the luxury of pretty paint. If something wasn't going to directly help us catch more fish, it wasn't within our budget. Our girl was going to have to look like she was in sweatpants the next morning until she could prove she could still perform.

When we purchased the vessel, she went by *Kawika*, named after a waterfall on Molokai that had sentimental meaning to the previous owner. However, that was not her original given name.

In a time before we came to find her sadly collecting algae in Kewalo Harbor Basin, she was born as *Ao Shibi*, a name derived from "ao," meaning blue, the color of her hull, and "shibi," meaning tuna, like the ones she would catch. Shibi is a general reference for any tuna under 100 pounds in Hawaii, whether it be a bigeye or yellowfin. The offshore boats primarily catch shibi.

We now had our new boat and our new gear. What we didn't have was a new boat name. Given the name had already been changed once, we didn't fear the bad luck known to be associated with changing a boat's name. In our minds, that line had already been crossed before our time. So, it was someone else's *kuleana* (responsibility). As we sat in our living room considering the different name options, we found ourselves staring at a list of names classically commercial, classically sportfishing, and hybrids of both. I wanted the boat to have a name that included my mother's name, like was done traditionally in New England. Brett couldn't have disagreed any harder on the idea of having his mother's name on the hull. Childhood scars would not be washed away, regardless of how much saltwater we encountered.

We toyed with names that involved things that sounded like the action or excitement we associated with our love for fishing. Brett really loved "Strike Anywhere," which honestly is a great name, but it didn't capture the romance I felt for the ocean. It had all the great components associated with fishing but lacked that missing piece that draws us back to land.

The boat names we always agreed upon had a double meaning that referenced boat-related life and something inappropriate. The problem was that we were pretty certain we couldn't get away with some of them legally, and certain people in the industry might look down on the other names. This could ultimately impact our image of professionalism and income. Examples of names we agreed upon were the words I've uttered a million times, like "Always Fucking Something" because shit always breaks on boats and we were always trying to get laid on land.

We laughed at "Smoking Ice" because we burned through tons

of ice while out at sea and often were surrounded by ice heads in our industry or ones at harbor trying to get a free fish or steal something. These types of names were fun to play with, but we knew we would never put them on a hull.

After hours and hours, we were still at a gridlock on our new boat's future name. That was until my ex came home and administered one of her world-class tongue lashings and ass chewings. Brett had violated the most holy of holy rules in our household — he had worn his slippers inside. (Side note: Slippers, pronounced "slippahs" in Hawaii, are what East Coasters call flip-flops, Australians call thongs, and the Bible call sandals).

What made matters far worse than his sin is that I had done nothing to stop this atrocity. The slippers were merely the fuse for the bomb we had unknowingly set off, culminating in the conclusion that I was a pretty terrible guy. All of my worldly faults were highlighted with a succession of blastings not seen since World War II. When the smoke had cleared and the final explosion rang out in the form of our bedroom door being slammed, I found myself in my recliner rubbing my temples. "Man, it's a vicious cycle," I sighed.

Brett paused. "That's a great boat name!"

"What? 'Big Cunt?'" I replied.

We had already written down that one in reference to what our Australian fishing friends called huge marlin.

"No, seriously," he said "'Vicious Cycle.' Think about it. It has a double meaning as it applies to life on land and life at sea. It's perfect!"

Brett was absolutely correct. Thanks to my ex's recent rant of tyranny, we had a name for our boat. The *Vicious Cycle* was born.

Luck always plays a significant role in any new business venture. We were so spoiled with luck at the beginning of our business that we took it for granted. It was a great time to be an offshore handline fisherman or any fisherman in Hawaii, for that matter. The fish came easy and even more so did the money. Not to say we didn't create a lot of our own luck because we certainly did. We were going hard on back-to-back trips and working around the clock. I became so obsessed with filling the boat with fish that I had periods where I would stay awake for seventy-two hours in a row just to get the job done.

I drank Red Bull like a normal person drinks water. In fact, over the course of that first year, I hardly drank a bottle of water on a trip, if at all. I became so immune to the impact of Red Bull that I'd drink three cans at a time just to give my heart a kick start in the morning. Most days, I didn't really need them, but I enjoyed the warm sensation they gave me as my heart raced as my mind tried to keep up while looking for birds or working the lines. I liked how it made everything feel important, sprinkled with an intense amount of focus. I also liked how I knew I was doing something a lot of people couldn't do, putting one great trip together after another. For the first time in my life, I finally felt like I was really good at something of value. My passion was not only filling boxes and my wallet but also my heart. For the first time in a long time, I felt like I had a purpose. It appeared I had found my calling. I loved feeding the people of Hawaii fresh fish, and it turned out I was pretty good at it.

The money continued to get better and so did the fishing. The trips were getting shorter, and the average fish on the sea mountain we routinely fished continued to get larger and larger. So large in fact that the longest running captains, Mike Aobi and Joe Dentley, said our take was the best class of fish and fishing they had seen in their careers on the mountain.

We slammed the boat full, one trip after another. In a month and a half, I had repaid my loan to Diamond Dave with 10 percent interest for his goodwill. Incredibly, within three months, we had made back our initial investment in full. With Brett's help, I had finally created a revenue stream that would allow me to purchase a home, build up retirement accounts, and provide for my hoped-for family. I was very happy. Ironically, I had found a sense of certainty and success in a place of never-ending uncertainty and change. I loved this boat, and she seemed to love me right back.

# CHAPTER 2

# BAR LIFE: DROWNING ON LAND SIX OUNCES AT A TIME

Despite what many may believe, your life as a fishing boat captain in Hawaii, or anywhere for that matter, is much more than just driving a boat, listening to Jimmy Buffett, and sucking down tropical-flavored drinks neatly ordained with tiny umbrellas. Aside from navigating and properly maintaining a vessel, being a captain also means being a therapist, a doctor, and a problem solver for your crew while still trying to manage the shitshow that is your own personal life. The riskier the fishery, the greater the monetary gamble or the lack of monetary gains, the greater the number of issues a captain has to deal with. We call them "boat marriages," referring to the amount of time a person works a particular boat. These short-lived relationships can often be a fickle undertaking. For a variety of reasons, lots of people come and go from fisheries. The onboard relationships between captains and their crews can be a very capricious thing. The wildly different temperaments and vast levels of education can make for an array of unforeseen challenges.

One of the most difficult tasks for a captain doesn't actually occur at sea. Rather, it happens back on land. Often, the people and personalities willing to work in these unique conditions of the offshore lifestyle are also the types of people who immediately scurry into the darkest corners of the city like cockroaches once the lines are tied off. Getting every one of these crew members back on board after making landfall is often more difficult than trying to herd cats. The undesirability of the offshore lifestyle often leaves you working with characters that society may consider undesirables themselves. Gamblers, drunks, addicts, and former and current criminals are no strangers to the offshore scene. For these reasons, the most unlikely of stories occur on a routine basis around the fishing docks. In the end, this is a place where yesteryear pirates still have a place in modern-day society.

The phone call had come in a little after three a.m. I had done my best to ignore it. However, the caller was relentless. The insistent and seemingly endless vibration of my cell phone finally got me out of my bunk. I rubbed my eyes and ran my left hand across my face as my right hand held the phone. I looked at the blurry-eyed screen, still partially drunk from the evening's activities. *Who the fuck is this at this time of the morning? What the fuck do they want?* I did not recognize the number. *What the fuck now?* I already wasn't in a particularly great mood, having been absolutely horse fucked on our fish prices the previous morning. Now my phone was blowing up like the Kīlauea volcano on the one morning I actually got to sleep in.

After a week offshore, the prices on the auction were so cheap that we didn't even cover our operating expenses. Even our 7,000 pounds of ahi tuna wasn't enough to cover the ice, bait, and fuel, let alone have any money left for any one of us to make a dollar for our efforts—another week of around-the-clock work for free. This was the third trip in a row of terrible prices despite great catches. The extremely low market price had a grave effect on our economies, quality of life, and morale. Generally, a man surrenders to his vices in these types of situations, finding comfort in a distraction even if it's harmful to his health. I was no different. My coping mechanism was a bottle of Crown Royal on the rocks. Alcohol and disgust filled my nostrils and breath. The purple pill, what I call the lovely purple bag the bottle comes in, had once again done its job. No part of me wanted to answer that goddamn phone.

"I suppose I better answer the fucking call," I said out loud despite no one else being on the vessel. Maybe one of the crew got arrested again. I wondered who had gotten into a fight or had gotten a DUI. I answered the call with a "Yahhhhh, go ahead" like I was on a VHF radio. A woman's unrecognizable form of Asian

English came in rapid succession. She was clearly angry. I listened on with absolutely no idea what the fuck she was going on about. That is until I heard her mention the clearly recognizable name "Shaky." *Oh fuck,* I thought. *What has my train wreck of a crew member gotten himself into this time?*

Shaky, who earned his nickname for the way his hands would shake when his blood alcohol level wasn't properly polluted, had been hired and fired, rehired and refired more than any man in history. Shaky was a bit of an anomaly. He possessed higher than average intelligence yet succumbed to his demons easier than any other man I've ever met. Shaky, or Shake Dog as he was often called, came from a good family. His parents were hard working and successful, one a teacher, the other a doctor. Shaky had attended private schools and even played sports at the collegiate level at an East Coast Division I school. He was well traveled, a master of sarcastic humor, and displayed a surprising wealth of knowledge while sober. There were two versions of Shaky—one we called Good Shaky, and the other we called Bad Shaky.

Copious amounts of drugs and alcohol were generally the catalyst for the latter. Of course, you would know none of that by looking at him walking down a street. He dressed in half-opened thrift store Aloha shirts and worn-out board shorts. He had stained clothing and an unshaven beard on his sunburnt face. Although arguably a handsome man, he had a large nose that was further accentuated by his extremely wiry build. This feature gave him a ratlike appearance, which was perfectly fitting for his lifestyle and activities upon the land. Shaky possessed one of those rare full-blown alcoholic bodies, where despite drinking everything in sight he only weighed about a hundred pounds soaking wet. No matter how much we fed him, he was nothing but skin and bones. While fighting large tuna on handlines, he was routinely dragged back and forth across the deck, hopelessly trying with all his might to hold on.

Back to the phone call. I couldn't understand anything this angry woman was saying except the words, "Fucking Shaky. Fucking

Shaky, pay now. You pay now, money, motherfucker, now, now money." These words were strung together between a storyline I couldn't understand whatsoever. I had the basic gist that Shaky owed this woman money. The only thing Shaky loved more than drinking and cocaine was whores. What might not be common knowledge outside of Hawaii—but is widely known here and is right out in the plain sight of day—is that Honolulu is absolutely full of whorehouses and the streets of Waikiki are littered with prostitutes.

Prostitution is everywhere in the city. A single man can hardly get in a taxi without a cabby trying to drive him to a whorehouse so he can collect his commission from the mama-san for bringing a patron in. Fluorescent neon-lit signs adjoin on random apartment buildings. Massage parlors that don't offer massages are commonplace. The Century Center Building has hookers working right alongside family residences. Ke'eaumoku Street and Ward Avenue are synonymous with hand jobs and rub and tugs. A man can get jerked off in a hundred different "drinky drinky bars" in this city. Honolulu is truly a Disneyland for the whore connoisseur, and Shaky might as well have been the head of the Mickey Mouse fan club. He longed for hookers and had a place in his heart for any and all of them. "The cheaper the better," he would proudly proclaim.

After minutes of the angry woman's incoherent rambling, I finally asked if I could please speak to Shaky. "You bring money now! Now money! Shaky die! We kill Shaky." *Now that's pretty good English*, I thought. Apparently, Shaky was trying to shortchange one of the knob shops, and they weren't having it. I would have just laughed the whole thing off if not for the fact I could hear Shaky in the background pleading in a tone I had never heard before. This notorious smartass was legitimately begging them not to hurt him while also yelling for me to please come and help him.

Apparently, he had really crossed the line this time. I knew Shaky was an addict and a lout, but I always thought of him as a harmless lout. He had a big mouth, but I never really thought of him as a bad guy, just a walking dumpster fire. I asked where he was, and she kept saying, "Orchid." I knew exactly where that was—a run-down whorehouse surrounded by another whorehouse on each side. It also served as a two-story dive bar. I had dropped many a deckhand both young and old off at this Ward Avenue address with the advice to "wrap it up, and don't bring crabs back to the boat." Now, I don't condone prostitution in any way, but I'm not these guys' parents either. They were going to do what they were going to do. So, I merely provided a sober ride to a place they were going to find themselves at anyway.

"You come now. You bring lots of money," she said.

"How much?"

"Many hundreds. Thirteen!"

*Oh fucking great. You've got to be kidding me. How the fuck did he rack up a $1,300 tab at Mama-San?* I thought it was a pay first kinda program. Did the idiot break something in a rant of anger? I was on my way. I scraped together all the money I had on the boat, about $600. I hoped they would settle with me given the time of the morning. I called a taxi because I was still clearly cocked. The last thing I needed was to be driving.

I told the taxi driver where we were heading, and he smiled, figuring he would be getting a commission for bringing in a patron. I told him I wasn't going there to get a girl. He understandably and empathetically said he didn't judge, which is when I realized he thought I was implying I was going for a lady boy. No, no nothing like that I told him. He released a very disbelieving "Yeah sure, I believe you."

*What the fuck has my life come to?* I thought as I watched streams of water race horizontally across the moving car windows fed by a driving Oahu rain. I wished I was in bed lying next to my wife on the Big Island, just hours from kissing my babies good morning. It's amazing how one can live two wildly different lives. Here I was in the darkest part of the city to support my beautiful family a little over a hundred miles away. Why was I surrounded by people whose derelictions and addictions made me shockingly look like a saint? Not an easy thing to do by any means. I was really getting over this shit. *Fucking Shaky. Fucking, fucking Shaky,* I thought. I was groggy and tired, angry and disappointed, as much in Shaky as in myself. *Why do I care about this fucking clown? Why can't I take a break and stop fishing? I want to hold my wife between trips, but instead I'm holding a whiskey bottle at night. Chasing a payday that refuses to come no matter how hard I work and no matter how much fish I put on the auction floor.* Sadly, the only ray of hope was that I knew time ensures things get better. But I was dependent on men like Shaky to survive until that day arrived. What a vicious cycle indeed.

When we arrived at the whorehouse, the cabby parked the car and followed me right up the stairs despite the fact that I had paid him and told him I wasn't there to fuck. He didn't believe me. He was convinced a meal was coming, and he wasn't planning on missing his cut. The building's lighting reminded me of a second- or third-world health clinic. The building seemed sterile but breathless. I thought of all the terribly sad things that had happened in it. The walls were plain, and the air smelled of Lubriderm and Vaseline. Nothing seemed inviting about this place whatsoever. Antiqued couches held half-awake and half-dressed Asian girls in frumpy nightgowns of all varieties. Mama-San greeted us at the door. "Hello, hello come in (which sounded more like 'hero, hero'). Me have nice girl for you. Whatcha want? Tall one, short one? Big one, small one?"

"No, no. I'm here for Shaky." At that point, all the niceties ended. Her jovial smile turned into the frown of a pit bull. "Ah, you fucking Captain Shaky friend."

"I suppose you could call me that, but at moments like this, I'd like to think of myself as more of an associate."

"You come now!" And so she turned and gestured for me to follow her. I followed her down a hallway adjoined with cheap wood panel doors on each side. I remember thinking you couldn't pay me to turn one of those germ-riddled handles. The farther we got down the hall, the more it smelled of sex faintly masked by Febreze. Shaky was sitting on the floor with his back against the wall. A man who strangely resembled "Top Hat" from the James Bond movies wore a wife-beater and sat contentedly in a dirty recliner watching some type of early morning Japanese infomercial. He didn't pay us much attention when we walked in. Ole Shaky had clearly been slapped around pretty good and looked even worse than his usual self after an onshore bender. Though Shaky was generally disheveled, he looked straight-up defeated today. He was leashed to a pipe with a set of handcuffs like a dog to a tree. I immediately wished I had used this same technique to keep him on the boat.

"What the fuck have you done, Shaky?" I disapprovingly said.

Shaky was trying to indicate it was a simple misunderstanding, but that sentence was stopped short when the Top Hat-looking fellow shoved a gun straight in his mouth. The barrel loudly clanked off his Clorox-treated teeth as it made its way inside. Shaky dipped his toothbrush straight into household bleach to brush his teeth. He claimed this was the same thing as a dentist bleaching them. I routinely assured him it was not, but he couldn't be convinced otherwise. So he performed his weekly or biweekly hygiene ritual using a gallon jug of Clorox. I had to admit his teeth looked pretty damn white compared to a gunmetal black.

I said, "Come on now, he's a fucking loser no doubt. But he's not worth killing over $1,300."

Mama-San looked in my direction with piercing eyes and said, "No $1,300.00; $13,000.00."

Shocked, I looked back at her and said, "Well in that case, fucking shoot him."

Shaky's face suggested he could accidentally swallow that gun whole right then and there. He was clearly worried.

"Okay, okay," I said. "I'm joking. I'm sure we can figure this out."

I asked how in the fuck did he run up a $13,600 tab, and learned that the debt had been incurred over the past three weeks. We had been on land six days total out of the last twenty, so the numbers weren't adding up. But apparently, Shaky was a top-notch customer, routinely spending thousands of dollars a day in the confines of the establishment. He had been known to spend five or six thousand dollars in a weekend, so Mama-San hadn't questioned his story. She had fronted him a few thousand in the past, and he had always made good on paying his debts. The problem was Shaky's whore fetish now greatly outweighed his current paychecks. Just two months before, he was making around $5,000 per week, so his appetite for multiple whores at one time had been happily satisfied and easily financed. Now, the money and pussy had run dry. It was time to pay. Mama-San wisely didn't trust Shaky's word. She smelled a rat. It was time to pay the fiddler. I explained to her that I didn't have the money and fishing was slow.

"She no care," Mama-San said. "Money now."

I took out my wallet and produced the $600 I had scraped together. Mama-San quickly snatched that, along with my wallet, out of my hand. She started fishing through all of its contents. She stopped at my license, holding it up in delight. "Ahhhhh yah." She walked my ID over to an ancient Xerox machine and proceeded to make several copies of it.

"Shaky's problem now your problem."

I said, "Hold on a minute. It's not my fault you let Shaky run a whore tab."

"Too bad. Your problem. Now your family problem too! You have kids, wife? You like them, then problem now too."

"Wait. Are you threatening my wife and children?"

"Goddamn right we are," said the second-rate Top Hat.

"Okay, just trying to make sure I thought that was what you were saying." I continued, "Look, I don't have the money. But if you release Shaky, I will put him to work and vouch for him that we will pay back the loan with interest on top." They asked for a down payment for good faith.

That's when I found myself in the backseat of the same shitty taxi. The driver, still convinced of a kickback to come, scoured the city for an open ATM. I maxed out my daily limit at one ATM, then another, and another. When I returned to Mama-San, I offered her $5,200 I'd acquired through ATM shopping. I confirmed she would leave my family alone for enough time to satisfy the debt. As luck would have it, Mama-San was an honorable businesswoman and had agreed to take the good faith payment and not kill Shaky on the spot. I worked out a deal that each week I would personally deliver Shaky's pay directly to her until we cleared the debt. I was as much worried about someone seeing me frequent this type of place as I was Shaky staying around long enough to pay what he owed. But I didn't mention either. As we left, Top Hat's cousin threw Shaky down the approximate twenty-step stairwell for good measure. His ragdoll-like figure tumbled down the stairs, landing like a crumpled up piece of paper. If he was any worse for wear, I couldn't tell nor did I care. He started to explain his side of the story as we got into a taxi. I told him to shut the fuck up. Fortunately, he obliged. We enjoyed an awkwardly silent ride back to the boat together.

Over the years, my own battles with drinking, women, traveling, and gambling had cost me a fortune. But none of that money ever felt ill spent. However, everything felt totally wrong about being responsible for someone else's fuckup. I would now be living in constant fear of my wife checking the business account and seeing the series of strange withdrawals late at night. I had a story prepared if she asked about the withdrawals, but I had no interest in lying to her whatsoever and I had no interest in telling her the truth either. So, I just prayed this situation would go unnoticed long enough that I could bury it under multiple transactions.

Shaky, a man of more or less decent morals while clean and sober, didn't grumble much during his time of indentured servitude. Fortunately for both of us, the fishing stayed consistent and the prices greatly improved and stabilized. Immediately following each trip, I would religiously take Mama-San a five-gallon bucket of ahi fillets and Shaky's would-be crew share minus enough money to get him cigarettes and a case of Coors Lights. For the most part, he kept his head down and did his job without complaining much. It seemed a good slapping around was just what the doctor ordered to keep him on the straight and narrow, at least for the time being.

Shaky paid off the whorehouse debt he had incurred. I actually fronted him the last $500 as a final parting gift. Shaky had been the best Shaky he could be for as long as he could be. But a Shaky is a Shaky. So, despite the fact that I only gave him enough money for a few cold ones and some smokes, he had managed to find himself a bag of blow. I caught Shaky red-handed doing a gagger on watch, which was the nail in the coffin for our time fishing together. It was one thing for a man to be a fuckup on land. It was a completely different thing to be a fuckup at sea, where the same common misstep on land could leave you and/or the rest of your crew dead. I have always had a strict zero-drug policy on the boat, and Shaky knew it. We parted on good enough terms, and I wished him nothing but the best.

I would still see Shaky from time to time on different boats and around the harbor. Honestly, I had no hard feelings for the guy. I just didn't want the risk or liability of the circus that came along with having him on board. He was generally drunk and always in need of money for cigarettes. Shaky went from boat to boat until eventually and unfortunately, he landed on one that condoned drug use. It seemed that on this vessel, he discovered the next level of drugs. Without "seahab"—a term fishermen call the time out at sea away from their vices, a place where we generally find clarity and/or sobriety—a good fisherman eventually becomes no fisherman at all. It seemed that without the balance of seahab in his routine, the pressures of his demons had won. When the boat Shaky was working on was repossessed by the original owner for failure to make payments, Shaky was once again forced to find a new home.

He first started living on one of the derelict fishing boats in the harbor with the other meth heads, crackheads, and heroin junkies. When the state dragged that crack house of a boat out to sea and sank it, he then moved under a set of stacked up docks in the Keehi Harbor parking lot. When those were deployed into the water, he moved underneath the overpass on Nimitz Highway. It was really hard for me to watch. He was in need of professional help I couldn't offer. He would sit before you, drinking a beer looking high while telling you he hadn't touched a drink in a month. I went as far as hunting down his parents. When I finally got ahold of them, they denied that their son had any type of drug problem. The flat-out denial of his habit sounded like the words of those that had totally given up on their son. I would guess that his parents had tried in the past and felt like they had lost that battle long ago.

Despite my own piss-poor financials at the time, I purchased him a plane ticket home to the mainland to try to get him help. Sadly, he no-showed for the nonrefundable flight. I didn't speak to Shaky for a few years after that. I began selling fish exclusively in Hilo on the Big Island, and so our paths did not cross again for some time. Sadly, when they did, he was so fucked up he didn't know who I was. I don't mean he didn't recognize me. I mean he had no fucking clue who I was. He was completely gone. He scratched at himself incessantly and bore all the stereotypical signs of a meth head.

For several reasons, I always found Shaky's story particularly troubling. For one, I liked the guy and I don't like seeing anyone I care about in hardship. He wasn't a fool. He was smart and well educated. I had some of the deepest and most thought-provoking conversations with him at sea while he was coherent. He was sharp and funny. He was a very good fisherman and a good person sober. He even had earned himself a captain's license in his time before commercial fishing. He used to take people out fishing both in Key West, Florida, and Kona. He had so much wasted potential and didn't seem ashamed of it. He often wore his demons like a badge of honor. He passionately spoke of his derelictions. He truly coveted the nights of debauchery. He wasn't openly embarrassed about them for the most part.

However, there were moments when I saw him staring out a cabin window and I could tell he wanted more. I could tell he knew he could do better. He didn't let many people see that side of him, but I spent so much time with him that he couldn't always keep up the front. He was better than the Shaky he chose to be, and he knew it. He always said he wanted his own boat, and he honestly could have had it and been very successful if he could have just overcome his addictions.

The other part that has always scared me about Shaky's plight was that it could have unquestionably and easily happened to many people I know, including me. But, I've never had a hooker or drug addiction. Despite admittedly sampling both, neither were my cup of tea. I've certainly had a drinking problem and an equal appetite for chasing women. I have battled with drinking since I was twenty-one years old and equally or more so struggled with relationships and depression long before that. I drank a bottle of Crown Royal nightly during the height of my drinking. I do not say that proudly, rather just matter-of-factly. A man can hate that which he does yet still do it night after night. That is the burden of the alcoholic.

We all kill ourselves with our decisions. Even when we know better, we oftentimes are hopeless against the magnetisms of our vices. Why can't we protect ourselves from the pain we all know? This remains one of life's greatest mysteries. We are given the keys to drive our own destiny. Yet, time and time again we knowingly drive it straight off the road into a head-on collision. One could arguably question whether free will is our greatest ally or our worst enemy. Is free will the most powerful and yet the most deadly tool we are given in our time here on Earth?

Once you get to a certain level of drinking and mastery of the art of functioning with a lack of sleep, you actually feel great the next day. Maybe it's the sugars still pumping through your system or the false feeling of accomplishment that you feel both the night and day. Maybe it's knowing that when you wake up feeling like you're on rock bottom you can only go up. This feeling and the comfort of a random woman's skin upon my skin kept me drinking and going to bars for years to fill the inexplicable void that traveled everywhere I went.

So, night after night, I scoured the bars and nightclubs looking over the glass-filled fishing grounds for what would hopefully be my latest catch. The reality is that nightclubs are nothing more than a sea of lost souls searching for something that cannot possibly be found within their confines. We go to these places for we lack other direction, momentarily appeased by distracting sounds, flashing lights, and the prospect of pleasures of the flesh. Again and again, we confuse these stimulants for something worthy of our time. We drink in these places to pretend like we aren't individually awkward, an irony we all share.

A man can be surrounded by people and still be very much alone. I would drink, and I would drink heavily in order to counter this feeling. Liquor is called "liquid courage" for good reason. Alcohol breaks down the barriers we build in our minds about whether we are good enough, smart enough, a good dancer, and pretty much every other limitation. Liquor temporarily breaks the chains that often hold us back in certain aspects of our everyday lives. It's a lubricant for otherwise awkward introductions and hard conversations. Not all the walls alcohol breaks down, of course, are good walls to be tampered with, such as the "I'm strong enough, I am tough enough, and wonder if I can fly off this building" walls.

I became an alcoholic because of the interactions it created with women. Without alcohol, I felt out of place in almost every crowd. I never quite felt like I fit in anywhere besides a fishing boat or along a shoreline with a rod in my hand. I always felt awkward in a crowd of land dwellers. I could not participate in casual conversations about popular trends and the like. My knowledge base was extremely limited to fishing and the happenings in the fishing business. I don't watch television, and I don't know other sport-related happenings aside from the Boston Red Sox (who I passionately follow). I almost never know what's happening in the news and don't understand the infatuation with celebrities. So, for the greater part of my life, right back to my school days, I've never really ever felt like I belonged or was a member of society.

I discovered an interesting thing when I drank. I wasn't an outcast anymore. I was a drinker—a damn good one. It turned out that I was genetically gifted to consume large amounts of alcohol. It also turned out that I loved to dance and wasn't half bad at it. Above all, it turned out I was pretty popular with the ladies between being able to dance and having my self-doubt stripped away, something this young man who generally felt lost on land never felt before. I ended up being pretty damn good at pulling women from bars. I would drink and wake up with these women again and again who were so physically out of my league I couldn't believe it. Not to say I didn't slay a few dragons to get to all the princesses because I certainly did my share of swordsmanship along the way. Being a diehard fisherman, I discovered I had a very broken way of looking at relationships for a very long time. The satisfaction came in the pursuit of the women and less so anything more meaningful. A fisherman rarely looks much at his catch after stuffing it in the box.

I had been hurt by a succession of women while trying to attempt "normal" relationships before my bar days. I wouldn't realize I was carrying those scars with me until I was much older. That is the very reason I naively continued this empty process for years. That ability, if you want to call it that, kept me from confronting my own internal demons for nearly two decades.

My honeymoon phase with drinking started to fade, like all things. Even strange pussy gets boring and meaningless when you've had enough of it. I began to find myself drinking for effect and not to be social. I was drinking now to hurt myself. I was lonely when I was sober, and I hated myself and didn't respect the trove of women who dropped their pants when I drank. Admittedly, this was a double standard, but like I said, I was broken. I wanted something meaningful. I wanted someone who could love the sober me. I wanted someone who loved the real me, not the guy who fucked someone else's bride the night before her wedding. I wanted real love. I didn't want the kind of love where I watched a wedding party comb the beach in front of my house looking for an engagement ring all while it sat on the dresser beside my bed.

A typical night a Lulu's consisted of me starting with Coronas and getting pretty well hammered before moving quickly onto Crown and cokes. At some point, things were probably going to get blurry with a round of tequila shots and Irish Car Bombs speckled in. As my tolerance rose higher and higher, I would hear from folks that they didn't even know I was drunk. I didn't either, I would tell them. However, the truth was that I was often a functioning blackout drunk who didn't remember parts of the evening until the following day or didn't remember them at all.

For example, on one particular night, I was noticeably drunk enough where my friends took my keys after last call. They had decided it would be best for me to get a taxi ride home. But taxis were so unreliable that I didn't know how I would get one. So, I was able to convince my friends to let me sleep in my car. In the morning, I told them, I'd have a friend pick me up. I realized my friends were looking out for my best interests, but I had no intentions of sleeping in the parking lot like they thought I was going to.

So, I put on my best act to make them believe I was going to get a night of slumber in my car. I nestled into my front seat in the fetal position and put out my best yawn and closed my eyes. Satisfied with my performance, I heard them say their goodbyes to one another and stub out their night's final cigarettes, shaking hands, and finally getting into their vehicles to depart.

I patiently waited until I saw the reflection of their car headlamps leave the parking lot. I looked around my Chevy Corsica, which I had purchased earlier that year from another fisherman. I affectionately had come to call her the Puerto Rican sweet ride, an homage to its overly excessive chrome tape that seemingly held it together, along with its ridiculous plastic chrome tire rims that reflected the sun so brightly you had to look away.

What my friends did not know but I had discovered is that the Puerto Rican sweet ride was so bitchin' you didn't even need keys to start her. Fumbling around the car one day, I learned you could start it just by turning the outside of the ignition where the key is supposed to go. I never gave it much thought, and nothing surprised me given the overall state of the vehicle.

So, as my friends exited the parking lot, I sprang up in my seat and looked over my shoulders like I was in a spy movie. I hummed the James Bond theme as I turned the whole steering column, causing the sweet ride to roar to life. I turned on the headlights with the makeshift knob made from a small pair of vise grips and about ten rubber bands. The song "Escape" came on. I turned a hard right out of the parking lot heading south on Ali'i Drive while scream singing to the chorus of "If you like piña coladas! Getting caught in the rain!"

It didn't take long for the blue lights to come on behind me, illuminating the whole car and early morning sky. *Fucccckkkkkk man.* My heart started racing. All I could think about was my captain's license. Getting a DUI means you'll lose it. *What a fucking nightmare. Okay, be cool. Be totally cool.* Adrenaline flowed through me, and suddenly my mind got stone-cold sober even if my blood alcohol level was not.

So, I pulled over to the right side of the road, stopped the vehicle, and waited. I sat there composing myself the best I could. A female voice from what seemed to be about six feet behind me said, "Sir, could you please pull to the side of the road." At that point, I realized I hadn't actually pulled over to the side. I had only turned into the lane I should have been in in the first place. I clearly had been driving in the wrong lane! *Ohh man, now I'm really fucked.*

A million thoughts filled my mind. However, the number one thought was that I wasn't going to go down without a fight. I did my best to throw myself together as the seconds raced past. I chugged a bottle of water and fired Visine eye drops indiscriminately all over my eyes and face. I prayed like a motherfucker that I wouldn't go to jail. I sat in wait while stressed out of my mind doing my best interpretation of a sober person. *How could I be so stupid? God, I'm so fucked.*

When that female voice finally reappeared, it was much closer and holding a brightly lit flashlight that cut threw me like a laser beam. I had to cover my eyes and retract from it like a cockroach scurrying away from a freshly flipped patio light. "License and registration please," she stated.

"Good dayyy, madam. No worries, love," I replied as I handed her the documents I had already organized as part of my smoke and mirrors defense strategy.

"Australian?" she asked.

"No, no. But I just got back from living there, so that's why I was on the wrong side of the road, just really tired I guess." I hadn't been to Australia for eight months, but she didn't need to know that.

I glimpsed the officer when she shined her light down on my paperwork and away from my eyes. She was a large Samoan woman, roughly in her late twenties to early thirties, and stuffed very tightly into a uniform clearly made for a man. I remember thinking that that's probably exactly what an elephant would look like if one ever tried on a human suit. She had a jovial face and dark black hair. Her name tag read, "Officer Happy." *She doesn't look too happy*, I thought.

"Have you been drinking tonight?"

"Wellllll, not technically."

"What do you mean?"

"Well, it's two thirty a.m., so really tonight hasn't actually happened. But if you mean last night, then yes, I had a few drinks after my friends called me to get a ride home from the bar because they were drunk. I had already been asleep, but when I showed up to the bar I couldn't find them so I had a couple drinks as I waited to be their designated driver."

She looked at me in disbelief. "So you're the sober one of your friends?"

"Yes, ma'am, that's right. I'm the DD."

"So where are your friends then?"

"Well, that's the funny part. I never did find them."

"Your eyes are really red."

"Oh well, yeah. It's something in the air. I think I'm just wicked allergic to the vog right now."

She asked me if there was any reason I couldn't take a field sobriety test.

"Well, yeah. Funny you should ask," I said with a smile. "I've got this really achy hip, this other bum knee, and, to be honest, both my ankles have been really bothering me lately. Did I mention I think my blood sugar level was low and I had bit of a headache?"

Her hard face was shifting, and she was smiling and slightly shaking her head laughing. She asked me to step out of the car.

"Sure, just one minute. Let me find my cane."

She asked about my cane.

"I do use it on occasion. Yes," I replied. I spent a solid five minutes looking for this fictitious cane and in reality just consuming every breath mint and Tic Tac I had squirreled away throughout the car. I even managed to finger-brush my teeth as rapidly as humanly possible with a travel-sized toothpaste tube I found while inverted under the back side of the passenger side of the car as I desperately searched for this mysterious missing cane.

Having no luck finding the alleged cane but having attempted to sneakily inhale about 100 Tic Tacs, I looked at the officer. "No luck. You'll have to pardon me if I am a bit shaky. My arthritis has been really acting up lately, and I've got a kink in my neck ever since I fell off the roof last week rescuing an elderly lady's cat. You know, real hero stuff." I caught a giggle out of the corner of my eye again. I'd seen that look before on a woman. I was winning. I'm not sure any part of me thought she believed I was sober, but I was entertaining the idea that she did or at least I was doing my best to be a nice guy and entertain her.

I heard hooting and hollering when I stepped out of the car. Laughter and cackles were clearly defined. At this moment, I realized I had been pulled over directly in front of a narcotic and alcoholic rehab facility. The windows were filled with onlookers who had great advice to shout at me, such as "Don't drop the soap tonight because you're going to jail." I actually laughed at that one. I thought it was helpful and probably true.

To the joy of the crowd, I then proceeded to fail all the officer's monkey tricks like an absolute champ. I knew I was blowing it hard, but I did it with a smile while cracking jokes and making her laugh. One might even suggest I was being a bit flirty. We now had a fun little dialogue going on about how it looked like I'd be yelling out of those windows soon enough.

It looked like all my winning was about to come crashing down when a second cop car arrived on the scene. *Shit.* She told me to stand next to my car and just be cool and she'd be right back. She asked if I could handle that.

"Just call me Mr. Cucumber," I replied.

"What?"

"Never mind. Yes. I can do that."

As I leaned against the car doing my best to act sober and natural, I slipped farther and farther down the side of the car as my treadless three dollar pair of slippers slid out from under my feet on the sandy road. My feet were getting farther and farther away from me and the car. I slid lower and lower until my neck was holding me just by the flare that covers the wheel wells. I looked back at my now-female friend leaning inside the other cop car talking. She briefly peered back, her eyes wide as saucer pans, giving that look women give when a man is fucking up. Then again she turned her head back into the car. Behind her back, hidden from the sight of the other officer, she frantically waved her hands in a "get the fuck up" gesture. I composed myself the best I could and climbed back into the standing position while kicking off my slippery-ass slippers that attempted to escape from me again at the same angle the moment I stood back up.

The second cop car drove off, and my new officer friend returned. "Can you park your car on the other side of the road?" she asked. No problem. She informed me she'd be giving me a ride home. "Sounds great," I said. After a bit of fiddlefucking, I finally got the ole girl fired up. For some reason, the drive shifter was being particularly stubborn. I put old reliable in gear and proceeded to reverse straight into the officer's car, slamming into it with a solid thud. *Fuck!* In my haste, I had not double-checked that the touchy gear knob was in the right place, which was sometimes the case with this luxurious vehicle I drove.

I looked back out the window to see the officer waving me on. *It's okay, it's okay,* I thought. *Man, I'm fucked now.* I swung my car around to the other side of the road and smashed my passenger side rear view mirror clean off on the rehabilitation facility's welcome sign. *How fitting.* Truly nervous now and not wanting to have my car too far out into the road in case some drunk driver came along, I accidentally grinded it against the rehab facility's stone wall, causing sparks to fly like a rooster tail off a boat.

I stepped out of the car to a roar of laughter and catcalling from my adoring public. *Man, now you're really fucked.* I walked straight to the back of the officer's car, convinced I was going to be arrested after that amazing display. "Your keys please," she requested.

"Well, that's the funny thing. I don't actually have keys."

"Wait. What? How come?"

"My friends took them away."

"Which friends? Wait, how did . . . does the car even start without keys?"

"Ummmm" and a shoulder shrug was all I could come up with.

"Never mind. Just get in," she said.

Up to this point in my life, I had never been arrested. I assumed that what was happening now was just normal Hawaiian police protocol, as the Big Island can be pretty laidback. I went to hop in the backseat. She motioned for me to ride in the front. *Holy fuck. Is this really happening?* She went into the car by foot, and I flew around to the passenger side. My charm had won. She could see I was a good guy. I stepped up extra high so all of the onlookers could see me getting in the front seat without handcuffs on, offering a most liberating and self-serving middle finger to the crowd. On the ride home, I greatly thanked her. We talked about nothing in particular.

When we arrived at my house, I thanked her profusely for the ride. As I was about to step out the door, she said, "Well, aren't you going to now help me out?"

"What do you mean?"

"I just let you off on a DUI that would have cost you thousands."

"Ohhh, money right. Well, I don't really have much money. But I'll give you what I have. What does this kind of thing usually cost?"

"I don't want your money."

"What do you mean?"

"You know what I mean."

"I'm not sure I do." I swallowed hard.

"A girl has her needs."

"Ahhh, I see," I said while allowing the severity of the situation to sink in.

"You'd still fail a breathalyzer right now," she noted.

Taking all that had just happened into account, I decided to do the right thing.

"Park your car over by the fence, and I'll go pour us a couple drinks."

"I don't drink when I'm at work," she replied.

Okay, well I'll drink them both, I thought, because this is going to take some serious alcohol to make this happen and twice as much to make me forget. I got to the liquor cabinet and couldn't figure out what to drink—that was until I looked at Officer Happy settling into my room and removing her uniform. That settled it—straight tequila it would be. And lots of it. I cracked open my new bottle of Patrón and started guzzling it until I could take no more. Eyes watering, body gagging, I wiped off the remaining tequila from my chin.

"Fuck it, go big or go home," I said.

I found Officer Happy lying on my bed just in her underwear. I knew friends who claimed to have a cop fantasy; however, I was betting none of them ever envisioned it looking like this. Checking my watch and still having to go fishing in a couple hours, I knew I had to figuratively and literally dive straight into this thing. I went straight for her pillowcase-sized panties, slowly pulling them down as I kissed around the tops of them. The farther I pulled them down the more I found a wildly overgrown pubic hair forest. There is no way this thing had ever been trimmed.

I imagined what the Amazon would look like if man had never started clear-cutting it. When I finally arrived where I was going down there, I was completely distracted and had a hard time focusing on the task at hand because this Afro of pubes was so long it actually curved around and tickled the inside of my ears. I'd never experienced anything like this before nor did I want to again. True to my work ethic, I stayed and finished the job in every sense of the word. Officer Happy had sexual frustrations, and she took every one of them out on me. Never before nor since have I ever been so wildly manhandled. She was very strong, and I had no idea I was so very weak. I have never felt more beat up and broken in my life on land. I was a prop for her, and she did as she wished with me. In the morning, Officer Happy dropped me back off at my car, still legally drunk.

Somewhere around nine a.m. while applying sunblock, I discovered Officer Happy had also come fishing with me that day in the form of two massive pubic hairs that somehow didn't come out in the shower. I found this while applying lotion to my ear; the other I discovered straight underneath my visor sticking out like a Jheri curl.

I would like to tell you this was the end of the story, but unfortunately, I would find myself hiding under my bed and in closets when surprise visits were sprung on me. This game of cat and mouse lasted for about three weeks until I left for Australia. I never again returned to that house, but I heard from my old roommate that Officer Happy had checked to see if I was around a few times. For this reason, even today, I always get nervous when a cop car is driving behind me.

This was also the reality check that I needed to work on getting my life in order. I could have lost my captain's license by getting a DUI, a piece of paper that was my most prized possession for a number of years. Far worse, I could have killed someone with the stupidity of my actions. The gravity of the situation was not lost on me at the time. This experience proved to be a great motivator and true wake-up call. I wasn't living my best life by any means, and I realized it. For the first time in my life since a bartender served me my first drink, I put the bottle down and walked away from the bar. I buried myself in self-improvement and my work.

I see the results of that decision in my life today. I was very lucky, and I did not let that fact go unappreciated. Not that I don't still have recurring battles with those demons, because I do. I'm still only human. However, today I try to be far more conscious about the possibility of the repercussions of my actions. I don't drink anywhere as much as I used to, and I absolutely never drink and drive. As for women, I thought I had beaten that demon. I remember the day I got married, thinking that I would never again be alone. Oh, how wrong I was on that, but that's a whole different story for an upcoming chapter.

# CHAPTER 3

# WORKING ON A SHOESTRING AND PRAYER: THE UNLIKELY FRIENDSHIP OF MIGHTY WHITEY

When I was first introduced to Brett through our mutual friend Tiny, I didn't particularly like him. I found him harsh and extremely cocky. He was loud and had a "know it all" air about him. He was just off a recent million-dollar fishing tournament win as the angler of the boat. Brett captured the largest white marlin in the White Marlin Open out of Ocean City, Maryland. From this win he inherited his nickname, "Mighty Whitey," that follows him to this day. It is often shortened to just "Whitey."

The Ocean City achievement was just one of his many wins in his sportfishing career. In fact, he had won more prize money and more tournaments in a matter of months than I had in my entire life.

It is still a little blurry to me how Brett and I grew to be such close friends. That might partially be because of how much we were drinking with each other at the time. We somehow began fishing together, first on *High Noon*, the sport boat I was running, and then on *Makana*, the commercial boat I was running. We even ended up becoming roommates somewhere along the line and living in three places together over the years.

The thing about Brett was that once you got past his hard exterior he often falsely projected, you saw that he had an absolute heart of gold. The more I got to know him, the more I came to understand that his hard exterior was a defense mechanism from his past. Despite my first impression of him, he had grown to be one of my very best friends in the world. I absolutely loved the guy, even though he rubbed every woman I ever had in my life the wrong way.

I loved fishing with Brett for several reasons. For starters, he is the most meticulous tackle person I've ever met. He ties the most beautiful knots you've ever seen, and his attention to detail is second to none. You wouldn't see preventable tackle failures happen on his watch. He is a thinker and an innovator when it comes to boats and boat systems. I still regularly use some of his innovative tackle ideas. Second, Brett is an animal on the deck and one of the hardest working people you will ever meet. At a time when the other crew members I had were falling like dead branches, Brett stood alone as the tallest and strongest tree in a forest of men who fancied themselves as being pretty tough. He worked circles around the average man. Like me, he valued fish more than sleep. We were a very good team and we caught lots of fish, both day and night. Trip after trip, we would often charge out as just the two of us, mostly because we had trouble finding a third person to relentlessly go on back-to-back trips with us.

Brett also liked to cook. He was amazingly talented in the kitchen, and there is nothing better than a good cook out at sea. It is a very highly respected attribute, as most men would likely go to bed starving rather than take the time to cook a meal for themselves or others. Brett would routinely manufacture meals the likes of which you would see in a fancy restaurant. This was definitely not the status quo in an environment where a hurried fist full of Cheetos and Mountain Dew was often considered a man's lunch.

You often don't really know the people who will forever change your life until that moment actually passes. I would have laughed had you told me the prick sitting in the front seat of my buddy's Jeep would one day end up being one of my best friends. But, here we are brothers-in-arms, close friends and business partners working hard for one common goal. I was laying it all on the line, and Brett was right beside me, menacing grin and bloody gaff in hand.

We left Honokohau Harbor on the maiden trip of *Vicious Cycle*, the boat still without its name on the side of it. Totally strapped for cash, it didn't seem like a very high priority to us, especially knowing we had a 0 percent chance of seeing the Coast Guard around the Big Island. In all the time we had fished offshore, we'd never seen the Coast Guard around the west side of Hawaii Island except on the Fourth of July weekend, when they put up a police presence for all the boaters and participants in the big marlin fishing tournaments to see. Also for this very reason, we spared no expense on safety equipment, knowing damn well it would be a long while before any help would be on its way if something ever did happen.

As we passed the green buoy that marks the entrance to the harbor at three thirty in the afternoon, I blared out Eminem's "Lose Yourself" via my iPod Nano plugged into the stereo. Our food box overflowing, bait box filled to the rim, ice holds completely stuffed, and our bank accounts totally empty, we were ready to go. Aside from our sea anchor, we were totally out of parachutes. There were no lifelines, bailouts, handouts, loans, nothing. We had officially tapped every single resource available to us. We were 100 percent balls deep. We were properly outfitted to safely go fishing. We did not have enough money or credit for another trip's worth of expenses if something went wrong. This would be it. One shot.

Brett had set out our two trolling lures as soon we left the harbor. I plotted the 138-mile steam to the Cross Seamount. When I finally got done fiddling and syncing the new autopilot with the GPS, the old girl was already instinctively headed right on track down to the very degree. This old girl still remembered her way home. I wondered which one of us was more valuable than the other—the one recently and unceremoniously let go or the one who had lay in chains after many years of faithful service. She rode deeply and confidently, pushing water out of the way rather than going over it. Like a double malt whiskey, she was strong and powerful yet remarkably smooth. She was a proud workhorse and eagerly went back about her trade. I could almost feel her determined stare pass the horizon as she effortlessly hauled her nearly 20,000 pounds of ice, bait, and fuel. She too longed for something one would not find on land. I gave her an extra 100

RPMs to help satisfy our insatiable craving to go after that which lives in the distance.

I stared out the starboard side window from my chair. My right hand lightly wrapped around the base of the throttles, I steadily tapped away with my middle and index fingers, a nervous twitch I had inherited while running the charter *Bunny Clark* out of Ogunquit, Maine. This was the first boat I had captained at age nineteen. I would take that twitch all over the world and repeat it countless times on any vessel's throttles I got my hands around. We chugged passed Kawai Point, a barren rocky edge that drops swiftly into the depths of the sea. With forty fathoms, a mere stone's throw from land, and 1,000 fathoms only three miles farther out, not only was it the most western point of the island of Hawaii but also at times one of the best fishing spots. It was going to take us anywhere from eighteen to twenty-four hours to get to the sea mountain, depending on the weather and the current.

Brett walked into the cabin and loudly said, "Yeah, buddy," as he firmly gave me a Hawaiian handshake, a hybrid of a high five and a handshake that more or less looks like arm wrestling in mid-air. We were officially doing it; we were fulfilling a lifelong dream. While I didn't have a cent to my name, I didn't have a worry in the world. I was totally confident in fishing because fishing had always been totally confident in me. Whenever my life was in shambles, feeling like the world had given up on me, fishing always got me back on my feet not just financially but emotionally as well. Since I was a young boy, I have lived and died by my catches. Fishing has been a caliper for my personal happiness and success for as long as I've truly understood the concept of emotions.

The sea can gauge your mood better than a thermometer can gauge your temperature. The sea is a teacher and a doctor. She gives you what she believes you deserve in dosages, prescribed by her liking. What you believe you need for your ailment may be exactly the opposite of what she believes you need. You may believe a slam job trip will fix your problems, yet she may believe a broker is more important to the lesson you are supposed to learn. You'll find no better therapy when both the patient and doctor are on the same page. I was hopeful we both agreed that a slammer was in order.

I cannot speak of organized religion nor if there is just one God. I can only speak of the religion I understand, the religion of the sea and the almighty power she has had over me since I was a young man. I truly believe you can find your soul somewhere between the horizon and the ocean. One need only play a favorite melody and set a loose gaze upon her to access the mirror of their life. One can find themselves in the ocean's glory like no other place on Earth. As we steamed into sunset, my undying faith in the ocean allowed me to be completely fearless of my empty bank accounts. To be successful at life and/or fishing, you can do neither scared. You must be fully invested and committed to the process.

The slow days at sea weren't created for boredom; they were created to thin the weak and hone the skills of the loyal. The doldrums weren't meant to break men; they were created to clearly determine the true bloods. Any man can fish when the conditions are easy and the fish are on the chew. It's the attention to detail when fishing is difficult that makes the measure of the fisherman. The details are what ultimately adds up to success.

You can spend a lifetime at sea. Your present and past surround you as sure as the salt air. One does not stare out to the horizon and eventually not see themselves staring back. The farther we go out to sea, the deeper we go inside our mind. The spirit of the ocean is a living, breathing thing, as alive as any of the creatures who inhabit her waters above and below.

To be good, you must be consistent. And to be consistent at sea, you must be experienced. To be experienced, you must have lived. To have lived, you must have found both tremendous success and failure. The information we compile from our wins and losses ultimately determines our character, and our character determines our fate. You are given a chance to change your destiny every day at sea, whether you realize it or not. The course we sail, the heading we change. The birds we do or do not notice. The splash in the distance we manage to catch a glimpse of. All of these small details weigh on your trip's final outcome.

Since age thirteen, I had envisioned this moment of running my own boat a million times. Even then, none of the dreams felt as great as the reality. The warm sea air filled my hair and my heart. I admired the final moments of the setting sun over the notoriously calm waters off the Kona coast. I couldn't help but think how blessed I was. Brett cooked us steaks for dinner, and I took first watch after we ate. We rotated time at the helm, watching the radar and the engine gauges every three hours. As usual, there was no traffic off the Big Island coast. The steam out was, fortunately, uneventful.

We arrived at the Cross Seamount around eleven thirty a.m. the following day with all our brand new shiny fishing gear ready to go. We thawed four of the thirty twenty-five-pound cases of anchovies we brought for *palu* (chum), chopped down our first fish box of ice, prepped to take brine and fish, and trolled four lures off the stern. These were two chrome trolling jets with single 10/0 hooks, approximately 100 feet behind the boat off hydraulic fishing reels known as "Bandits." We set another two slightly larger chrome trolling jets off twenty-four feet behind the boat by the stern cleats. These lines consisted of two fathoms of rope connected via a 1,000-pound ball bearing swivel to two fathoms of 700-pound test monofilament and a large double hook known as a fang hook that looks like an eagle's talons. Eight twelve-inch rubber squids hung in pairs from four metal poles known as dangler bars. Two dangler bars were located on each side of the boat; one was a few feet forward of the stern, and the other one was a few feet forward of midship.

We set up the squid with four feet of rope and three feet of 700-pound monofilament, connected by a 1,000-pound rated ball bearing swivel. The squid were armed with an even larger fang hook in them, roughly the size of a grown man's palm. We set the squid up to just touch the water when slow trolling (dangling) from the bars. The squid appeared to dance on the water when set at the proper height and proper speed.

The water was its normal rich purplish blue. The sea was flat, and the air was unseasonably muggy. Sweat sat on my temples as I searched the distance for birds or any other sign of life, all while constantly monitoring the fish finder for marks or schools of fish. The squid danced exactly the way we liked them in the calm water, doing what we called the skeet, skeet, skeet. They hopped enticingly along. The engine gauges all looked good. The boat sounded perfect. Everything looked good except the fishing grounds. The more we looked around, the more we discovered absolutely nothing. Not a bird in sight, not a splash or bait fish to be seen. The fish finder had remained ominously blank all day, not even a scratch.

Despite not catching a thing, let alone even seeing a fish, we weren't discouraged. Perhaps it was going to be a night bite. A thousand times before, I'd seen the scenario where the mountain appeared to be a desert during the day, only to reveal an ocean absolutely teeming with fish at night. This was commonplace, as was the opposite scenario of sometimes not being able to catch a fish to save your life at night and the fishing being wide open during the day. For this reason, we fished twenty-four hours a day once we got to the fishing grounds. In our business, you can literally catch thousands of pounds of fish in minutes, but you may miss this if you aren't awake and trying in the period when the fish are biting. The way the fish bite differs every day. Some days, they bite all day. Sometimes, they don't bite at all.

However, it is very common for the fish to only have a twenty-five to forty-five-minute bite window per day where they really go off. You can catch 5,000 pounds when the fish are really biting. For this reason, we had to be absolutely relentless in our pursuit, as any moment of the day could make your whole trip.

Daytime and nighttime fishing techniques are very different. We do most of our fishing during the day through slow trolling and being constantly on the hunt for a large pile of tuna. At night, we fish on a sea anchor while making drifts in hopes that our path and the fish cross. At night, we illuminate the water with an underwater light and throw a steady chum line in hopes of increasing the odds of the tuna finding us. In Hawaii, we call this fishing style "ika shibi" fishing. "Ika" means squid and "shibi" being tuna. It literally translates to squid tuna. The reason for this is that fresh ika is the primary and number one bait at night. We jokily say ika shibi is ancient Hawaiian for standing in the rain because of how many nights we find ourselves working in a downpour.

We spend hours and hours targeting and catching fresh ika for bait before actually attempting to catch tuna offshore. Fishing for ika can be far more difficult than the actual tuna fishing. But the ika are most valuable when they are the hardest to catch. We fish for ika around an underwater light that we submerge off the side of the boat to attract them. They feed on smaller baitfish, and the ika themselves are drawn to the light. We use custom glow-in-the-dark ika jigs we personally make and fish them off light tackle spinning rods most commonly used by freshwater fishermen for bass and trout. Our jigs do not have conventional style hooks like those used for catching fish. Rather, they have two to three circular rows of twenty-four sharp prongs to impale the squid's tentacles on the bottom. Ika fishing is a whole art within itself. Every fresh ika is worth a fish when the tuna are biting at night, so it's very much worth all the extra effort and time.

Unfortunately, frozen or older squid do not work anywhere near as well as same-day-caught ika. So unfortunately, you can't sidestep this crucial step if you want to be competitive. The better your bait, the better the fishing. We made short work of loading up on fresh ikas. They were snapping wide open so much so that we didn't have to drop the jigs below surface. We only had to cast three feet of line off the rod tips, which we rhythmically worked back and forth, a technique we call "the magic wand" because of its similarity to a magician waving his magical wand about. Perhaps the ease at which we caught the ikas should have been foretelling. However, as a fisherman, you have to be painfully optimistic no matter what cards it appears the ocean has dealt you. We pulled the sea anchor and started our roughly thirty-minute steam through the darkness toward where I planned to set up for our first ika shibi drift.

At sea, the darker the night the closer you will get to your past. The music you decide to play is the radio dial of your history. Van Morrison's "Have I Told You Lately" played as I stared at the setting moon. This is a song that always transports me to a New Hampshire backroad of my youth. Her name was Katie. She was tall, blond, and wore the girl next door look like an angel. She was smart, funny, and kind. She infatuated me from the moment I met her at Wentworth Marina. She was the daughter of two well-to-do doctors from upstate New York. It was her plan to sail around the world, and she wanted me to join her. "Just to mate" she would always say with a wink.

She told me, "Pull over, pull over. I love this song. We have to dance." So I found myself with goosebumps despite dancing in the warmth of the summer air. The sky around us filled with the flashing luminance of fireflies, and it seemed like we were dancing in the heavens above. You could almost touch the music as it drifted out of my truck windows. I will never forget the look in those crystal-blue eyes as we danced to that song alongside my Dodge Ram pickup. Little did I know it would be the last night I would ever get to look into them again.

The following day, I was supposed to be her designated driver home from a party, but I downplayed that role's significance to myself. I presumed she would be able to find a safe ride from someone else or she'd spend the night at her friend's house. I called her several times, but I was never able to get through to her, each time leaving a message letting her know I had decided to go on an overnight fishing trip and wouldn't be able to get her. When I returned to land, her slurred messages would be the last words I would ever hear from her. She didn't have difficulty finding a ride from an intoxicated driver, who killed himself and everyone else in the car when he went off the road.

The irony of depression is that I drowned myself in the very thing that killed her as reality sank in. I took full blame for not being there to give her a ride home. I climbed into a bottle that would take me years to climb out of. Completely ashamed of myself, I told no one of my claimed responsibility in the accident. People could sense a change in me, but they couldn't place it. They could tell I was drinking a lot more but had no idea why. I didn't speak of the incident or her again until 2017, when I gave away a lure she had given me. I had toted that lure all over the world, but I'd never had the heart to run it. Deep down, I always feared a fish would take it away and I would lose the last part of her I could still hold.

The thing about lures is that they are born to run, as we are born to live. I could no longer bear to carry the full weight of the cross from that evening. I had to keep living, and that lure needed to run. It was with a heavy heart that I left it with Jack Craft, a young fisherman that I saw glimpses of my younger self in. I suppose I could have run it, but I thought it better to give it to a person with more time left on the planet than me, someone who still possessed the innocence of youth that Katie held in those eyes on our final evening together.

I slowed the engine as we arrived in the area where I wanted to start fishing. Bob Seger's "Night Moves" thumped through the speakers. It was one of my all-time favorite night fishing songs, a song that always seemed appropriate as we lurked through the darkness. I threw the sea anchor back out into the ocean as my foot tapped along to Seger. We finally came tight against the parachute, and our bow was now facing directly into the wind. We set out our four handline baskets. In the front of the cockpit, we ran two float lines, each consisting of sixty fathoms of three-strand nylon rope connected with a 1,000-pound ball bearing swivel to eighty fathoms of a stiff, waxed ropelike line known as bloodline. Each line had a four fathom 400-pound monofilament leader rigged with a circle style hook baited with a fresh ika.

One float line was set shallow and the other deep. We tied both off via doubled up size 105 rubber bands. Small fish would just stretch them, but large fish would crack them off. The blastoff is one of my favorite sounds on Earth. The port rear line was a lead line. A lead line has the same makeup as the float line except it has a four-pound copper-filled pipe with a swivel on each end, known as a banana lead, that then goes to another four-fathom piece of blood line before attaching to the monofilament leader. We set up the line to fish straight up and down, and we strategically placed it to have its bait a few fathoms below the starboard side line, which had either a cone bag or a maki dog on it.

We tied off those lines with doubled up size 105 rubber bands. A cone bag or a maki dog's job is basically the same, but their delivery technique is different. Each is used to create an underwater chum slick and present a hook in the chum. A cone bag is a much faster system where one just stuffs chum into the bag followed by their baited hook and then places more chum on top of the bait. The cone is then dropped to the desired depth and then generally pulled up the length of the leader so the bait sits in the middle of a chum slick with the remnants of the chum in the bag drifting over the bait. Both the cone and maki dog are weighted, and the cone bag has a pyramid style lead on the bottom of it.

The maki dog has a flat weight that goes inside of it, known as a pancake lead. Maki dogs differ in the fact that, as opposed to the cone with an open top where chum starts coming out, the second it hits the water the maki dogs are a flat piece of cloth that are totally enclosed inside with the chum. The cloth is folded over the contents from all four directions and then wrapped up with the blood line that attaches to the maki dog. First, it's wrapped one direction, then wrapped the other. It appears to make a plus sign on each side of the dog.

It's then closed off with a slip knot designed to open up when the fisherman yanks on it or stops it at a certain depth, releasing its contents. This technique, also known as dropping stone, dates back to the earliest days of fishing in Hawaii where fishermen would take smooth stones from the shoreline and wrap the *palu* (chum) and a baited hook in tea leaves with the handline. The fisherman would then open them by stopping the line at a desired depth. The difference was that the leaves and stone would sink away versus the modern-day maki dog that is attached to the line and used over and over until it is either broken off or, more commonly, made into a delicious treat for a shark who can't believe its good fortune. Maki dogs are much more time consuming but far more effective for fishing deeper depths when the fish are being picky. Cones are more effective for shallow depths and rapid firing.

We made a disturbing discovery on our first drift. No matter how high we put up the gain on the fish machine, we couldn't mark the lead line let alone the chum that usually floods the screen when you drop a cone bag. Our boat's fish machine didn't work. We could survive night fishing without a machine by just working as if there were fish under the boat, constantly checking the lines and working the chum. However, it's still always better to have a working one. It's nice to know if fish are coming under the boat, even if they aren't necessarily biting. You can use that information to help make decisions like whether you should move or stay in a particular location. We had done five drifts as the sun rose. We had covered nearly ten miles of ocean and had almost as many ikas as when we started in the evening.

We weren't going to survive daytime fishing on the sea mountain without a fish machine unless a miracle happened, and I knew it. After witnessing what nighttime had to offer, I wasn't confident nighttime was going to carry us either. We drove around until about three p.m. on the second day, again without seeing a single sign of life on the surface. No birds, no splashes, no bait, nothing at all. Now, that doesn't mean we didn't drive over giant schools of tuna as we hunted around. It just means we couldn't see them without a working sounder. If we did drive over them, they weren't aggressive enough to charge our trolling lures without being seduced by chum. Another problem was that we routinely found large schools of tuna on the fish machine with no signs on them on the surface, yet we simply just had to stop on top of them and let down our chrome-plated diamond jigs we use on 400-pound monofilament handline spools a mere 10-20 fathoms down. In some cases, we could catch thousands of pounds out of a school by working the jigs like the fleeing of a hurt bait fish. Tuna's instinctive trait of hanging around flotsam often leaves them following the boat for hours or even days as we harvest fish from the school. Without a fish machine, we were driving around totally blind. As Brett put it, "We are fucking Helen Keller out here."

I had to make a play. That play wasn't going to be retreating like a loser back to land to get the fish machine fixed with money I didn't have. It was time to roll the dice. I said, "Brett, we have to go fishing somewhere where we don't need a fish machine to catch fish. I only know of one place we can do that, and that's around a weather buoy. Given the time of year, I only know one buoy that has a likelihood of having any fish on it. That's buoy three."

The National Oceanic and Atmospheric Administration (NOAA) has weather buoys strategically placed around the world's oceans to monitor the weather and natural disasters. These buoys act as a warning system for significant events such as hurricanes and tsunamis. Hawaii has multiples of these large buoys surrounding it offshore. At times, these buoys can be absolute goldmines for us handline fishermen.

Acting like an oasis in a desert, these structures gather fish around them, as fish are naturally attracted to floating objects. A weather buoy will have the complete food chain living around it when it is fishing really well. This goes all the way from microbait to the apex scavengers' sharks and apex predators' marlin. In addition to tuna, we also catch lots of mahi mahi and ono around the buoys. At the weather buoys, you will encounter the most spectacular big fish action and equally the greatest strikeouts. You can easily travel all that way and not catch a fish there. My most epic weather buoy fail was leaving from Honolulu Harbor in Oahu to check weather buoy four, positioned 205 miles southeast of Hilo off the Big Island of Hawaii. The steam was a total of 405 miles, and it took sixty-two and a half hours to get there. When we arrived, a three-pound mahi mahi jumped off our trolling lure. We stayed there for twenty-four hours, and that would be the only fish we would encounter around the buoy.

Weather buoys come with another potential problem besides the chance of totally striking out and the fact that sometimes you have to do battle with unrelenting sharks and endless harassment from large marlin: You can catch the most beautiful looking load of fish you've ever seen on the exterior only to discover they cut out chalky or white in color.

There are two reasons for this. The first is due to the natural instinct of fish to hang around the structure. Sometimes, a massive pile of fish will hang around a buoy that may not have enough additional other life around it to support the school's dietary needs. So the longer the fish hang around the buoy, the meat quality degrades on a poor diet. Sadly, these fish cut out terrible, and we get paid awful for them, if anything at all, in really bad cases. On the other side of the coin, sometimes a buoy rich with smaller bait fish will see large schools of tuna arrive. We call them racers or runners. These are fish that have just migrated a long way and have used up all their fat stores and are tired. When they first arrive, they look long and skinny and cut out terrible. However, after a couple of weeks around a nutrient-rich buoy, they will fatten up and actually start cutting out better and better each trip until they ultimately leave on their own accord or are aggressively forced away by the toothed whales. I have witnessed false killer whales, pilot whales, beaked whales, and even orca whales pillage the buoys. When the whales come through, they can totally wipe the whole buoy clean, driving every single living thing away. It can take months or even a year for a buoy to come back to life after a whale attack.

Buoy three would be another 134 miles to the west and put us a total of 272 miles from Kona and 211 miles from the closest point of land on Oahu. It would take us another eighteen- to twenty-four-hour ride to get there. That would make our ride back to land approximately thirty-six to forty-eight hours, depending on the weather and current. It would also double our growing fuel bill. The last report from buoy three was about two weeks old. The buoy did have some fish on it, but they had cut out terrible and Kona Fish, our fish buyer at the time, wasn't interested in another load of chalky fish. We had been advised to stay away from it. Given our situation, we had no choice but to hope that more fish had arrived and the grade had improved.

After an uneventful eighteen-hour steam, we got the first glimpse of what we thought was the weather buoy. As we neared, we were disappointed to discover that what we initially thought was the buoy was actually another boat already next to the buoy. It had a foreign outline to me; I didn't recognize it as a handliner. As we got closer, we saw that it was a sailboat. *What the fuck?* As we pulled right up next to the buoy and with a closer inspection, we found some type of old fishing schooner. They were actively hauling longline gear right next to the buoy when we arrived.

The three-man crew enthusiastically waved at us as they went about their work of hauling gear. We drove around the buoy and saw absolutely nothing. *Just fucking great. Totally awesome*, I thought. I positioned the boat directly down current of the buoy and pulled her out of gear. In the greasy flat water, we hardly moved, drifting less than a tenth of a knot to the south. The water clarity was absolutely as good as it gets in the ocean. Brett lackadaisically tossed in anchovies, and we watched them slowly drift farther and farther down until eventually slipping out of sight. *Looks like no one's home today. Guess we better hope something lives around here at night.*

The *Kiami Kai*, the sailboat already fishing, finished hauling their gear. The captain hailed us on VHF radio, introducing himself as Pauly. After some idle chitchat about our boat, we learned he actually had worked on it in years gone past. I put two and two together and figured out I actually knew the captain. However, this would be my first formal meeting. I had fished next to him for years, and unbeknownst to me at the time, we would come to fish around him a lot in following years. Although he was unaware of it, we always referred to him as the token white guy. He was tall and lanky, and his complexion was very much Caucasian. He stood out like a sore thumb on the back deck of the boat captained by a local Japanese man and otherwise crewed by Micronesians and Hawaiians.

We eventually got around to the only subject I was truly interested in and really was concerned with. I inquired, "How was the fishing?" Pauly reported that a large pile of bigeye tuna had been coming and going from the buoy. But they weren't really biting. They had caught some big pieces on the diamond jigs over the last couple of days right before sundown, but that was it. Pauly claimed they were primarily focusing on trying to catch larger yellowfin on their longline gear and were having marginal success, some sets catching some, some sets nothing. However, they had caught over a hundred nice mahi mahi. We shared a couple more exchanges and said our goodbyes.

At about the same time I hung up the microphone, Brett excitedly blurted out, "Yo, yo." I knew what that meant. He saw some fish. I eagerly put on my gloves. I came out of the cabin to see a sight for welcomed eyes—bigeyes in the teen- and a twenty-pound class eating anchovies. They weren't big, but they were fish. And we needed fish. We started to catch them on our palu lines, which basically are the same exact thing as the float lines we use at night. But they aren't tied off. We fished them side by side directly out of our hands. Generally speaking, we'd throw a handful of anchovies out at the same time that we tossed our line, which is also baited with an anchovy on a circle hook, the idea being that multiple free meals will drive competitive feeding amongst the schooling fish. They'll overlook the hook until it's too late.

We were steadily catching teens when suddenly three bigeyes appeared. They ranged from eighty to ninety pounds, and they greedily came to the surface pushing the small fish out of the way. We each hooked one immediately. The palu lines screamed through our hands. "Fuck yeah!" I yelled in pure joy as we each gaffed and dragged our fish over the low sides of the boat minutes later. The beautiful fish glistened side by side, and Brett and I fist-bumped each other in approval while squishing tuna blood and anchovy juice from our yellowish-orange outer gloves, known as snot gloves for the clear rubbery plastic honeycomb grip with which they are coated. We'd also sometimes call them Cheeto gloves, because your hands would look like Cheetos when they were brand new. We wore these outside of flexible yet strong blue PVC rubber gloves for additional grip and protection. We refer to them as our power steering units, mostly because of how much more control they give you on the line (as opposed to just the rubber gloves or cloth gloves alone). I knew men who fished bare-handed, attempting to prove something I've never understood. Although they got the job done, they were never as efficient as those of us who used gloves. They'd eventually get hurt on some level and could never take as many back-to-back trips as we did. Remember, as a fisherman, your hands are one of the most important tools you have. So, I've always done everything in my power to protect them.

As the fish flopped around on the boat, we clubbed them with custom Amazonian hardwood bats that looked like war clubs. Brett had made them for us while marlin fishing down in Brazil just the winter before. We then bled out the fish by cutting the collars behind each side of the gill rakers.

I competitively noted that Brett's fish were larger than mine. The best crews with which I have fished always seem to have that competitive desire to catch more and larger fish than the guy standing next to his mate. I didn't have to mention the fish-size difference to Brett, as I'm sure he already noted it as well. We are all on the same team, working together in the big picture, but it's that additional motivation and desire that ultimately adds up to bigger loads and bigger paychecks for everyone.

We continued to steadily harvest smaller fish on the surface until it was time to finally pack them away. We had caught about a thousand pounds of bigeye in about a half hour on just two palu lines. Unable to truly know what was under us besides what we could see on the surface, we had no idea of how large of a pile on which we were sitting. Since I didn't have a working fish machine, I feared putting the boat in gear and possibly losing the pile. A school can be very temperamental; sometimes, you can't shake a pile no matter how fast and hard you go. But more often than not, they don't respond well to boats changing speed while side drifting. I wouldn't have a fish machine to get back on top of them if they bolted. So, with all these factors in mind, I conservatively drifted, not attempting the big hit with a dangle rush. We processed and packed the fish away. We then pounded down a victory Gatorade and threw some more anchovies onto the surface. However, after taking a break, nothing came to the surface to feed.

*Jigs perhaps?* I thought without mentioning a word. I dropped my chrome-plated A67 diamond jig down on my all-monofilament jig spool. I dropped the jig to the first inline swivel that marked twenty-eight fathoms of 400-pound test J line. It was the length of one whip of that brand of monofilament and coincidentally my favorite depth to start jigging at. It always worked out perfectly as a marker to gauge my jig's depth. I wrapped the line once around my right hand, preparing to jig it toward the surface like a fleeing fish. I just barely flicked my wrist once, slightly twitching it at depth, and it got piled on by a freight train.

The swivel went blistering around my gloves despite my best effort to slow it down. It shot off my gloves like a rocket. It quickly took me through two more sets of swivels and then into the final section of the handline that we call the ohh fuck line. We call the final section that because 99 percent of the time those are the words that are coming out of your mouth if the fish has gotten you down that far into the spool. You are desperately trying to survive the fish run at all costs. It's the last ten fathoms of 800-pound test that you have before hitting the spool. In that ten fathoms, you need to either take it or break it, so to speak. You either need to get the fish heads turned or get ready for something to break, preferably not your hand. On the ohh fuck line the most dangerous shit happens in our business as you do everything in your power to not have the spool ripped out of your hands.

The ohh fuck line rarely ends well. Gloves are in tatters, hands are smashed, profuse swearing is a given. Spools launch up and smash people from every angle. Gloves get ripped off at 100 miles an hour. In my years of running an offshore handline boat, two crewmen have been yanked over the side of the boat, both entangled in the ohh fuck line. Thankfully, each person made it back into the boat alive—both shaken and fairly beat up, but alive all the same.

This fish got me into the final fathoms before I could finally get a quick set of double wraps on my left hand as my right hand was giving its all to slow the line down. I dumped the single wrap off my right hand before the two hands met, twanging off my glove like the sound of a 22-caliber rifle. I grabbed around my left hand with my right, locked my body and knees under the covering board, and assumed the position for something to break off as my arms got stretched out as far as they could without being ripped off. Then it happened—much to my surprise, I turned her. She didn't break off as predicted. She broke before the line did. I stood up and started painstakingly pulling her bulky mass to the surface, one single wrap at a time, alternating back and forth between my right and left hand.

A few times, she would rip a couple of fathoms off, but she would never again regain the momentum of her initial run. Foot by foot, inch by inch, I pulled her up. She swam in large circles that got tighter and tighter as she tired and neared the surface. She was big. I could see her ominous blue-silver glow from twenty fathoms down. Her lovely shine got brighter and bigger as she ascended reluctantly to the surface. When her head popped out from underneath the boat, it was confirmed—she was a slob. I fired a metal slap gaff straight into her massive head. I could barely get her over the rail on my own. Brett could not help me because he too was now yanking on a large fish. It took little more than two seconds of my fish ripping line out of my hands before my man Brett had a jig descending. Brett had also hooked up instantly. He was now reefing on his fish.

Brett possesses the physical trait that is known as being "retard strong," also sometimes stated as one being retardedly strong. There generally was no way of telling how big of a fish Brett was pulling on because of the way he absolutely put the wood to them. Brett could kick a fish's ass on a jig like no one I've seen before or since. A combination of being a world class wireman and having a grip that could smash walnuts made him a worthy adversary to even the meanest tuna.

Our good fortune continued as we drifted slowly away from the buoy, catching one large bigeye after another on the jig. We caught ten more fish in a row that weighed over eighty pounds. There was no sign of any other sailboat in sight; they must have been taking the afternoon off. We got lucky. So we again stopped. We gilled and gutted our fish and packed them into the icy brine. As I stuffed the final body cavity of the last fish from round two, my heart nearly stopped when I heard that job-stealing Lazy Boy clear as day calling us on the VHF. Sure enough, he had snuck into the buoy when we were packing our fish away.

I had the unfortunate job of reporting to him how terrible the fishing had been and that we hadn't even marked a fish yet. The second part was at least true anyway. I told him how Pauly was also here and how he was napping the afternoon away in hopes that some fish would show soon. Lazy Boy grilled me intensely about what we had been catching, most likely probing for irregularities in the story. He was most concerned about whether we were sitting on a pile. He knew a pile was hanging around just last week, so it concerned him that it had suddenly disappeared. I emphasized that we all knew how hit and miss the buoys are. Now, he could have driven a mere thousand feet and called my bluff, but living up to his nickname and reputation, he instead decided to leave the buoy after only trying for five minutes. He had driven 272 miles to only take one lap of the buoy and then leave. We were laughing our asses off. We knew he was a burnout, but this was next-level lazy. "What a lazy fucker. Gets what he deserves," Brett said matter-of-factly. Brett called him a fucking dickhead for good measure as he gave the boat the finger with one hand and grabbed his balls with the other as he steamed out of sight.

Lazy Boy now gone, we went back to absolutely kicking the shit out of the eighty-plus pound bigeye on the jigs, catching and packing nonstop, slowly drifting farther and farther from the buoy. The tuna loyally stayed with us. The jig bite was absolutely phenomenal. One or two slight twitches, and you were on. Another boat showed up on the horizon somewhere around the 5,000-pound mark. However, this boat came from the west and was considerably larger than us. So we just assumed it was a longliner heading to Oahu and didn't pay it much attention. For the most part, large-scale longliners can't be bothered to fish around weather buoys. So we went about happily jigging and catching the fuck out of them.

Then we heard a voice calling us. We immediately recognized it. The voice referred to our boat by its original name. "*Ao Shibi*, you on this one? Hello, hello, *Ao Shibi*, you on this one?" It was Joe Dentley. Joe, with the biggest handline boat in the fleet and who also happened to have longline gear. As the boat neared, the distinct catamaran design came into focus. Surer than shit, it was old Joe. What the hell was he doing coming in from out west of the westernmost buoy? I called him back on the radio, and he was surprised to hear my voice. He didn't know I wasn't still on the *Makana*. Apparently, he was lurking around the buoy the day before and had only caught a couple of fish on his longline gear; and since Pauly was around, he had decided to try throwing his longline gear on another Seamount about twelve miles west of the buoy.

He caught a few otaru, a couple of spearfish, some marlin, and one yellowfin. This was definitely not enough fish to be worth his time, so he was double-checking the buoy to see if the fish had come back. Joe is the oldest handliner in the fleet. He is no pushover. He's been doing it so long he literally invented dangler bars. He's also one of the most aggressive people you will ever see on a pile. He will make full-speed trolling passes with his eighty-foot catamaran literally three feet off your bow. He had the real potential to fuck this up for us.

The biggest problem with Joe coming at your pile is that he doesn't stop and work with you. Being in his late sixties at the time, Joe wasn't going to be drifting side by side working a jig. He was looking for a trolling or dangling bite. Joe has dragged a pile off my bow more times than I can count. Sometimes, he catches fish doing it. I remember one time watching him catch twenty-one big ones just trolling off our bow. However, most times he just fucked the fish off, totally ruining it for us. I couldn't afford that right now. So, I lied and told him we hadn't caught shit in order to keep him from getting too close. I literally had Brett stop pulling on the fish he was yanking on and sit down like he was doing nothing, all while he actually had a nice fish double wrapped on his hand cleated off like a boat to a dock.

He made it look effortless with his retarded powers. Fortunately, Joe didn't come right in like he would have had he known we had a pile. Not to say Joe fully trusted us, because he didn't. He watched us like a hawk with his binoculars while Brett nonchalantly sat on the fish box with a look of total boredom and an eighty-pounder tugging on his line. I kept engaging Joe in meaningless conversation so he would step back inside his cabin and put down his binoculars he had pointed at us. After about forty-five minutes of this charade, Joe was equally convinced the buoy was dead and he headed to the mountain.

We had survived the competition. As night fell, we had about 7,500 pounds of fish. Several fish weighed over 100 pounds, even with the gill and guts removed. This was an awesome class of fish and an awesome load for our fishery, seeing our average fish was generally twenty-five to forty pounds. We caught a couple more fish right before sunset. Brett made dinner as I now worked the ika shibi lines with the ika from a few days earlier. After two hours without a bite, we wrapped the lines up and went to sleep gambling on the fish still being under the boat in the morning.

I woke the next day very sore and very much in need of relieving myself. As I sat on the five-gallon bucket doing my business, I reached over and grabbed three anchovies from an open case of bait that was within arm's reach and winged them over the side. All three anchovies were consumed by fish in the fifty-pound class.

I woke Brett up, cracked open my daily Red Bull breakfast, and put my orange Grundens rain pants on over my same very filthy, very lucky shirt that I couldn't be bothered to change before I had passed out in my bunk the night before. I excitedly told him about the fish still being under the boat. I hauled in and stowed away the sea anchor in the bow anchor locker as Brett got ready. Once I had the sea anchor put away, I hurriedly ran back to throw bait. But this time nothing came to the surface. *Damn. What a tease.* I kept throwing palu, but nothing came up. *Well, looks like we are back onto the jigs.* The jigs worked, but it was a much, much slower pick. The fish varied in size, mostly on the smaller size. The bite had completely shut by ten thirty a.m., and we wondered if anything remained under the boat. We now had about 8,200 pounds of fish. It was a great trip. We would have loved to fill up on our first trip, but we came close.

I put the boat in gear for the first time in over twenty-four hours. I pushed the throttles up to about 1,000 RPMs and had the wheel at about twenty-one degrees to starboard. The boat made a hard circle at about three and a half knots. After tossing out the trolling lines and danglers, Brett now steadily and rhythmically threw anchovies in a constant stream, one at a time, making a chum line of bait the fish could follow right up to the danglers if they so desired. It didn't look like it was going to happen after a few full circles. I was glad I hadn't attempted it sooner and fucked the pile off. I was about to go inside the cabin and punch in the course for home. But then it started, first as a large boil far back in the chum line, then another and again another. "Here they come!" I said as excitedly as a man can speak about anything that involves wearing clothing. The trolling lines went off first, peeling line off the hydraulic reels with unusual ease.

I took over the chumming, and Brett ran back to start yanking on the lines, but he never made it that far because about five anchovies later all hell broke loose. Every dangler had an eighty-pounder absolutely losing its fucking mind—the best kind of chaos. Fish frantically threw white water higher than the canopy and all over us. The blood flowed like champagne on New Year's Eve. The bats sounded like warmups at Fenway Park, each home run swing determined to clear the green monster. These gorgeous fish were sacrificing themselves to feed man's appetite along with our souls. Despite the desire of the fish to aggressively feed, it was obvious we had to stop and assess our ice and room situation.

We pulled all of the lures out of the water and again pulled the boat out of gear. When we finished packing the fish, we were absolutely hatched for the amount of fish we could carry. Larger fish take up more space and leave more voids in the boxes, especially if you don't have smaller fish to fill the gaps in the brine. We could carry over 12,000 pounds with a full load of smaller fish and mixed sizes. However, we ended up with a little over 10,200 pounds because of the size of the fish. It was an absolute awesome start. We couldn't have asked for a better outcome. Larger fish are usually worth more money per pound than small fish, but sometimes the market dictates otherwise. Larger tuna generally holds a higher value because not only is the meat quality usually better but also because the larger loins are viewed as being more aesthetically appealing for sushi dishes. Sushi chefs and other high-end restaurants and their chefs prefer working with the larger loins for the visual appeal on a plated dish. We were excited about our load.

With the boat on autopilot, we cranked the Counting Crows's album *Films about Ghosts*. It remained on a steady loop as we scrubbed away happily for hours. We laughed and joked all the while. It was an uncommonly flat ocean that resembled an infinite tabletop. The visibility was endless and so seemed the possibilities. The old girl sat much lower in the water but clearly was standing again a little taller. She contentedly steamed home, feeling heavy and validated. When I finally found myself again behind her helm, I cocked my head to the right and leaned onto her cabin wall like a high school sweetheart does on one's shoulder.

I was falling in love.

# CHAPTER 4

# THE GIRL IN THE GREEN HAT

In 2007, I had just completed another season on the Great Barrier Reef. While in Cairns, Australia, I worked on big game fishing boats for giant black marlin. Cairns is home to the greatest heavy tackle fishery in the world, with anglers catching more fish here over a thousand pounds than any other place in the world. In a typical season, one in five fish you catch in Cairns will often surpass the 800-pound mark. No other marlin fishery in the world compares to these statistics and monstrous fish. The fish and the crews that ply these waters are things of legends. If you fancy yourself a fisherman, it would be a cardinal sin to die with enough money in your bank account to have fished the Great Barrier Reef, but chosen not to have done so.

Having gotten hammered drunk on Bundaberg Rum and shacked up with a Swedish backpacker on my last night in Cairns, I managed to miss my flight home. Apparently, I misread my itinerary whilst half in the bag the evening before. Instead of boarding my flight home like I should have, I instead found myself leisurely drinking a flat white at this girl's hostel while trying to tune out some French douchebag name Peri who wouldn't stop trying to engage me in a conversation about President Bush and US politics, like all French men seemingly do. It was time for me to leave after enduring as much earfucking as one could possibly handle. I said, "Listen, Frenchy, you'd be speaking German if it wasn't for my grandfather and his homeboys coming to the rescue right now. Try not to forget that." He looked totally disgusted. I tipped my lucky Red Sox hat, said "God Bless America," and never looked back at that cock.

Upon my arrival to the airport, I discovered that I had completely blown it on my flights. Due to airline scheduling, I would now have to take the four-hour flight south to Sydney and spend the night there in order to fly out the following evening. What can you do? The flight to Sydney was uneventful, and, without a problem, upon arrival I found midlevel accommodations not far from downtown.

Never a man to stay in for the evening in a foreign place, I went out for a nice early dinner down by an area called The Rocks. I dined at an open-air restaurant and indulged on prawns followed by Moreton Bay bugs, all chased down with a Jack Daniels neat. The perfect air temperature made for a very satisfying meal. As my extremely cute Australian waitress covered all the fun things she recommended I do this evening in town, I recalled thinking how much I truly loved the people and country of Australia. If I was ever to have been born in another country besides the United States, I would want it to have been here.

Following my waitress's recommendations, I went down to the Sydney Opera House to catch the remnants of sunset. I sat upon the fabled steps, admiring the view with countless others from all around the world. Together, we stared at something and yet nothing in particular. When one looks at the horizon above any body of water for long enough, they often find self-reflection in the distance.

A man will forget many things in his lifetime, but he will never forget the moment he bears witness to the most beautiful woman he has ever seen. For me, that moment occurred on those very steps. She had chosen to sit a little more than four feet away from me. She was slim but not too slim; tall but not too tall. She was very well endowed, curvy, and strong. She had the complexion of a perfectly tanned angel. Her hair was long and naturally blond, drawn back into a ponytail she wore below a large green sunhat that looked like it belonged at the horse races. She wore a flawless all-white mini-dress with midrange high heels that accentuated the muscles on her calves. She appeared to be a goddess.

I tried to look away, but I kept finding myself staring, in awe of her. She caught my glimpse and said, "It's beautiful, isn't it," gesturing toward the setting sun in an accent that sounded like she came from somewhere between South Africa and Australia. "You most certainly are. I mean, I mean it certainly is," I said, stumbling out my words like a total idiot. I closed my eyes and faced straight ahead, confident I'd just blown it. *Really? That's the fucking best you could do?* I sighed. Clearly it was audible enough for the girl in the green hat to hear. She said, "It's not that bad, you know."

"What's that?" I replied.

"You calling me beautiful."

"Oh yeah. Sorry about that," I said.

She smiled. "Well, mate, I did decide to sit next to you and not the other way around."

"You most certainly did," I replied, the blood now flowing through me like a hit of adrenaline.

Now, I have been very fortunate for some reason—and completely unbeknownst to me why—to have had some extremely attractive women come into my life. But this one took the cake. She was a whole different animal by any metric. We hit it off like a house on fire. We talked and talked a little bit about everything and a whole lot about nothing in particular. We laughed and laughed and laughed some more. We thrived on each other's sarcasm. I introduced myself and told her my friends call me "Captain K."

"That's cute," she said, never once volunteering her name. I didn't press the issue.

Somehow, we landed on the subject of what I did for a living. The idea of catching and releasing fish as a livelihood made no sense to her whatsoever.

"So, like you just torture them and let them go? I mean, I understand catching fish to eat, I get that. But why would people pay all this money just to hurt a fish and then let it go?"

"Well, it's like going to South Africa to hunt. But instead of killing all the animals, we only keep a handful of very special big fish for either world records or if we're trying to boat the elusive grander for someone who wants to keep one," I explained. She asked about the term "grander." I explained that long before my time, someone had coined the word, referencing a marlin over a thousand pounds. It has since become a metric by which one measures their fishing accomplishments in the industry, both as an angler and part of a crew. It is a special thing to actually kill a grander. It's very easy to say you released one just by touching the leader and getting it boat side. It's a whole other animal to actually put one in the boat.

When she asked if I had accomplished that goal myself, I spoke about how I had finally been part of a team to accomplish that very feat this past season. However disappointingly the sensation, it was nothing like I had envisioned it would be. She wondered what I meant.

"The actual capture was awesome," I explained. "That part did not disappoint. I was fortunate enough to be the one who got to feed her and hook the leviathan when it came up to consume the freshly rigged twelve-pound scaley mackerel we pulled as a skip bait."

I went on to tell her the rest of the story, explaining that the grander was a difficult fight, displaying the characteristically stubborn marathon-runnerlike qualities black marlin are known for and the amazing aerial acrobatics more commonly associated with her sprinter cousin the blue marlin. She was beautiful yet possessed beastly qualities. She was graceful yet her stancher opposing. Though her voice silent, as she leaped from the sea she appeared to roar like a lion from a cavernous void that was her mouth.

Her giant head and mouth looked as if it could have swallowed a fifty-five-gallon drum if she so desired, I told the girl in the green hat. She jumped alongside the boat not as if in fear but as if to stare down and threaten her opponents. The slight gulp in my throat and the foreign shake I felt in my hands and knees let me know it was an effective technique. She was incredible, humbling, and truly deserving of freedom, and most days she would have easily won it. But not on that day. On that rare day, years of man's experience, waiting, wanting, and luck would be with us, not her.

The captain of the vessel, Ross Finlayson, masterfully chased and outmaneuvered the sea monster as she attempted to go farther and farther out into the depths of the Coral Sea. The other crewman, Brad Fergus, a world-class wireman who possesses wiring skills far superior to anyone else I've ever fished with, did an artful and skillful job of wrapping the final thirty feet of 040 galvanized wire around his gloved hands to get the fish within gaff range. Brad incredibly held on through a series of breathtaking boat side jumps without breaking the 400-pound wire that may very well have been his Mona Lisa. I remember thinking I was watching a man paint his masterpiece.

Once Brad shortened the distance enough, I satisfyingly sunk in the first gaff just behind her massive shoulder. Our good friend and renowned marine artist and photographer Craig Smith sacrificed his own craft to help insure ours. He put down his camera and picked up a gaff, perfectly thrusting the second, flying into the desired spot upon her hump. With some difficulty, I managed to cleat off the first two gaffs. Ross ran downstairs and fired the third of the four gaffs that would eventually find their way into her.

She went hard on the flying gaffs, making the cleated off ropes ache and creek like a vessel tied to a dock in a storm, her giant forked tail a shovel for the buckets of water, which she forcefully cascaded over twenty-five feet in the air. After a long succession of death blows administered by a large hardwood bat called a donger in Australia, this brightly glowing creature was finally subdued. Marlins turn an unearthly electric blue when they pass on. I believe that blue-light glow is truly the fish's soul shining one last time to remind us of its significance and importance. I'd never seen a fish shine more before nor since. All these years of yearning for this moment seemed encapsulated in that shine—a shine that was over in minutes but still glows in my mind today. I was excited and grateful. The physical capture was everything I could have ever hoped for and more.

The part that left a bad taste in my mouth, I explained to my now-rapt listener, was the unappreciative angler that went by the nickname the Big C. He was a fat New Yorker who was a total pain in the ass on the boat and no good for his word. He spent the majority of his days either sitting on his ass wearing his billboard sized T-shirts he had custom made to say "Big C" in large lettering or antagonizing me about something. He was so large he couldn't properly wipe his ass in the small head of the game boat, leaving one of our daily tasks to clean up his shitballs off the floor or wipe the streaks off the wall. Now, I have never marlin fished for the money, but rather because I truly love it.

But our shipmates promised us a big tip if we captured the grander Big C was searching for over the course of thirty years. At a bare minimum, it's industry standard to tip each member of the crew a dollar a pound for the weight of a grander. This is on top of the regular tip the crew would normally receive, regardless of killing a fish or not. So, in our case, we each should have gotten $1,102 plus a sizable tip because it was a sixteen-day charter. Industry standard is a hundred dollars per crew member per day, minimum. That put us on the low end of looking at getting $2,702 per person. Since Big C promised a huge tip between the moments of bragging about owning a 288-car collection and the rental income his skyscrapers captured in New York City, we figured we were looking at the sky being the limit. Now, I certainly never normally judge a person by the size of the tip they leave unless they are the asshole type who brags about money the entire trip like our good friend Big C here did.

It wasn't even how little he left us that really got to me. It was the way he placed it in my hand and said condescendingly, "Now, don't go spending it all in one place like you deckies always do." Big C never even said thank you for all our hard work. At the dock you wouldn't have even known a crew was on board to help him capture that fish.

I then explained to my new friend that I took his measly 700 Australian dollars that he had painstakingly weeded out from be-tween two inches of solid Benjamin Franklins with surgeonlike precision. I placed them behind my driver's license in my ratty old wallet my ex-girlfriend had given me my freshman year of college. I was now saving this money to do something special and prove Big C wrong about all us deckies.

After relating this story, I suggested we go out for a drink. She agreed and grabbed my hand, taking the lead. I followed her down the stairs to a taxi cue. I would have followed this woman straight into the gates of hell if she asked me to. I was in total awe of her—not just her looks but also her confidence and demeanor. She stopped traffic and turned heads as we walked. I knew I was punching way above my weight with this one. She was a total absolute smokeshow. We entered the taxi, and she informed the driver that we were heading to the casino.

We got to the casino and ordered some drinks. We then walked around, drinking and losing. We had some drinks at the craps table and lost money there. We had some drinks at the slot machines and lost a little more over there. Our drinking and money lasted longer at the blackjack tables, but even there our drinks and winning streak dried up. The more we drank, the flirtier we became. Although I was hemorrhaging money like crazy, I was the luckiest guy in the casino.

It would be at the three-card poker table that we would call it a night. We were about a million drinks deep at this point, getting more and more handsy along the way. I had happily blown about a quarter of all my season's wages that evening. I was flirting on the edge of losing all my available money in my wallet, aside from Big C's money that was still stashed behind my ID. I had $503 in chips in front of me and now the most attractive woman I'd ever seen nibbling on my ear. I played a $100 hand with the one-dollar bonus kicker. I lost.

"Do it again," the girl in the green hat whispered in my ear. She breathed heavily on my neck, making every hair on my body stand up. Like I already said, I would have done anything this woman asked me to. So I did. Again, I immediately repeated the bet and lost.

Kissing on my neck, she told me to put all of it in this time. I stuck my one piece on the dollar bonus and pushed my remaining $300 out to the wager circle. "No," she said, grabbing me firmly by the crotch. "I want it all in, and I want it all in now," she said. She had my full upright attention as I sat down. "Now is the time to put that fat ass's money on the line," she said. "Give it to me. Give it to me now." She was extremely convincing, so I took out the $700 I had saved for an occasion exactly the opposite of this one. The dealer cashed me in for another $700, and the girl in the green hat pushed the money straight into the wager circle with her available hand to join my other remaining $300 in chips. "Don't worry," she whispered in my ear. "Don't you know, Captain K, the third time is always the charm." I honestly did not give a fuck. As this woman held me, all I could think about was taking her back to my hotel and fucking her. By my logic, the sooner my money was gone the sooner that was going to happen.

The dealer dealt the cards, and I watched only halfheartedly as the girl in the green hat ran her fingers through my hair. I wanted this girl so bad. The first card was an ace. *Good start*, I thought. Then another ace to make a pair. The final card was yet another ace. *Holy fucking shit!* I had just gotten the best possible hand with the bonus dollar in place and a thousand-dollar bet. A pit boss came over and instructed us to keep our hands away from the table as they would have to do a video camera review for security purposes. When a muffled voice came through the pit boss's earpiece, he confirmed it was a clean and legitimate win. The casino paid me two to one on the wager and an incredible forty to one on my wager for the three-aces bonus. I jumped up in celebration, and the wall of alcohol apparently hit me all at once.

I woke up in the most comfortable bed I can ever recall sleeping in with the best-looking woman I had ever laid eyes upon lying naked beside me. We were in the nicest suite I'd ever seen, and I had the worst fucking headache imaginable. The bedside radio alarm clock played Ben Lee's "Catch My Disease" and pointed out that for the second day in a row, I had missed my flight. I couldn't have cared less. I'd have to fill some gaps in from the evening, but those could wait. I went to the bathroom, hopped back in bed, and threw my arms around Lady Luck. I wouldn't wake again for several hours.

Both awake, she was feeling frisky. So, we did what adults do. She explained that because of the severity of my intoxication, I had stood up from the table and immediately fallen over. The casino comped me a suite generally reserved for whales and high rollers. Also due to the large amount of money I had on the table, they had locked my chips in the cage for my protection. *What a night,* I thought, as I lay there half groggy and in half disbelief.

The girl in the green hat called down, informing the casino that Mrs. Geer and her husband wished to again gamble tonight if the suite was available. As luck would have it, it just so happened that it was available for the next two nights. The casino obviously wanted to win their money back.

"Mrs. Geer, huh?"

"Someone had to sign you into your room," she said with a smirk.

"What is your name anyway?"

"My friends call me Helen."

"Helen what?"

"Helen Day."

Helen and I had the greatest time over the next thirty-six hours. We never even left the room. We enjoyed room service, watched movies, talked, and bonded. We seemed to connect on every level. She was very well traveled, and she loved to do all the things I liked to do. She seemed to come from money but didn't speak of it directly. I found her absolutely intriguing. I couldn't believe my luck on so many levels—the girl, the money. Just incredible.

But her exit was to be as mysterious as her arrival into my life. I caught her leaving in the middle of the night, her body just a silhouette covered with that big signature hat.

"Where are you going?" I asked.

She said it was time for her to go.

"Go where?"

"Home," she said.

"Where is that?"

She said nothing.

"You weren't going to say goodbye?"

"I don't do goodbyes," she said.

"Well, what about farewell then?" I smirked.

"I'll never forget you, Captain K. Will you forget me?"

I told her I would as soon forget the ocean as I would ever forget her.

We embraced in a kiss that still lingers. She sauntered gracefully down that hotel corridor with a giant piece of my heart that I knew I was never getting back. I would search for this Helen Day for many years by every means available to me, never once finding anything. It appeared this lady of mystery had given me an alias.

I never went gambling again on that visit with anything other than my heart. When I checked out of the hotel, I still had over forty thousand Australian dollars, which converted at the time to roughly a little over 29,000 USD. The remaining balance of the girl in the green hat's winnings made up the majority share of the money I was able to save toward purchasing the *Vicious Cycle*. I had only known her for mere hours, but she forever changed my life.

# CHAPTER 5

# THE HIGHS AND LOWS OF A FISHERMAN'S LIFE

Even when the offshore life proved difficult, it was hard to argue its beauty. Dawn on the Penguin Bank was often surreal, with the cliffs of Diamond Head to the north and the sun rising over the hills of Molokai to the east. Pink Hawaiian skies, highlighted by streaking beams of light, accentuated an array of vibrantly painted clouds of all shapes and varieties. Dark, rich purple water and greasy flat sea conditions made a living oil painting not only for the eyes to indulge in but also for one to physically touch; light sea sprays upon the skin were as comforting as a distant hug. Hands and fingers ran through these gleaming waters, bringing joyful memories of warm childhood baths.

The hordes of elegant humpback whales were returning from their yearly pilgrimage from Alaska and the Pacific Northwest, a beautiful caliper of another year gone past. These giant, majestic creatures going airborne while breaching was awe inspiring, something to behold. There truly is nothing like the sight of a forty-ton marine mammal jumping repeatedly in and out of the water like a child in a puddle. Their sheer mass could possibly make them seem imposing, but their overwhelming grace makes them more than welcoming. The whales return to one another, always feeling more like a reunion than a casual happenstance.

In my early twenties, I was free diving while working on a moored boat running gear in the crystal-clear waters of Kailua Bay. As I steadily worked away on the shaft zincs that needed to be replaced, a shove from behind startled me. I thought it was the quasiresidential tiger-shark local nicknamed "Tony the Tiger" or simply "Tony." With my heart just about pounding out of my chest, I turned around to find, to my extreme surprise and wonderment, a juvenile humpback whale literally six inches away inquisitively looking at me like a cat would watch a bird from behind a window. It was turning its head back and forth as if to get a closer look. I had to swim around the whale from underneath the boat to get to the surface to take a breath. Though fairly large compared to a human, it was the smallest humpback I'd ever seen. It must have been very young, and I most likely must have been the first human it had ever laid eyes upon.

The whale followed me to the surface and began slowly circling me while gently bumping me in a playful manner all while trying to figure out what the heck I was. As my heart rate returned to normal, I noticed junior wasn't alone. His full-grown mama sat under him like a submarine, her watchful eye on her baby from about thirty feet below. I couldn't believe what I was experiencing. A baby whale is large, and a full-grown humpback appears as a behemoth when you're in the water next to it. Baby whale did slow passes past me, and I ran my hands along its smooth sides. Despite the water actually being fairly chilly that morning, I was completely warm all over. Eventually, Mama whale also came up for air right beside me, carrying her baby close on the wing. I was wearier of her movements and actions, as her raw size alone demanded respect. She had the elegance of a lady, but I knew like all mothers she could be a lioness if she felt her baby was in peril. I felt small but not insignificant. The ocean being my religion, I knew I was witnessing godliness.

Unbelievably, the whales continued to circle me. Eventually, I was even able to run my hands down Mama's back several times. Her black skin felt much tougher and tired. Remnants of barnacles made her skin rough in patches. She seemed more hesitant of this human. Perhaps she had firsthand evidence of man's horrible actions and treachery. I didn't blame her for her concerns. I had come to trust fewer and fewer humans myself. Her giant eyes possessed wisdom only found in the passage of time and miles traveled on long journeys. This once in a lifetime experience lasted approximately an hour and forty minutes, which is many life-times in length when it comes to interacting with nature on this level. The experience ended just as magically as it had begun. Though Baby was reluctant to leave, Mama made it clear it was time for me to return to the boat from which we had drifted a great distance away. She signaled for this by coming alongside me and effortlessly pushing me away with her massive fluke. It was clearly different than any other interactions we had. She didn't have to say anything, as I knew exactly what her actions meant.

Mama sank down to about sixty feet with Baby in tow. Three powerful fluent pumps of her massive tail and slight angle change and Mama breached so close that her splash pushed me away and completely consumed me. It was like a tidal wave washing over me. I couldn't believe how little energy she seemingly expelled to go completely airborne, her mass literally displacing tons of water from the ocean upon her reentry. Afterward, Baby quickly re-joined with Mama and I watched the whales swim briskly out of sight, continuing on their journey as I retreated back to the boat. I wondered if they would remember me as knew I would never forget them.

The rugged and secluded northeast coastline off the island of Hawaii, with its countless cascading waterfalls, imposing cliffs, and lush green valleys, was my favorite part of any commute I had over the years. I found its inaccessibility and raw beauty en-chanting. No roads. No buildings. Untouched and unmolested by man. Only pure nature as Mother Nature herself intended it to be.

I admired the large number of the handsome Hawaiian long-tail tropic birds that resided in this area. These tiny white birds left the comforts of their homes on these daunting cliffs to travel far out to the sea in search of food. I found their commute relatable and admirable. Though my work may have been closely mirrored by the lives of these determined birds, I saw my own reflection in the albatross, their large-winged cousin that also frequented these waters. These massive birds are awkward and clumsy on land. More often than not, you'll find them alone at sea. With six-foot wingspans and giant flippers for feet, you will only find their true grace offshore. At sea, they effortlessly glide just above the waves like a fighter jet. Upon water, they graciously paddle like a cruise liner. They are perfectly designed to be the rogue voyagers they are. I have often thought if I were an animal, I would like to be an albatross—that is, until one day when I realized that perhaps I had in fact already become one.

I've always felt the most comfortable in the grand presence of an albatross. This giant seabird has so many striking things in common with my own life that I wondered if I was actually look-ing into my own eyes when I stared into their dark brown eyes. Of all the albatrosses I loved, there was always one above the rest. The logbook of our first meeting read, "The most bizarre albatross you've ever witnessed followed the boat all day repeatedly land-ing on it. In a horribly awkward crash-landing sequence, I had to wonder each time if it survived. You would think it was trying to commit suicide. It has no interest in leaving the boat and gets up-set when you attempt to release him back in the water. It falls about the boat getting covered in blood and then spends hours contentedly preening. He enjoys being hand fed anchovies and poking at the tuna we catch. I have never seen this behavior be-fore. He has a band around his foot that reads B125. One is metal, one is plastic. Must find out what these mean."

This same bird would visit me time and time again that year. We nicknamed this odd duck "Pig Pen." I recall a length of time when Pig Pen didn't visit with us. In 2011, the logbook read, "Well, well, guess who is back? Good ole Pig Pen!!!" Piggy would visit with us for three trips and not be seen again until 2015. In July of that year, the logbook read, "Got the absolute living hell scared out of me while taking a leak. My old buddy Pig Pen came crashing in under the canopy, sliding under and hitting me from behind. It's truly the strangest bird ever." In its typical fashion, it would be around for a couple of trips and then nothing.

After a four-year absence, on March 3, 2019, I was reunited with my old buddy. *Nahh, it can't be,* I thought as this graceful yet clumsy bird strangely circled the boat. *How long do these birds even live?* I wondered. In the time it took me to get my camera out, ole Pig Pen was already piled up in a heap on the back deck. My buddy had returned, still gorging itself on all the anchovies it could handle and preening away for hours after rolling around in the action.

As luck would have it, when I returned from that trip, an ornithologist would stay at my Airbnb. He connected me to the right person to find out about my old buddy. It turns out my buddy was eighteen years old and banded as a chick at Midway Atoll. Pig Pen's sex was unknown. I also didn't know if he had ever been sighted at Midway again. My heart skips a beat, hoping that my old friend has once again returned whenever I see an albatross on the horizon gracefully flying low over the water like a B-52 bomber.

At night, fishermen are paid for their hard work with one of the Pacific's greatest views—the gates to the heavens above. Hawaii's remoteness to the rest of the world leaves the skies unpolluted by man's industrial byproducts and artificial light known on the mainland. A man can actually look back in time when he gets far enough away from the shores of Hawaii and leaves modern society behind. He will find a sky above him before the hustle and bustle of mankind, a place where a stunning display of rhythmically twinkling stars are the norm and planets lay boldly pronounced. Shooting stars are commonplace and so is the humbling feeling a man gets when looking at this masterpiece before him. The boat churns up neon-green phosphorescence that glows in the water below like fireflies. When the ocean is calm enough and the moon dark enough, it is completely impossible to tell where the earth ends and where the heavens begin.

Few would ever witness these experiences, and sadly others would take them for granted. Common of most truly beautiful things, moments like these were often the shortest despite leaving the longest lasting impression. The life of a fisherman is lived in epic highs and tremendous lows. The tabletop flat water on one occasion is often countered by seas of agony the following day. A fisherman is often rich one day and poor the next. With so many uncontrollable variables, your finances have the same certainty as a roll of the dice on the craps table. The weather, the moon, cyclic trends of the fish themselves, and, of course, supply and demand all play variable roles in the cycle of your life. A full boat doesn't guarantee riches nor does a small load ensure poverty. Fish pricing at the hands of fishmongers is much like a drug deal, giving you just enough money to go out and try again. Amazingly, the prices were always strong when you had little fish, however they always seemed to crash when you came in with a big load. Despite no evidence to back up the claims, word of big catches elsewhere would drive your price down. If it wasn't one side of the island rumored to be biting, then it was both.

The greatest moments of stress for me never actually happened out at sea. They occurred back at the fish auction. Fishing itself is pretty straightforward. You go to sea and try your best to bring in the highest quality load of fresh fish as quickly as you can. That part is pretty simple. I've always said that catching fish is the easiest part of the business. If you have a hard time catching fish, then you're never going to survive the rest of the business. If you don't have that part down, then the economical roller coaster and the unrelenting crew problems and maintaining your vessel will most likely break you in short order.

I have watched countless pipe-dreamers come and go from the fishing business. Most people who watch you unload a large load of fish have no idea of the real cost of catching them—the thousands of dollars in expenses, the years of devotion to get the necessary experience, the children's birthdays you missed, the holidays you unknowingly celebrate alone at sea, the damaging habits you inherit, the vices you call upon during the times of slow fishing, and, of course, the divorces and broken homes.

Tonnage of fish back at the dock is a false narrative of the life of a fisherman. Delusions of grandeur are commonplace around fishing piers all over the world. Land dwellers often wrongly think a boat is what makes you money. The truth is that a boat is merely a platform to carry the heart of a fisherman to the place that it belongs. A great boat is a lot like having a lot of money—it accentuates who you are as a fisherman, but it doesn't make you the fisherman. If you're an asshole when you're broke, then you're going to be an even larger asshole if you have a lot of money. If you're a kind, charitable person without money, then you're only going to be an even kinder, more charitable person with money.

If you're a great fisherman without a great boat, you're just going to be that much better of a fisherman behind the wheel of a great boat. You can give the poorest skilled fisherman the greatest boat in the world, and he will still be a failure, whereas you can give a true fisherman a shitbox and he will make do with it until something better comes along. The vessel you run doesn't make the fisherman; rather it is the fisherman that makes the vessel.

Just about every harbor in the world has an incredible fishing machine just rotting away in it. Often purchased by some rich parent or grandparent for an undeserving wannabe or perhaps for themselves, it seems people that don't earn their boats by working their way up the hawse pipe are always the first to fail out. What real incentive does a man working with a handout or spare money have to press on when the night is dark and the prospect of success even darker? If you want to survive in fishing, then you have to have the heart and tenacity to go straight back out fishing even after you've lost. If you should head out and lose again, be prepared to go do it all again with a smile.

We fishermen adapt. We create new markets. We fish smarter, and when all else fails, we work even harder. We are relentless, not because we are greedy but because that is who we are. We fanatically clean parts of our boats that no one else will see. We craft and engineer new fishing gear that may or may not work. We dream of fish when we sleep and speak of them when we are awake. The ocean haunts us and leaks into every avenue of our lives. That is fishing; that's how it works. We create our own luck. We write the story, and we don't sit around to hear about it. If you want to bathe in the ocean's riches, then you must be prepared to be flooded by her misery.

The Honolulu Fish Auction is both exciting and heartbreaking. You can make a small fortune in a day with your catch when the stars align. But when the cards do not play out favorably, you can find yourself dry heaving in stress as your hundred-pound ahi tuna is going for twenty to thirty cents a pound. A man will even begin to question his life's work when he loses hard enough or enough times in row on the auction. If you've never worked a month straight around the clock for no pay, it would be hard to explain the stress this can place on your family and your crew. If you've never stuffed your boat full of fish, only to owe money for the trip expenses after being up seventy-two hours straight, then it may be hard to rationalize why fishermen do this on a regular basis.

Loved ones will beg you to stay home but in the same breath refuse to stop mentioning how much money they need. They want you around more but want the all-mighty dollar just as much. So, though you may long for your warm bed at home, you know it will be freezing cold if you don't come home with money independent of how many blankets you pile upon yourself. Just because fish were worthless this month doesn't mean the mortgage or price of groceries was adjusted to reflect how terrible the auction was.

Fishermen don't play to fold. They will always play the bluff no matter how hard things get. We throw the dice no matter how broke or how leveraged we may be. Like any true gambler, we know the dice will eventually get hot again if we throw them hard enough. It's just a matter of surviving long enough to throw them enough times to find a winning streak.

The hottest the dice ever got for me was on September 12, 2012. It would be the icing on the cake for the largest money-making month of my fishing career, the timing of which could not have been better. I had been out of commission from fishing for nearly three months, which felt like a lifetime. Some asshole had decided to put muriatic acid in my fuel tanks when I was gone for the weekend visiting my wife and young family on the Big Island. This cowardly act of sabotage cost me tens of thousands of dollars in downtime and damages.

The muriatic acid ate its way past the filters and got into the tip of an injector, blowing the end off. The blown injector tip went through the head of the engine and totaled my six-month-old engine. I couldn't figure out who or why someone ever decided to fuck me over like this. I can only assume they were unaccomplished and a failure in our business, most likely blaming their poor fishing and prices on us. At that point in my life, I was religiously dropping off a load every week at the auction. I also thought the perpetrator might have been another jealous fisherman who had found out the auction had fronted me the money to buy the new set of engines. I knew the auction had declined loaning other fishermen money, but even then I had asked for help. In my experience, Frank Goto, the head of the auction, was a man of few words. But when I had asked him for the loan, he had said, "Yep. No problem."

He nodded in approval, and I shook his hand profusely. Just like that, he agreed to my $60,000 loan. Frank Goto was the real deal. He built the auction from the ground up. He was a fisherman's advocate and a good man. For this reason you'll never hear me say a bad word about the auction. Although I've left the auction feeling absolutely gutted, I truly do believe they have the fishermen's best interest in mind. The hardest part for a lot of fishermen to understand is that the market has really changed over the years. At one point, I could have been the auction's poster child, dropping off my load somewhere between Thursday and Saturday each week. I was making a lot of money, and I loved that place. It's extremely professionally run, and you get paid the same day, which is a huge advantage to the traditional seven-to-ten day pay period of most fish houses. For years, I sang the auction's praises.

When I finally got the boat back together and started fishing in the beginning of September, we kicked off the first trip of the month strong, grossing a little over $20,000 for five days. By any standard, this was a great trip for us. It also was what I needed to get the wheels turning in the right direction after the malicious act of terrorism I experienced. We loaded the boat right back up and left the same morning we unloaded, which was common for me at that time.

What happened next is a little blurry, as in my mind the actual catching was overshadowed by the amount of money they threw at us when we landed. It wasn't my greatest catch by any means. It wasn't my fastest fill-up, though we did fill the boat in one day. I don't even recall the tuna fishing being very exciting, and a one day fill-up is usually very exciting. The only thing I recall making my heart race was the barrage of large marlin attacks that trolled on our path to the tuna grounds. We rigged two chrome jet heads for catching tuna, and those big, angry marlins absolutely hammered them. The first marlin we caught was the only one small enough to keep on the ride out. Once it was gutted back at the auction, it weighed 390 pounds. We went on to release three other fish I estimated at 500 pounds, 700 pounds, and 750 pounds. I couldn't justify burning ice on these low-value fish. So, after steadily winding away on them, we got these magnificent sized fish alongside of the boat, removed the hooks, tipped our hats, and watched them gracefully swim away.

We hooked and lost another fish around the 500-pound mark, and that's when I told the boys to keep the lures in. The amount of big marlin in that section of water was absolutely ridiculous. It would be a sportfishing dream, but as a commercial fisherman it was actually a burden I couldn't afford. At the rate we were going, we were never going to make it to the sea mountain. Although the action was incredible and certainly the best day of marlin fishing I ever had off the Hawaiian coast, I was broke; and catching near worthless marlin wasn't helping the nagging from our homes. Although I love catching large marlin when I'm sportfishing, I just as soon not have to deal with them when I'm commercial fishing. They somehow always seem to know this fact and get in the way. Over the years, it's amazing how many big marlins I've caught in the middle of nowhere that it didn't make sense to keep. Instead, I would have loved to have hung on the scales if I were on a sport boat.

My boat had a good load for weight when we arrived back in

Honolulu, with a little over 8,500 pounds. There was nothing particularly special about the size of the fish or sheer overall weight. It was just an average catch, nothing more. With all the marlin delays, it took us thirty hours to get to the fishing grounds. But once we arrived, it took less than twenty-four hours to fill the boat with tuna. At the dock that morning, I knew there was going to be something different about that day. The fish buyers, who rarely could be bothered to come to the boat when you offloaded nor generally cared what this handline boat had in it, circled above us at the pier like vultures above a kill in the desert. They appeared desperate, and all inquired about what we had on board. My responses were converted into scribbles on sheets of paper and hand-covered cellphone conversations.

Apparently, the buyers needed these fish. Though my load was average, the prices they offered were not. When my first fish, a seventy-six-pound yellowfin, went for $13.90 a pound, I knew this wasn't going to be any ordinary day. It was strange in itself that the auction house put the less desirable yellowfin in line before the larger more desired bigeye tuna. The bigeye always went first on the auction. This was the only day I ever saw otherwise, but then again it was a one-of-a-kind day. My first bigeye went for $15.80 a pound. The prices were on fire. When the smoke settled, we had grossed a little over $62,000 for our actual day of fishing. Even our least valuable fish by price per pound, which was the marlin we caught on the way out, went for $4.20 per pound. This still stands as my best trip for money versus effort. Since I was 50 percent owner of the boat and the captain of the boat, I walked away with a little over $28,000 for one day of fishing and two days of driving.

I called this trip my "Rolex Trip," as I had always said I would buy myself a Rolex if I ever landed a pull on that little boat worth more than $50,000. I envied my sportfishing friends who had received them as bonuses and tips for great fishing or tournament wins. In my years of fishing the ole Casino, I never got close to winning a Rolex. So, one day I decided I would set a high goal and reward myself with one if I ever achieved it. At the time, I set the goal of a normal trip between $13,000 to $14,000, so $50,000 was a stretch but achievable if the stars aligned. When the moon was finally in the right place to make the dream a reality, my heart was in another place all together. With an eight-month baby at home, it seemed ridiculous to buy something so extravagant for myself. I went as far as even going to the Ala Moana Mall and trying on the green Submariner I desired. I looked at it from a thousand different angles, rotating it back and forth on my wrist. It certainly shined from every direction, but no matter what angle I put it at, it just didn't sparkle like the eyes of my little boy when I held him.

I left the mall and headed to the bank, still wearing my tired dive watch. Despite being scratched to hell and having fish scales and dried blood in every crevice, my old watch somehow seemed to be looking particularly proud this day. I was feeling proud too. When I deposited that check into my savings, I remember thinking, *This one's for you, Kandiddy*, the nickname I'd given my son Kanyon.

This trip was so financially awesome that I often overlook that I had my second-best trip ever just four days later. That trip grossed over $42,000. Within just one week, I grossed over $100,000. I would drop off five times in September, never once grossing less than $22,000. I hoped the person who spiked my fuel tanks was watching karma in action. His devious deed set my fishing into perfect calibration, setting a record twenty-two trips in a row where I wouldn't get less than $20,000 for my efforts. Even if the auction price was weak one day, I would kill it the next. I could do no wrong; it was unbelievable. It seems funny to say this, but if it wasn't for that asshole sabotaging me, I would have never been aligned for the best run in my fishing career. The amount of money I made in the months to follow surpassed any money I lost from the attack. Even if the following twelve months had been just an average year, I more than doubled my normal income.

I learned in those months that great things generally only last for so long, like the sunrises on the banks. It was to be no different on the auction floor. With the amount of money that was going daily across the auction, it was just a matter of time before bigger players arrived. I was filling a niche market when I made a lot of money on the auction. I was the local poke and sashimi guy. My fish weren't flying all over the world. I caught a nice grade of fish for domestic use but not much for exportation. Our handline-caught fish were staying right here in the islands for the people living and visiting Hawaii. Our handline fish, although far fresher than the longline fish, didn't have the shelf life that the longline fish generally had. We catch a great local product, but it has a much shorter shelf life for the buyers to work with. So, we always run second string to longline fish when they are available.

However, fish buyers happily used our local-caught fish when longline fish weren't available. When the handline fleet was doing really well on the auction floor, the Honolulu longline fleet basically consisted of about eighty-eight active longline vessels. Most were older and aging. The present day number is just short of double that, and the average-size vessel has greatly increased along with the amount of gear thrown into the water daily. With new and better boats came better technology. I would say that the satellite charting technology has been the single most powerful tool in capturing more tuna than in the past. With trained eyes supplemented by water temperatures from multiple depths, currents, salinity, plankton counts, and a plethora of other information from satellite charts, fish don't have many places to hide anymore. As more and more boats came with better technology to Honolulu, so came more and more longline fish arriving at Pier 38. I and the other handliners no longer had a niche to fill. Not only did the auction have its steady supply of longline fish, it was actually flooded more often than not. I and the other handliners were no longer needed or wanted. We started routinely seeing our larger fish going for less than a dollar a pound, commonly around fifty cents. Our smaller fish were going for the auction minimum of ten cents a pound.

If the influx of longliners wasn't bad enough, we were also

fighting the imports. This is the true kiss of death to all local fishermen. While we have had imports coming into our market for a very long time, the foreign-caught fish have completely infested our local markets today, so much so that most consumers don't realize they are eating foreign-caught fish. In fact, many restaurants don't even realize they are serving foreign-caught fish when it's substituted by a less than reputable fishmonger.

Local fishermen always do better when containers of poke cubes aren't readily available. We thrive in the years that massive shipping containers have a high rejection rate because of failing histamine testing at the port of entry or other foreign countries outbidding US buyers. Although modern society touts supporting local fishermen with fun hashtags like #supportlocal or #supportlocalbrah, they don't back it up with their spending. Those same people who would rant on social media about the evils of big business and the oppression of the little man will spend their money in poke markets that have the best deals or the cheapest fish. Foodland supermarkets, "Hawaii's home for poke," uses imported carbon monoxide-treated fish from Vietnam and Indonesia in its poke. Eating foreign-caught ahi in Hawaii is a slap to the face of every fisherman and all things Hawaiian. Hawaii has a long, rich tradition of being a community of fish-eating people, with the average resident eating two and a half times the yearly consumption to our counterparts on the mainland. Even early on, ancient Hawaiians understood the necessity of sustainable fishing. It was written early into the laws of the land, detailing what species can be harvested and when. From a very early time, they understood and respected spawning cycles. The original settlers of Hawaii had a far better connection and understanding of their environment than the droves of blue hairs and mainlanders who came later.

Thinking of tuna as a cheap food source takes away the whole significance of harvesting one of our truly last wild resources. The ocean is doomed until we get that idea out of consumers' consciousness. Until we value what we harvest, we will only encourage dirty fishing practices overseas whose final end products land right in America's lap. It costs money to do things the right way and the sustainable way. If you want the best product and the best for the ocean, you can't pick the cheapest. As anyone who knows anything about fish will tell you, cheap fish isn't good and good fish isn't cheap. The truth is that the foreign-caught fish tastes like shit to anyone with a discerning palate. However, it's generally saturated with other overpowering ingredients, so most people don't seem to notice or know any better.

Eating foreign-caught fish also comes with another price. You're not only gambling with your health from a lack of health regulations and histamines, but you're helping to pull the trigger on killing whales, dolphins, turtles, seabirds, and other marine life. Don't like the idea of killing a whale or whacking the fins off a shark just to watch it helplessly sink? Then don't eat foreign-caught tuna. Foreign fleets aren't highly regulated like the United States fleet. The Hawaii longline fleet is the most highly regulated longline fleet in the world, ensuring the best handling of your fish as well as the most sustainable fishing practices. The local Hawaiian trolling and handline fleet is probably the cleanest tuna fishery in the world, with next to no negative marine mammal interaction.

Foreign-caught fish don't come with that promise, although some areas might be doing it the right way. How would one know? The imports come with zero traceability, dodgy bills of lading, and the blood of marine mammals. Many foreign longline boats aren't worried about hooking a whale because they are going to keep it and kill it to sell if given the opportunity. Turtles are apparently just as tasty as whale and seabird. The Hawaiian fleet takes tremendous caution to protect and serve the safety of other mammals and birds. Sea life is as cheap on foreign boats as human life is back in their own countries. They care not what they leave behind, only of what they take. They think not of the future, and leave the ocean raped and bare.

The Honolulu auction today is a very different place than it was in the early and mid-2000s. I, like the other handline vessels, was forced to move back to the Big Island, where the prices were always more consistent and fair; but this place was much more difficult to run a business out of due to the lack of infrastructure for fishermen. The biggest problem is that we have the back-breaking job of physically loading our boats with fifty-five-gallon trash cans of melting ice we've driven halfway across town in Kona traffic versus just spraying the ice directly in the boat like is the case in Honolulu. For that reason, today we often take the 142-mile steam to Oahu to load up on ice and bait. The downside to this, of course, is that every five to seven days we spend commuting costs us the same amount of opportunity at sea.

For a few years after working off the auction, I fished for a company out of Hilo called Suisan. They had one particularly great fish buyer named Kyle, who worked really hard for us and the company. Kyle was a hustler. I watched him fill every and any job description required to get the job done. Aside from his mate Kalani Lewi, a hardworking and longtime employee of Suisan, he was almost always short-staffed. Kalani had been around as long as any modern fisherman could remember. Kyle and Kalani would start unloading 8,000 pounds of fish alone almost every time because not one or the other revolving doors of employees would show up for work. It was truly amazing to see those guys do so much work for so long without any help. This is rarely seen in a place that lives on "island time" or "Hawaiian time," a concept that being late is okay and things can always be done tomorrow. Suisan was really lucky to have these two. They are definitely what made that relationship and business work. Once Kyle left the company, they could no longer handle anywhere near the weight a sea mountain boat brought in and the prices either dropped when they had fish or they wouldn't greenlight enough fishing to make a living.

It's funny how life works out sometimes. My current fish buyers were also my first fish buyers as a boat owner. I was loyally selling fish to Kona Fish and Hilo Fish when I bought my first boat; however, they didn't need our sea mountain fish because of the large quantities of big yellowfin tuna coming in from the inshore fisherman around the island when summer came around. When the large yellowfin run inshore, everyone and their brother catches them. This tapers the demand for our fish from offshore. During this time frame, I generally go marlin fishing, traveling, or both.

The thing that wasn't common that summer was that not many imported containers of poke cubes made it into Honolulu. Word on the street was that a bunch of the refrigerated containers weren't passing health standards inspections at the port. A couple of the fishermen I knew from Oahu bragged about the big money they were making on auction. Since we were currently out of work, I enjoyed dangling tuna more than fishing out of Kona. I decided to take the gamble. The first thing I did before ever untying the boat was to call Wes at Kona Fish. He was the main guy, and we dealt with him to make sure it wouldn't be a conflict of interest. I didn't want some summer fling to ruin my marriage back on the Big Island. He said it wouldn't be a problem since they were currently dealing with lots of big yellowfin.

I had no idea that summer fling would go on to last years. The very first time I dropped in Oahu, I got a $4.89 per pound average on my load. That was my biggest trip in my career to that point, and in summertime on top of all that. It was at a time when most offshore handliners generally either didn't work or were killing time on land somewhere else. The prices remained strong and steady for a long time to come. But, one day it became undeniably clear that the heyday of the auction was over for us. I actually called Kona Fish first to see if I could drop off fish to them. They said they didn't need the fish, and that's how I found myself selling at Suisan. I sold to them for a while. When Kyle left, the best days at Suisan left along with him. Then I found myself back at the Kona Fish doorsteps hoping they would let me fish for them again. I had heard they weren't very happy I was selling at Suisan, one of their direct competitors. Fortunately, and thankfully, they took me back.

Life had gone full circle from Kona Fish to Kona Fish. The company has really grown since I first started selling to them all those years ago. They have more locations and more selling power than ever before. They are even located on the mainland now and are definitely a dominant force in Hawaii seafood. Though part of their business is the importation of seafood, I've been really impressed with their commitment to using local fish from around the islands when available. I've also been very impressed with the pricing to the fishermen, especially when I know they could have bought fish cheaper from the longliners in Oahu. It's a great feeling when you know you're being treated fairly when you've been in a business long enough to have seen all the ups and downs. I feel very fortunate to be doing what I love and being paid fairly for it. I think that's all most real fishermen want. We aren't on the ocean to get rich, but we do want to feel respected.

The fish market is a forever changing thing, especially as consumer desires change along with supply and demand dictating market value. The thing that doesn't really change is the life of the fisherman. Sleepless nights, howling winds, and the endless gamble are a constant. Nautical miles traveled are measured in blood, sweat, and tears, not on an odometer. Giant paydays are great, but loser trips are gut wrenching. Consistent pay is rare, and steady fishing is even rarer. The freedom of working in an environment that has no roads is what draws us back. A place that is forever changing. A place where every day truly is a new day. The day before offers no guarantee of what tomorrow will bring and tomorrow no reflection of the day before. One day you are celebrating the beauty of the ocean by swimming with the most immaculate creatures you've ever seen, and the next you are standing on a concrete slab praying that your week's bounty will put food on your family's table.

The ebb and flow of life often matches the ebb and flow of life as a fisherman. The ocean giveth, and the ocean taketh away. But lucky for each of us who are forever inexplicably tied to the deep blue sea, it gives so much more than it takes. The highs often seem just so high, and the lows seem lower than the ocean floor. Even then, we continue ahead. We do not quit, and we sing praise more than we curse shortcomings. Simply put, that is the life of a fisherman. You are literally riding the wave. Even knowing all this, a fisherman still religiously goes to sea, not because he doesn't know any better but because being a fisherman is not what a man does but who he is.

# CHAPTER 6

# DIVORCE AND THE RAIN

It would seem that every major moment in my life involved rain. Perhaps it was the universe's way of crying for me the suppressed tears we as men aren't supposed to show for either joy or sorrow. From a young age, society teaches us men that vulnerability is a weakness. Don't cry! Lord knows I probably needed to cry a hundred times more than I did during my divorce. Not to say I didn't cry, because I most certainly did. It seemed I couldn't allow myself to cry as much as I really should have, mostly due to the potential fear of outside judgment of my masculinity. While my whole world was falling apart, I felt I needed to at least hold on to what I thought it meant to be a man. I needed to believe I was doing what a man would do in a time like this. This false belief completely backfired on me, especially as the pressure continued to mount. Eventually, the stacking of life's weights on my back finally sent me down a spiraling hell. I was totally lost.

In my early and midtwenties, I believed rain was the world's way of giving me a clean slate or a new beginning. In that context, it was quite romantic, the tears of a lover I hopelessly tried to wipe away in a rainstorm outside the departure terminal of the airport, the droplet-covered blood that seemingly dissipated as soon as it came out of the wound. It would seem that with every incredible woman I ever met, I either accidentally bumped into her in a full-on downpour with a makeshift newspaper umbrella in hand or she was dumping my sorry ass while it drizzled outside a bar. Yes, the rain—it would seem to be the only constant part of any relationship for me. I would long for it when my life was in the shitter, oftentimes just standing in it when it finally arrived.

I would stop in midstride and just stare into the heavens between heavy blinking from the droplets flooding into my eyes. I'd look to see if I could see what the future had in store for me. More often than not, a soaking wet set of clothes revealed the only secrets to what the future held. Ironically, when I was in a better place in my mental state and my quality of life had improved, you would find me jumping in puddles and "singing in the rain" like a child. I would come home covered in mud with an ear-to-ear smile, which by most social standards would make a grown man playing in the rain seemingly insane.

And yet, at other times when my relationships, work, and life were apparently going great, I'd stand in that same rain and it would seem freezing cold. I would again look into it, asking, "Not now. Not this time. Please let this be good news." On the good rains, life simply improved, and I appreciated catching the drops on my tongue. They hydrated my mind, body, and soul. The sun would come out, and the world would seem fresh and rejuvenated. However, the bad rains left hard nipples, a soaking wet shirt, and chafing blue jeans as evidence of the shitstorm to come.

The darkest raincloud of my life arrived the night I finally realized our divorce was truly imminent. I went through the whole emotional spectrum. I was first shocked. "You're fucking kidding me, right?" Then I was angry. "You fucking cheating bitch, how could you, after all I've done for you and this family?" Then I groveled and begged. "Please think about the kids. We can work this out. What about counseling? A trial separation? Anything, anything at all please?" But, she had already checked out. She was gone, baby. Fucking gone.

I was lying outside on the cold-tiled porch of our guest apartment that I was recently sentenced to like a prisoner in my own home. I imagine I looked like a dog hit by a car. I felt paralyzed. My heart literally hurt so bad that I was in physical pain, a feeling that would become all-too familiar in the following months. I moaned in agony like a cow giving birth. To add insult to injury, my beloved soon-to-be ex-wife would walk by emotionless and cold like I was just another piece of furniture on the patio. The only thing she ever said to me was "What's wrong with you?" I didn't reply.

My two young children would come and jump on me like a beanbag chair, lifeless and soft. They would ask me questions, but I heard none of them. They eventually got bored of this worthless blob on the porch and moved on to more important things, like drawing on the walls, which I discovered from the bitching that echoed through the house windows. This gave me a slight momentary grin. Minutes became hours, just staring at the gray siding of my home with the only changing scenery being an occasional ant that would scuttle by. My eyes would flood, but the tears refused to fall. I was officially broken, none of my basic functions working, not one at all. I had become obsolete, just another part of our disposable culture.

The first raindrop hit my cheek in the late afternoon, and my eyes instantly widened. When the second drop hit in almost the exact spot, I scratched at it. The water felt as trapped inside my facial hair as I felt inside my own mind. My five o' clock shadow had recently turned more into something like a five-week shadow. Depression seemed to force even the simplest of daily tasks onto the backburner.

*Well fuck me, it can't get any worse,* I thought. *Either I'm going to die and be put out of this misery, or something good is going to happen.* The rain continued to fall, and I continued to wallow in my own misery along with the puddle that now surrounded me. As Lake Kenton grew drop by drop, drip by drip, I wondered, *Where did it all go wrong? Why? What now? Poor kids, poor me.* Somewhere during the darkest cloud of self-doubt, my thoughts drifted to suicide. "I'll kill myself," I murmured. Like that would be the answer. My kids wouldn't have to grow up the products of divorce. I wouldn't have to live in the unspeakable embarrassment of my ultimate failure. My ex would receive my large life insurance policy we had in place due to my dangerous offshore fishing lifestyle, and this would ensure they had a good life. Dad would have actually gotten one thing right for once.

I lay in the rain as it made intricate rivers that flowed off my nose and along the peaks and valleys of my face. I could almost feel memories encapsulated in the different streams. Water pooled in the leeward side of my mouth after cascading across the rapids of my front teeth. In the previous hours, my jaw and mouth went limp from their newfound home on the ground. They now served for little more than a shitty birdbath. I wished the water would drown me. Somewhere after dark, soaked, freezing, demoralized, and completely defeated, my natural instincts reluctantly took over to survive. I swallowed my catchment of water and pushed myself awkwardly off the ground like a newborn horse stumbles for his first steps. With a loud "What the fuck?" I pushed open the door to my cell. Too depressed and sore to give a shit, I sloshed through my side of the house, wet fucking slippers and all. I remember thinking it looked like Frosty the Snowman's crime scene. I hopped in the shower to discover it was freezing cold, they had used all the hot water in the main house, and no one had bothered to flip on the electrical bypass for the solar hot water heater like we typically did on rainy days and overcast days. *Of course*, I thought. *Perfect. Just fucking perfect.* After an extremely brief shower, I wrapped up in my towel and jumped straight into the bed.

Despite never being so run-down in my life, my brain refused to shut off and my body refused to sleep. Tossing and turning, I cursed life. *Alcohol*, I thought. *That will do it. Yeah, that's the ticket.* My heart still literally burning in pain, I got up and trudged toward the liquor cabinet, sloshing through frosty entrails. The only thing I found was my last sacred bottle of Bundaberg Rum, procured from my last season of fishing on the Great Barrier Reef. A bottle of Bundy was the going currency amongst the sportfishing boats of my generation that made the pilgrimage to these sacred grounds for giant black marlin every season. Today, Sailor Jerry is the rum of choice for the young crewmen, but I'm old school and forever will be a Bundy man.

A bottle typically and traditionally is only reserved at my

household for special and auspicious occasions such as truly large fish, winning a tournament, or the news of a fisherman's death or of a fisherman's newborn child. This bottle in particular was specifically reserved for something truly special, like a grander blue marlin, a goal yet to be accomplished thus far personally. Feeling particularly low and depressed, and pretty sure I'd probably take my life sooner or later in the coming days and just writing it off as another failure, I wiped the thick dust off the rectangle-shaped bottle and put the warm bottle of sugary rum to my nose.

I deeply inhaled its contents. The distinct pungent smell hit me like a line of cocaine. The hair on the back of my neck stood up. I placed the bottle to my lips, hoping God would help me as I again reentered the vicious cycle of love and hate with drinking. After my first swig, I was immediately on the reef again, sunburnt and wind tattered, smiling from ear to ear below my proudly earned panda bear eyes from a lifetime in sunglasses. With the second swig, I was on my beloved commercial fishing boat, the appropriately named *Vicious Cycle*, which I lost in an accident while away on a vacation in March 2016.

I tapped on the glass bottle before me with all my fingers, grasping it from both sides like a baby bottle to ensure not a single drop of this magic elixir went to waste. The firewater coursed through my veins, artificially stoking my soul. Feeling slightly more upbeat, I turned on some music. I put my iPhone on shuffle. Johnny Cash's rendition of Nine Inch Nails's "Hurt" came on. I swallowed a mouthful of rum I had been vigorously swishing around like mouthwash. I closed my eyes and said, "I love you" to my wife. She couldn't hear me nor wanted to. The tears now flowed in place of the rain.

When those fucking feral Hawaiian roosters began crowing at dawn, my eyelids, which seemed to be clamped down with a 100-pound Danforth anchor, painstakingly unglued themselves to reveal I had downed the whole bottle in the evening hours before. I, unfortunately, survived to live another miserable day.

I was cursed with the inability to ever sleep in late, a habit inherited from years of working on fishing boats. Being drunk and/or being hungover has never been nor ever will be an acceptable reason for not being at work and doing your job on time. In some sick way, there's even a sense of pride from being able to party all night and work all day. Throughout my entire career, I and others alike in the industry were praised for this attribute. A talent that I often secretly wore like a scarlet letter of shame, I was blessed with an extremely high tolerance for alcohol, particularly whiskey. The problem with this is that it got me into a lot of shitty situations. I often found myself in questionable locations, with even more questionable company, doing even more questionable activities. It was a direct portal to a darkness that had haunted me since my teenage years.

From the outside looking in, you might not ever recognize I had an issue, mostly because the sadness was always behind closed doors away from the boats, away from the public eye. I was happy in those places. That's not where the darkness found me. The darkness cornered me when I was alone. After the drinking, when I was tired. When I was run-down. When I again violated my own moral codes. I had gone almost two years sober to help support one of my best friends who needed drinking out of his life. It also gave me purpose and an excuse not to drink. I would find out later that he only made it three months, but he and his wife didn't have the heart to tell me.

I had only started drinking again four months ago. As sad as it sounds, I only started drinking again because my wife told me I was no fun since I stopped drinking. Desperate to do anything to appease her and save my marriage, I reinstated a dangerous relationship with alcohol. The curse that seemingly would be the cure to my wife's unhappiness with me and our marriage would unfortunately turn out to obviously not be the cure we had all hoped for in our personal relationship.

At that moment, my three-year-old daughter, Vera, came into my personal Alcatraz that morning and delivered what I call one of her patented million-dollar hugs. It's a multistage hug, the initial "up, up," where she requests you to pick her up, the initial hug around your neck that grips like a vise, then the nuzzle were she buries her face ever so softly into the deepest part of your neck. When you think a hug can't get any deeper, she somehow magically goes there and somewhere in that space of time no matter what's happening in life, everything for at least that moment is at peace. I call them her million-dollar hugs because if I had a choice between a million dollars or her hugs, I would take her hugs every time. No amount of money could replace a father/daughter hug. And so, with that hug, I realized I better get my head out of my ass and figure out what the fuck I was going to do with my life.

Sweating profusely, I pounded water and searched the Internet for anything I could find to help me survive this divorce. I plugged in words like "help," "getting through," "advice," and "how to survive." I was totally inundated with ads for scumbag lawyers promising to get me what I fully deserved. What a racket, making money from another person's misery. The longer I searched, the more I got disgusted with everything I came across. When I finally did find articles on divorce, most were written by totally unrelatable people—some women therapists, some soft-cock doctors. They didn't speak in the blue-collar language I know and live by. They didn't speak to men, a recurring theme I would hear fellow divorced men echo nearly every time the subject came up. Perhaps the information is solid but often poorly delivered to a man who's either wildly angry, depressed out of his mind, both, or just plain fucking lost.

A few days later, no less confused but at least sober, Counting Crows "Rain King" played in my black Silverado pickup truck as I sat with my children in bumper-to-bumper traffic in an extremely unusual Kona rain squall. At the end of the first chorus, my son Kanyon announced that he would be getting a new dad. Immediately followed by that, he said he didn't want a new dad. Apparently, my little sponge of a son had absorbed a conversation his mother had had with her herd of friends.

"I don't want you to have a new dad either, buddy," was the best and only thing I could muster.

"Why are you crying, Dad?"

"I'm not crying. It's the rain."

Vera chimed, "Nah. You're crying, Daddy."

I was in fact crying again, and I had no idea how to make it stop or how to explain it to the children.

"Don't worry, guys. I'll always be your dad," I whimpered while I attempted to turn the music up.

Kanyon weighed in again. "But I heard Mom say she's going to get me a better dad."

"Well, Kanyon, no one could ever be a better dad. You're my children, and I love you more than any other person possibly could. You're my little opihis, buddy."

This answer seemed to satisfy them. We sat speechless in the rain, the music and the thunderous raindrops muffling my tears and heavy breathing. For the second time in a week, it rained both indoors and outdoors in my life. My heart was completely pillaged. I had nothing left. I was totally running on empty.

I got hammered drunk daily. I couldn't think about anything but the divorce. My wife leaving me completely consumed me. I was going crazy thinking about it. It was on my mind from the morning I woke up until the minute I passed out in a drunken stupor late in the evening. I was so stressed I lost weight like crazy despite drinking most of my meals.

I followed all the advice my mind could compute and digested it to the best of my ability. I'd run, work out, eat healthy, and then swallow a fifth of whiskey. The man cave below my home began to look like a recycling center for Crown Royal and Jack Daniels distilleries. I discovered that empty whiskey bottles made an eerily satisfying thud when stacked up like cordwood. The sturdy glass was much thicker and stronger than my own skin, and I admired their resilience to outside forces. I had been working on a charter boat since the tragic loss of my commercial boat, the *Vicious Cycle*, an accident that haunted me as did my divorce. I had the opportunity to purchase the boat back from the insurance company for next to nothing when it magically made its way home after drifting for twenty-nine days at sea.

There is truly no humanly good explanation for how that vessel returned all the way home when it capsized 178 miles offshore and was eventually towed into the harbor only a mile off Waikiki Beach. There is equally no humanly good explanation why I chose not to buy the boat back at my wife's wishes, other than that I was trying to be the best husband I could be. My wife was practically raising two young children alone as I financially provided for the family by working at sea. I was gone to sea a lot in search of the ole mighty dollar. Just to feed the family, I missed birthdays, parties, holidays, and practically everything else. The pressures of single parenting were understandably weighing on her. So I begrudgingly passed on purchasing back my beloved boat in what I believed was the best interest of my family.

The problem was that I didn't adjust well to land. We also discovered we had very different lives when we spent larger portions of time together. It turned out that a large piece of our past relationship success was actually distance. We both were very strong and stubborn personalities and collided nearly every day on shore. At sea, I was the captain. I was important, and I had a role. I ran the show. At home, I was the swab. I did the shit work, almost always unappreciated. I loved my family, but man did I hate being on land all the time. I tried my best, I honestly did. I really stepped up my game around the house to be the best dad and partner I could be. It just was never good enough. With no offshore fishing and encouragement at home, part of me was dead inside, the part that made me who I am. I missed my boat daily. Flashbacks were a constant. I daydreamed of foaming schools of tuna while washing bubbly dishes. I saw mahi mahi boldly charging baits as I folded brightly colored laundry. When I went jogging and my heart started pumping, I saw huge marlin going wild on the gaffs. Everything reminded me of the boat. I most likely honestly had post-traumatic stress from the whole ordeal.

When a man's dreams live past the horizon of the sea, his soul dies a little each day he spends upon land and each mile he moves farther inland until ultimately one day he is nothing but a shell, empty and dead inside. Like a shell, you can hear the sound of the ocean if you hold it close enough to your ear and truly listen. In the sound of the ocean, you can find a man's purpose and in his purpose you will find the meaning of his life. If you love this man, you'll bring him back to the sea and set him free. If you greedily wish to showcase this man like a trophy on your windowsill, he may shine for you at times. Perhaps even your friends will comment how wonderful he is, but trust that a storm is brewing within. Each one of his stares into the distance is foretelling of a voyage of freedom to come. When this storm ultimately hits, it will take all that you have to survive and more likely than not, you'll be separated in its gales.

Nobody cared to hold this shell close enough to listen. If they had, they would have heard the sound of a man's soul dying. Inevitably, the two typhoons living underneath one roof met full force and nothing remained but the remnants of what could have been and what never was. Devastation and hardship were my constant companions for months to come. Road sodas never seemed like a bad idea when I didn't have the children, and daytime whiskey went well with everything. Liquor bottles littered my life like palm branches littered the Florida Keys after being hit with a category five hurricane.

I know if I had kept the boat I would have at least kept my mind. Perhaps not the wife, but at least my purpose. A man's purpose is his most valuable possession. The worst thing in reality that could happen to me? Losing the house in the divorce. I have never valued a house as little more than a place to rest your head between fishing trips anyway. Plus, with my boat, I could easily rebuild any financial loss that would come from the separation of assets.

Now, I was boatless, wifeless, and worthless. I gave up that boat for her, and she gave up on me within months of trying to adjust to life on land. I was trying my best, I really was. But everyday life on land was very difficult. At sea, I was important. I was Captain K, the guy who always got the job done. On land, I was this socially awkward, middle-aged man who didn't know what a meme was and didn't fit in with his wife's partying friends. I thought that life was over when I got married. I thought we had grown up. I didn't want that life. I didn't care about fantasy leagues, Snapchat, and smoking pot. I spent the evenings staring at the moon, guesstimating where the schools of tuna were and what they were doing beyond the horizon.

When I had been at sea, she felt so close, yet now living full time on land in our bed she couldn't have been any more distant than the summit of Mauna Kea from the sea mountain. I longed for this woman beside me, like a first-time marathoner desires the finish line. I could envision the big picture; I saw us as old people holding hands and watching our children graduate from college. I was mentally prepared for the hardest of miles. In my mind, none of our problems were more than a mere hang-up in a lifetime commitment to something bigger than ourselves. Schooled by the sea, I feared not hard work, less than perfect conditions, or the hands of time. Accepting the temperamental nature of the sea and women, I expected this storm to pass as the others had before. She would toss and turn, relentlessly complaining about summer heat in our room, yet no number of blankets could warm me from her wintery chill. I had been over a thousand miles out to sea before, but after the accident, my side of the bed became the loneliest place I ever visited on the planet.

I was haunted by tuna and images of my old boat even before the divorce began. Someone even put an underwater picture of her capsized and defeated in the following year's tide calendar. I could only look away, disgusted with the sight. How would they like it if I posted a picture of their child raped and murdered for all to see? It was clear to me that the editor of the tide calendar had never known true love or had a stitch of saltwater in his veins. A true person of the sea would never let a fellow oceangoer bleed out like that showcasing their beloved boat like some type of sideshow act. To them, it was probably just a neat photo of something different to fill the mundane task of sloppily throwing together yet another shitty yearly tide calendar. To me, it was like being stabbed with a thousand swords.

Sometimes, when we lose something major in life, we squeeze too hard on what remains. Afraid we will lose that last part of ourselves with which we are still familiar, we end up strangling the very thing we wish to preserve. I smothered my ex in all the wrong ways. I was weak and needy. I was uncertain and lacked confidence. I'd lost my focus, and for lack of a better term, I was scared. I knew and wanted no other life than working the sea. What I found to be mundane everyday life on shore was painful to me at best.

It gets blurry where the story and the reality stopped overlapping in our marriage. Did we just get too comfortable? Too complacent? Just plain fucking lazy? Or did we grow apart because our relationship needs weren't, in reality, being met? Did we ever really get along in the first place? I questioned everything. Did we convey our issues properly, or did we just assume the other person knew? Ultimately, somewhere along the line our communication completely broke down and we found ourselves fighting over who keeps the fucking lamps and placemats.

If I wanted something bad enough my whole life, I knew the answer could be found in working harder, putting in the time, and getting the job done no matter what. Keeping your head down, staying painfully optimistic, grinding it out after the others have gone. Doubling down when others would leave. That has been proven to work in my business life. However, no matter how hard you try, you just can't make someone love you. I finally came to this realization and accepted this as fact as I scraped incessantly at a black and white Jack Daniels label with my fingernail. My right index finger worked frantically away as if I was following up on a stubborn piece of fish guts that even the toughest bristle of a scrub brush couldn't remove from gelcoat.

With that bottle of Jack, I determined that the things you love the most ironically have the highest probability of hurting you the deepest. Love and pain live in such a tight arena that it's often hard to determine which is winning as the battle rages. Often, it's difficult to tell who the good guy is and who the bad guy is. Sometimes, the things we view as the things we love are actually our worst enemies, and the pain we fear is actually the bridge to happiness when and if we are prepared to walk across that scary, narrow path.

Once I finished off the Jack, I added the empty bottle to the waist-high summit of Whiskey Mountain and stumbled down the road. I have no idea what I went out searching for. Maybe I was just trying to escape the house, or maybe I was trying to escape myself. Maybe I was looking for the scary, narrow path out of my living hell.

Cars flew by me. One missed me by inches as I staggered in and out of the road's shoulder. People honked at me, some because they recognized me and others to inform me to get the fuck out of the road. It was about a fifty/fifty mix of shakas and middle fingers. Eventually, a little more than a mile down the road, the probable happened and I passed out in a bush. I can't for sure tell you how long I was incapacitated in that shrubbery, but I can tell you that the downpour woke me up. The booze had masked the misery of sleeping in my thorny bed. Though I had scratches and cuts all over, I paid them no attention other than noting out loud, *Well that sucks!* I had difficulty scrolling through my phone partially because I was drunk and partially because the case covering the screen was saturated with droplets from the cascading rain. No one had called, no one had texted me. No one noticed I was missing or at least didn't care enough to check on me. I sighed heavily and wondered what the fuck I was doing.

I'm not going to sit here and tell you I was totally innocent of all wrongdoings. I most certainly was not. I was a total asshole during this time. I was absolutely losing my fucking mind. I swam in a sea of anger whose waters were far wider than I could have ever imagined, and I sank to depths I didn't know I was capable of reaching. I said the most terrible things. I hated her, and I hated myself even more for hating the one I loved. My whole life became just pissing in the wind. Everything I did backfired on me. My life was at a giant standstill, and I was standing in purgatory. Fuck, even lying in a bush during a rainstorm didn't feel strange. The crazy part was that it was more comfortable than facing the guy in the mirror at home. I came to hate my ex, but I hated myself the most. I was disgusted at who I had become. Who was this fucking broken down drunk in the bushes?

I painstakingly perused Instagram from my jungle waterbed, despite having a dry room in a half million dollar home up the street, often clicking on the wrong thing because of the rain on the screen. I came across a friend reposting an ad for the upcoming Cairns 50th Anniversary Black Marlin Tournament on the Great Barrier Reef. Somehow in that moment, I knew that was my call to action. The tournament was a tribute to a 1,064-pound black marlin that Captain George Bransford and crewman Richard Obach caught on September 25, 1966. It was the first marlin ever caught over 1,000 pounds in Australian waters. This whopping fish put this once sleepy little town on the world fishing stage. Almost fifty years later, tens of thousands of anglers had come to the holy land to try their hand at besting one of these giant fish thanks to Bransford's discovery. Today, Cairns remains undoubtedly unrivaled as the best place for an angler to have a chance at capturing a giant marlin.

I decided to go. I jammed my phone in my soaking ass pockets and trudged back up to my dungeon home, booking the flights and applying for my visa online. I didn't ask for approval. I didn't arrange a hotel. I didn't have work lined up. I wasn't sure if I could even get on a boat at all. I hadn't been to Australia in almost seven years. Maybe I was delusional and living in an old man's "back in my day" story. The only thing I was certain of was that I was going.

I went to the bathroom and put each hand forcefully down on opposite sides of the sink. I looked straight into the mirror before me and stared at the person I'd been ignoring for some time now. I didn't have to say much. I already knew all this person's demons. I shook my head in disapproval. The alcohol and hate were killing me. What they missed, the depression whittled at unrelentingly. My whole life I had been told that I didn't look like a fisherman. All the while the only thing I wished to be was a fisherman. I screamed at the mirror in pure rage.

"Do I look like a fisherman now?"

"Dooooo IIIIIIIII looook like a fucking fisherman now!!!"

"Do I?"

My emotions completely changed, and my eyes erupted with tears. My strong arms became weak and my posture bent. *I'm a drunk, I'm divorced, and I'm a total degenerate.* "Do I look like a fisherman now?" I meekly asked through my tears. My nose ran, and my eyes poured.

I packed my bag and passed out for a few hours. The following day, I left with saying little more than, "I'm taking off," which was met with a "so." I kissed my beautiful children goodbye. I promised I would send them something cool, which excited them. I then went in search of that man who had become lost somewhere along the way. I hoped that Kenton Geer still lived on the Great Barrier Reef because he was dead in Kona.

I've always loved to travel. I can stare out of airplane windows for hours on end. The three connecting flights to Cairns were different though. I was looking, but it were as if I wasn't seeing. I supposed it was a lot like my marriage—I had been told I might have been listening but I was not hearing. My mind drifting back and forth from the present tense and the past, sometimes I would see things in the clouds that would make me smile. Sometimes, I saw things that made my eyes instinctively close. On most flights to Australia, I easily slept away or constructively worked on a future business plan. However, on this flight, my heart raced and my mind refused to settle. The only thing of value I accomplished was walking a young single mother's baby up and down the aisle until eventually the young girl fell asleep in my arms. I'd recently been wearing the same set of eyes the mother had, and I knew the pain behind them. I knew what someone who needed help looked like. The mother, at first hesitant for a stranger's help, was ultimately relieved and relished the break. I was happy to be useful to someone and appreciated being needed for something.

My final flight arrived in Cairns around ten p.m. I easily cleared customs with my haphazardly packed bag and, thanks to my iPhone, found a mediocre hotel on the outskirts of downtown. A rude Lebanese taxi driver tried to rip me off by attempting to take me on an endless odyssey of the suburbs, not realizing I was familiar with the area. When we eventually arrived at my fleabag hotel, I knocked the rust off my Australian lingual skills. Calling the driver a "cunt," I threw him half the fare the meter read. He barked a little, but we both knew the deal. He sped off, spurting some unrecognizable gibberish into the surrounding darkness.

Even at night, the air was hot and sticky as is often the case in Cairns. My clothing stuck to me, my forehead dripped of perspiration, and my mouth had an unquenched thirst. I checked into my hotel and showered. Despite being up for nearly twenty hours, I didn't think about sleeping. I got dressed and walked straight out to the bars to see who or what I could find.

The first thing I noticed on my pilgrimage was the dingy old park off of Sheraton Street. Ten years earlier, I cautiously had to navigate it because of drunken angry Aboriginals. But now, it was no longer a barren shithole. It was a beautiful outdoor concert arena with groomed fauna. I found this pleasing, knowing that I was now a much slower runner than I had been in my early and midtwenties and had no interest in getting mauled. The thought of being bashed hadn't really occurred to me again until I came across the former gauntlet where it was well known that many a poor victim had received a random act of violence. I personally had found myself high-tailing it out of that park more than once over the years. It looked like things were on the up and up around here now.

I went straight to an infamous pub known as The Woolshed. *The Lonely Planet* book on Australia, a traveling guidebook series, says of this establishment that if you can't get a root here you can't get a root anywhere on the earth. I can attest to this being true. I've never seen a place easier to get laid in my life. Between people either celebrating just arriving at the gates of the Great Barrier Reef or blowing off some steam before heading back home to the real world after traveling abroad, this apparently sleepy town has world-class night life due to the droves of travelers.

When I walked in, it reeked of spilled beer and bad decisions. Men at Work's "I Come from a Land Down Under" thundered from the speakers as hundreds of backpackers from all around the world sang in some type of drunken unison. Every inch of the large wooden tables that encompassed this barnlike-designed bar either had someone dancing on them or drunkenly stumbling off of them. I ordered myself a jug of Bundaberg and Coke. A jug is basically a pitcher containing four to six regular-sized mixed drinks. The drinks in Australia are poured extremely weak compared to American standards because they don't free pour. They have a government-regulated shot size per drink. So a whole jug would only have four to six standard shots in it. One measured drink wasn't going to get a man who had been snubbing 750 milliliters of whiskey a day very far, so I figured I'd prime the pump with a jug.

Nothing had changed at The Woolshed. I saw the same bouncers, the same DJ. The same endless stream of scantily clad bartenders. The same adolescents having the time of their lives. Christ, they were even playing the same music. The only thing different now was that I was the old guy in the room. I ran into fellow fishermen, but between the blaring music and being half deaf, these days we had no meaningful conversation other than the fact we would catch up tomorrow. We drank heavily. We danced, and somehow I even ended up fucking this large-breasted French girl who I thought was way hotter than she actually was. When I came back to my hotel room from a morning jog down to the boats, my sobriety proved to be a real eye opener.

Despite Snaggle Tooth's appearance without my beer goggles on, she was decent enough and kind from what I could make out from her broken English. I fucked her again and passed out in the air conditioning. She was still lying next to me when I woke up hours later. I had been married so long I forgot what it was like when someone actually wanted to stay around. Also having entered the world of adulting, I forgot that backpackers don't have shit going on and she could have just as easily been milking the air conditioning compared to staying in her hot, crowded hostel. Whatever the case, it was time for her to fuck off. I woke her and let her know I had to check out, which was a lie, but I was ready for her to leave.

I hadn't flown half around the world to shack up with a Cairns five. I was here for one reason: to find myself. In the first twelve hours, I had only found the guy I hated, the drunk who fucked anything that walked. The woman was adamant that I take her phone number and email. She scribbled down both on notebook paper. I grasped the sheet of paper, assuring her I'd be in touch. I gave her a final nudge toward the door and a final kiss goodbye, carefully avoiding her snaggle tooth. I closed the door, crumpled up the piece of paper, and fired it like a basketball at the wastebasket. I loudly proclaimed "Kobe" when it easily swished through the rim of the garbage can.

I made my way down to the Black Marlin Marina in hopes of finding a ride for the tournament that started the following day. Although I knew lots of people on the docks, everyone was already crewed up. My friends sent me on many leads, but they kept coming up dry. I repeatedly heard, "Oh man, I just got someone. Wish you were here last week."

"Me too," I kept replying.

Understandably, most of the boats had either their regular crew for the marlin season that was just starting or had prearranged a team with friends for this big tournament months prior. I was given a pass to the banquet that evening, but that looked like that was as close as I was going to get to the action. I had a great time catching up with all the boys and enjoyed watching the presentation, showcasing the fifty years of the fishery since the first grander was captured in these waters. I smiled proudly when, to my surprise, I saw that I was in a couple of the pictures in the presentation. As happy as I was to be back in Cairns, it seemed I had unfortunately come across the Pacific to only find the same failure I knew at home. I again was boatless. When the presentation ended, the others shuffled out of the auditorium, but I just sat in reflection. I was more or less only forty nautical miles from my favorite place in the world, and yet it was out of reach.

Suddenly, the massive arm of legendary Cairns skipper Billy Billison wrapped around my shoulder, snapping me back to reality. Billy had sat down next to me, and I hadn't even realized it until that moment. Though Billy is a mountain of a man, my mind had been far out to sea. I had fished with Billy in years past and was fortunate enough to have some incredibly good fishing with him, including a run where we hooked and caught a fish over 800 pounds ten days in a row.

"How's it going, champ?" Billy inquired, already knowing the answer because we'd spoken earlier on the dock about my lot in life lately.

"Well, you know, Billy."

"I do know," he replied. "I looked over and saw you sitting here. I know that look. I know what you're going through. I've been there. I can't leave you here. If you'd like to come with us, I'd like you to be part of the *Viking's* crew for the tournament."

"I would love to, Billy," I said so emotionally charged that I worried I might cry not from pain but from joy. There was nothing I could have wanted more than to be fishing the tournament with a highliner and a legend. I did not carry on to the pub with the rest of the fellows. Instead, I found myself happily walking back to my hotel whistling and singing, singing in the rain as the far North Queensland sky drizzled upon me. Every once in a while, I spun around a signpost and clicked my heels in my best Gene Kelly impersonation. I was going fishing on the GBR again, and that was enough of a high for me. Despite my excitement, I slept the most restful night of sleep I had for months.

The next morning, I arrived early at the boat to meet up with the crew. I eagerly met the charter from North Carolina that probably had no idea that I was more excited to go fishing than they were. The charter consisted of two brothers, Richard and Mike. Richard brought his young son Connor and a close family friend named Chase, a fellow professional fisherman from North Carolina. I liked all of them immediately. The other crew consisted of an Aussie who went by the nickname Wuzza. His real name was Warwick Anderson, a name I hadn't learned until knowing him for almost two decades. Wuzza was a well-respected Cairns veteran, an endless treasure trove of the most amazing adventures and tall tales that ultimately always had a way of being validated. He's just one of those people who inordinate is the norm. Wuzza is a master in his craft. He's an excellent fisherman and equally talented host for the guests. It's hard not to like him. He's quick with a drink and a hilarious story. His scratchy laugh and kindhearted humor is infectious. I had been drinking with Wuzza for years, and I liked him from the moment I met him. But this would be the first time I actually got to work alongside him.

The second deckie was a Cairns virgin, a friendly POME (Prisoner of Mother England) named George. I came to find what George lacked in deck experience he made up for in the culinary arts. George was a classically trained chef who made every meal a delight. He was charming and witty. Funny enough, I received a phone call and an ultimatum from my wife just moments before we untied the dock lines. The offer was to come home now to save this marriage or don't come home at all.

Morning dew artificially rained from the outriggers as I pulled down on the halyards, deep in thought. I got off the boat and paced up and down the dock. I looked back and forth between my phone and the light-blue hull of the vessel before me shining in the morning light. I sighed deeply. In my heart, I knew the truth was that the other ship back at home had already set sail. Heavyhearted, I looked one last time at the phone and jumped on board.

The tournament started with a sail past. Each boat lined up in a parade like a fashion show slowly cruising past the onlookers lined up along the wharf. The crowd consisted mostly of families and friends of the boat crews. I recognized a fair number of people whom I hadn't seen in years besides on Facebook. I happily waved back.

Once we passed by the wharf, we had to idle for a little ways down the leads of Trinity Passage behind the herd of slow-moving vessels transiting the no wake zone. Captain Billy's vessel, *Viking Two*, seemed naturally reluctant to move so slow. It always carried the air of places to be and fish to catch. She was a rocket ship in her day. The *Viking Two* is a custom-made war machine specifically designed to Billy's personal specifications for the Cairns fishery. The vessel, though decades old, was made with lines way ahead of her time. Even while sitting at the dock, she appeared to be going somewhere fast. She was sleek and beautiful. Pretty, yet strong. Of all the marlin fishing vessels I have stepped foot on, she was perhaps the greatest. Sure, I'd been on larger multimillion-dollar sportfishers with all the bells and whistles. But truly most of those aren't really great fishing machines. Sure, those rigs are comfortable for anglers, great for dock parties and cock measuring contests. But the truth is that most of those boats couldn't back out of their own way. The *Viking Two* was a real fishing machine made for battle.

Eventually, we were able to open up the gates for this mare, and she ran for her familiar pasture with grace and elegance. The Cairns air was thick and the sea was choppy, but this mustang effortlessly sliced both air and water like a knife slices hot butter. The first three days of the four-day tournament, the fishing was slow for the whole fleet. Most boats didn't even see a fish let alone catch one. Of the fifty some odd boats, many did not have a fish on board going into the fourth and final day. Luckily, we had managed to tag the two little marlin we had come across. Though it was not much, it still kept us near the top of the field in these difficult conditions. First place only had four tags and second place three.

Going into the fourth day, the fleet had only caught two larger-sized fish. Both fish had been estimated at 800 pounds, which by most people's standards is a giant fish. However, this was Cairns, the home of the sea creature. An 800-pounder, though a beautiful fish, isn't particularly rare in the water off of Cairns. The fish we desired swim in the four-digit category. Remember, a big fish here is the so-called grander. It's the magic number most fishermen will pursue for their entire lives. There is just something about that 1,000-pound mark that calls to your most egotistical desires. It's that crazy number that makes a man feel like a failure with a 999-pounder and a hero with a 1,000-pounder. A 999-pounder is a big fish, but it disappointingly just can't be called a grander. It's just a manmade number, but that number can be absolutely maddening.

At night, we anchored behind Opal Reef, an area affectionately coined by the game boats as the "Opal Reef Country Club." We rafted with fellow game boats. The food was good and company even better. The rum flowed and so did the fish stories. During the hours others were awake, I felt whole again. When everyone was asleep, I just stared into the spectacular night sky that covered the Great Barrier Reef from my makeshift bed on the bridge of the *Viking Two*.

The weather was calm and stagnant and so was the fishing. Slow fishing is the fisherman's greatest enemy, and I found myself battling within. I lay there nightly, wondering if I had made the right decision. I wondered if the ultimatum was real or just a guilt trip. My thoughts heavily leaned toward a guilt trip, but my broken heart was completely torn. I prayed to God for guidance for the first time since I was a child. Though I knew exactly where I was, I was totally lost. I prayed to God for some kind of sign to let me know I had made the right decision. Bundaberg Rum filled my nostrils, and thoughts of children filled my mind. *How can I be the best dad when I'm not the best me?* I was miserable not being an offshore fisherman. I passed out to thoughts of me taking the kids fishing at Honokohau Harbor back at home in Kona.

The sign I was looking for came as the sunlight cracked the horizon. It first came as a droplet. Then another, followed again by another. The light rain woke me as it gently massaged my face.

I stood up and just stared straight into the sky, hardly having to blink my eyes. The rain felt fresh and rejuvenating. It was cool yet comforting. It brought with it the promise of a new day. I inhaled deeply through my nose as if to smell what the rain had in store. I looked around the anchored fleet to find that no else appeared to be awake and stranger yet the source of rain was a small, friendly looking raincloud that only seemed to encompass our small boat. *How wonderful and yet odd.*

Rain is considered a blessing and a good omen in Hawaii. I knew I wasn't back at home in Hawaii, but sitting on that anchor behind that reef surely felt more like being at home than anywhere else I had been since my boat sank. It certainly felt like a blessing. This rain felt invigorating to my soul. I happily sat alone in the rain on the back-covering boards. I watched the red bass and spangled emperors loyally and patiently wait for our breakfast scraps off the stern of the vessel. I stared at them and wished I had anything that loyal in my life. Deep down, I knew today was going to be a good day. I could just feel it in this mysterious wet, cool morning air.

I started a pot of coffee for when the boys woke up and mentioned nothing of our blessed rain when they finally did. We started our fourth and final day of the tournament with unnoteworthy bait fishing, which is common when a fleet stacks up in an area putting a large amount of pressure on the same quasi-residential fish in the area. Because of the lack of any type of concentration of fish in the surrounding zone, Billy surmised that it would be in our best interest to cover as much water as possible to heighten our chances of encountering more fish.

Typically, we run two to three dead baits in Cairns. One is generally a swim bait, a bait that is rigged to swim below the surface, and the other or others are skipping baits. These are designed to skip or track across the surface. Though most skip baits range from five to ten pounds, a twenty- to thirty-pound tuna is not considered an unreasonably sized skip bait in the land of giants. These baits are generally pulled in the four- to six-knot range.

However, Billy wanted to cover even more water than that.

Surface lures afford you more speed and allow you to cover a lot more range but come with the cost of a far lower hookup ratio. Lure fishing is often referenced as drag and snag, meaning you generally are either on or you're off right away. The lure snags into the fish or it doesn't. Lures are designed to come tight against the reel's, drag right away before allowing the fish to feel the unnatural vinyl and or plastic, and drop it.

Naturally, rigged baits are designed completely opposite to this, allowing for the marlin to swallow the familiar feeling fish with a preset amount of slack, known as a drop back. The fact that the bait actually goes inside the fish's gob greatly increases your odds of penetrating a vulnerable spot on the fortified mouths of a beast that is ordained with a bill as hard as a baseball bat. These bills are designed to be fish-killing machines, and inadvertently nature's design has foiled many a man's dreams when their fish of a lifetime merely gets the bait or hook wrapped upon it. It's not uncommon to battle a marlin for great periods of time, sometimes even hours, only to have a hook that never penetrated the fish slide off its hooter. This awesome adaptation makes them both frustrating and mystical like.

Billy wanted the range of a lure, but he wanted the hookup ratio that came with natural baits. Billy, always an innovator in the industry, decided to gamble on deploying an unorthodox technique for the Cairns fishing grounds. He chose to use a technique known as bait and switch. Bait and switch is commonly performed in some waters but not the waters this far off North Queensland. These waters are known for big baits and even bigger fish.

The plan was to run a high-speed dredge below the waves from the port outrigger, an umbrella-looking teaser contraption that looks like a small school of fish tightly balled together. We'd also run two hookless lures from teaser rods. In this case, the teaser rods were custom designed to have no guides on them, like traditional fishing rods. Instead, the line ran up through the hollow center and came out directly from the top. The rigid fiberglass poles were designed so that a crewman could put the wood to them, so to speak, if a large marlin inhaled the lure on a sneak attack. The idea was to take the lure away from the fish at all costs if this occurred. It was preferable to see a fish come into the spread and rapidly pull it away from the fish in a natural fashion that kept the marlin's attention and excitement.

Bait and switch, like any fishing, is an art. Move the lure too slowly and the fish may inhale it and even in some extreme cases may actually take it away. Stories of empty teaser reels and leviathans that make this happen are not unheard of. More often than not, it's the unfamiliar feel of a lure that causes a marlin to lose interest.

The idea is to take the teaser away from the fish so that it will continue to engage the teaser closer and closer to the back of the boat until it perfectly crosses paths with natural bait. This would be bait the angler has deployed off the stern, and the fish switches its interest to higher hookup ratio bait. In theory, this can be the best of both worlds—the ability to cover the ground of a lure spread and the hookup ratio bait.

It certainly is a much more exciting technique for all involved, especially when it all goes according to plan. Traditional lure fishing, which requires a lot of patience from all parties, is not nearly as exciting as fishing with rigged baits. You're constantly doing something with bait fishing, whether that's rigging backup baits or changing out a washed out bait or replacing a bait that was chopped off by one of the razor gang—a wahoo, mackerel, dogtooth tuna, or a barracuda that mauled your most recent work of art.

Generally, two types of people are in the fishing community: People who fish with lures and those who prefer bait. You'll find these conversations in the smallest trout streams to the widest spans of open ocean. I love doing both in the right application. The vast majority of offshore tuna fishing I did was actually a type of bait and switch. We would throw palu over the side of the boat to lure the school to the surface. Once the tuna was there, we aimed to trick them over to eating the plastic mold craft squid we had dangling, called "danglers." So bait and switch wasn't a foreign idea to me whatsoever. No matter your preference, the cooperation of the fish is always the key ingredient for success with all things fishing. If the fish don't want to feed then there is not a damn thing you can do about it. I had an unusual feeling that Billy's idea to change things up was going to be the ticket.

I sat just below Billy's helm station on top of the ladder, watching our two perfectly running teasers rhythmically pop along the surface as we discussed the finer points of divorce. I found Billy's life extremely relatable on so many levels. It seemed when he was also at his lowest, fishing always had a way of pulling him back up. He felt more like a dad than a friend right then. I needed the kind words and his thoughtful advice as much as I needed a giant fish.

We had our shot about forty-five minutes after lines were in. The beast didn't give us any fair warning of the attack that was to come, never once revealing herself or her massive bulk before savagely inhaling an Aloha Lure XL beauty being run as a teaser like a gum drop. It was an epic crash tackle bite where the beast's head and shoulders protruded from the water. Though this creature had gotten the lure down its cavernous void, George did an expert job of getting the lure back from her snatches. Firmly and energetically, he bested the monster's grasp by yanking hard with his whole body. I'd like to think my encouraging words of "Pull on that fucking thing like you were pulling Wuzza off your sister" helped.

The lure resurfaced as George hurriedly pulled it away with perfectionist timing. The giant black shadow of the submarine-sized fish reappeared, stalking its prey like a U-boat does a cargo convoy. The lure was equally as helpless to this sea wolf. Several times, she batted the fleeing lure with her massive bill. Between George's flawless tease and our angler Chase presenting a perfect switch scenario, the fish sucked down the scaly mackerel Wuzza had rigged like a vacuum cleaner. At Billy's guidance, Chase followed up a perfectly placed bait with a perfectly timed feed. Wuzza and I cleared the remaining gear from the water to avoid an entanglement.

Chase slammed the drag up to strike, where at forty-five pounds of drag pressure the fish effortlessly stripped line from the reel like a child free-spools a kite into the upper atmosphere. The drag appeared to have absolutely no effect on the fish. The fish sped off straight down at unprecedented speed as Chase manhandled the cumbersome rod to the fishing chair. Once at the chair, we placed the rod with quite a bit of difficulty in the swinging gimble. Chase's forehead veins and his muscular forearms flared. Two quick snaps of the carabiner clips attaching chains of equal length to each side of a bucket-style fighting harness offered some relief as the primary load was transferred from his arms and back into his stronger leg muscles. Chase valiantly stood up in the chair, man against fish, fish against man. Despite all of Chase's resistance, his attempt to slow this fish seemed futile compared to the will of the beast. The fish continued to take line like a stripper takes a man's money.

I'd never seen a fish take such a deep dive on the initial run. The large Penn International 130 class reel had less than a quarter of the spool remaining before the reel began to show any signs of slowing. The fish now took a short, forceful burst of line, indicating it was shaking its mammoth-sized head far down below. The line was straight up and down, an extremely unusual position to be in after an initial run.

Oftentimes, when marlin are in duress, their first instinct is to frantically explode across the surface to try to relieve themselves of whatever is causing them pain. This fish didn't seem particularly bothered by the applied pressure of the line or the hook that now attached it to the sweating angler. Aside from an occasional headshake, she seemed content to just calmly and nonchalantly paddle slowly at great depth. She was a peculiar fish, not seemingly very troubled by the situation at hand. Billy instructed Chase to push up the drag to see if that would get a reaction. The fish now faced approximately fifty-five pounds of drag. The stress level above the water appeared far greater than below. Chase's legs shook, and perspiration soaked his dark blue T-shirt. The fish, seemingly unaffected, continued about its routine.

"Give it to her," Billy said, gesturing for Chase to put the drag to full sunset. Chase obliged, and little changed besides the increased shaking in our anglers' legs. Chase was giving her full smoke, and she was taking it like a champ. Billy kept the boat out of gear, allowing our adversary to appreciate the full strain of the reel at maximum tension. The fish swam slowly away from the boat. The rod moaned, and the line slowly crackled off the reel, making a god-awful sound. Each loud ping of the line made my heart skip a beat. Though completely confident in our fishing tackle and Wuzza's knots, I silently prayed that the line wouldn't break.

Few things are as impressive as watching a 130-pound-class fishing tackle being pushed to its absolute upper limits—unless, of course, it's watching a fish that doesn't seem particularly concerned with the severity of the pressure applied. The additional drag failed to break this titan's blasé response to the situation as she continued steadfast on her path to the east.

Chase muttered the likes of "Come on, you big bitch." However, Billy stood on the bridge like a sentry, quiet and focused. His body was at the helm, but I could tell his mind was swimming beside this great fish. I could picture these two physically imposing creatures staring each other down, neither one willing to blink, both animals stubborn and hardened by decades of being on the reef.

Billy wore that certain look only possessed by a man who has given everything to the sea. It's a converged look of pain, love, heartbreak, and joy. It's a look of battles lost and victories won. It's the look of the one who got away at sea and the one who got away on land. It's a distant stare on the outside that's focus is anything but far away. It's the look of a lifetime committed to something bigger than any one fish. Below his baseball style cap, nearly forty years of experience lay in wait for an occasion such as this. Billy called down to Chase, "Hold on, champ, we're going to drive away from her. We've got to change the angle; we can't catch her if she stays down deep."

Chase braced himself for our tactical maneuver by pushing his left hand down on the top of the reel and grasping the right-hand side armrest with his other. The lower a spool of line gets, the greater amount pressure that is asserted on the main line. Driving away from the fish to make angle change meant more line would be coming off the reel, so Billy had Chase back the drag down to about forty pounds of pressure. The line again went straight down off the spool in a steady clip before Billy even started driving.

Billy was clearly fearless of this fish and the emptying spool. One hundred percent confident in his tackle, he hammered down on *Viking Two's* throttles like he was trying to outrun a tsunami. Lines screamed as the engines roared. Black smoke came out of two rear wet exhausts, like the nostrils of a fire-breathing dragon. The beast above the water had decided it was time to retaliate. The clash of the titans had begun. Billy had run this boat so long that it was completely impossible to tell where the man ended and the machine began. Sometime over the years, they had become one and the same.

Billy performed a number of mind-blowing maneuvers, tearing circles around this fish in multiple directions, then backing down hard in order for Chase to crank. Our captain effortlessly swung the throttles in and out of gear, like a master swordsman swings a blade, his boat a lethal weapon unsheathed. The *Viking Two* was Excalibur within his hands. Chase was able to gain some line, but mostly we lost it.

"Don't worry. We'll get it all back," Billy calmly said when someone mentioned the lack of fishing line that remained on the spool. "I just need to find the right angle to get the line across her face and really piss her off."

After a number of failed attempts of backing and filling around this fish, Billy finally found the desired angle to irritate our nemesis enough to force her out of her comfort zone. The stress on the line began to ease as the lurking beast ascended up the water column. As the fish neared the surface, Chase was finally able to really gain some line.

What had initially started as one hard-earned turn after another was now a frantic race to turn the handle as fast as possible to keep up with the slack line that the fish's upward momentum was producing. Chase wound and wound, throwing his whole arm and shoulder into it as he painstakingly earned back every inch of the hundreds of yards of line the sea creature had effortlessly pulled out. The fish had pulled out so much line it was anyone's guess where she might actually be in comparison to the boat. Even though the line was straight astern of the boat at the moment, that didn't mean the marlin was straight astern of the boat as marlin create giant bellies in the line while transiting through the water column.

When the fish decided to take another run, the line screamed to the port side of the boat despite the beast boasting its hulking mass in a demonic display to the starboard. The once calm and reserved beast had lost its composure. She tore across the surface throwing a rooster tail like a speedboat. She porpoised in and out of the water, throwing water like a breaching whale. She would disappear momentarily only to explode out of the water like a depth charge moments later. At depth, she was a stubborn caged beast. On the surface, she was a runaway stampede. A startled school of flying fish took flight and fled like innocent pedestrians at the running of the bulls.

Above her lateral line she was blacker than night; below she was a metallic silver. Her physically perfect body represented both the heaven and hell she possessed. She had the lustrous lines of a young mistress and brought all the trouble that accompanies one in her devious black eyes. She teased us by exposing herself from the depths but refused to surrender to our desires.

Dreams and nightmares live in close proximity when marlin fishing. Billy drove, Chase cranked, and the fish swam. Wuzza waited with his gloved hands to get a shot at the leader once within reach. George devotedly steered the fighting chair, ensuring the line went directly off the roller guide rod tip regardless of what mischievous maneuver the great fish made below in attempts of besting us.

I stood by with the tall lancelike tag pole, waiting for my chance to do my part in slaying this dragon. All Chase's hard work and

Billy's jockeying would be for naught if I couldn't come good on getting the orange-colored monofilament tag into this creature, signifying the fish as being caught by the tournament guidelines. Being a tag and release tournament, this fish's massive size and unrelenting resolve was more of a burden than prize as far as the actual point scoring went. Long battles cost lots of precious time when trying to catch as many fish as possible versus trying to catch the largest. Small marlin are often tagged in a matter of a couple minutes; this fish had already battled for over an hour.

A marlin was a marlin in this tournament, regardless of size. Though this beast steadily ate away the play clock, it was definitely better to be fighting one versus trolling around looking for one. No one was going to complain about it, but when fishing is your passion you become competitive about it during tournament time. All size versus numbers scenarios start running through your head as minutes turn into hours. Though it would be far easier to capture a small marlin, the truth is that men don't return to the waters off the Great Barrier Reef each year to catch small fish. We come here with dreams of battling with sea creatures like the one we now had on the line. So, regardless of the tournament standings, in reality we were doing what everyone else in the tournament wished they were doing at that moment.

In all honesty, when the fish decided to take flight, displaying its jaw-dropping size, the onboard discussion quickly went to gaffing the monster versus tagging and releasing it. We all agreed it was over the fabled 1,000-pound mark. Aside from George, the rest of us wanted to attempt to kill it, but after several discussions, we all agreed with Billy's final ruling: It was in the best interest of the industry if we released it. This tournament was highly publicized, and killing a giant marlin in the public limelight wasn't going to do an industry that was already under heavy scrutiny any favors. Long gone were the days where a big dead fish was proudly put on display in town. The new generation of greenies and bubble-blowing scuba divers were extremely antifishing, many never even realizing that many of the dive spots they coveted, such as the world-famous Cod Hole, were actually protected by actions taken by the game fishing industry to ensure their future for generations to come. Some boats don't even take gaffs fishing with them anymore. The trend has leaned toward almost 100 percent catch and release for marlin off Australia, which is a wonderful thing in many regards, but this was a true sea creature and the feel of a flying gaff in my hand wouldn't seem inappropriate.

So, we would be tagging and releasing this fish if the opportunity was given to us. We still had to get the fish close enough for that to happen, and that was definitely not guaranteed. Even just tagging a fish wasn't a foregone conclusion with the highest likelihood of a hook being pulled out of the fish when additional pressure would be applied by our wireman, Wuzza. The Wuzz would grab the thirty-foot heavy monofilament leader to get the beast within range of getting a tag in her.

The sea was bizarrely calm for September, and the rich blue water's visibility appeared near endless. Rays of light from the sun directly overhead highlighted an assortment of unworldly jellyfish and other zooplankton-type creatures as we passed by them at a slow, steady clip in reverse. We continued to follow our foe farther and farther to the east. She had returned to this pattern at a much shallower depth following her impressive display of theatrics. Albeit slow, we now unquestionably gained line at this point. One crank here, one crank there. This real-life game of tug of war had now gone on for an hour and forty minutes. Chase was drenched in sweat, and I was full of nerves. Everyone had done their parts masterfully, and I didn't want this story to end with this Yank blowing it. Stories of some "Yank" or "sepo" missing a gaff shot, tag shot, or something along those lines, which resulted in losing a giant fish, were commonplace on the reef—a place where American and Australian crews have always maintained a friendly rivalry since an American caught and then weighed the first grander.

I had no intentions of being the fucking Yank who blew it. The longer the fight continued, the gravity of the situation started to sit heavier on me. I had a lot of losing in my life lately, but this would be a loss that I just couldn't bear. The world is full of women—I had a chance to survive that. But a fish of this caliber was truly something special. I have seen a lot of women in my life, and none of them have ever had me yelling at the top of my lungs in excitement at first glance. Wonder women are rare, wonder fish are twice as rare. This fact was not lost on me. I successfully pushed away the self-doubt, reminding myself that this in fact was the very type of moment for which I was born. I wiped the sweat that had begun to accumulate in my hands onto the shoulders of my shirt and again grasped the tag pole like a gladiator grabs a spear going into battle.

What first started as dark nebulous shadow far below grew into an ominous black figure that appeared to be rising from the deepest depths of hell. The once obscure beast became more and more defined as Chase continued to gain line. This fish was truly astounding even sixty feet below. One could clearly see definition on this massive fish. Every inch of line Chase earned made this behemoth appear that much larger.

It was finally Wuzza's turn to take over. Chase had done his part. He had gotten all but the last thirty feet of line out of the water. Wuzza's veteran hands made quick work of wrapping the leader around his gloves in a succession of double wraps that alternated back and forth between his right and left hand. Years of muscle memory made his actions look effortless despite the great skill represented. He masterfully led the fish closer and closer to the boat as Billy properly regulated the speed in reverse to match the fish's actions below.

The engines again roared in reverse as the additional pressure Wuzza had applied upset the beast. The fish raced astern as the Wuzz held on and Billy throttled up. Billy kept the boat in perfect time with the fish, masterfully engineering her actions like a Swiss watch. The first glimpse of a tag shot came within sight, although not particularly the one you would want. The first look I had at the fish was head-on. I was staring straight down at her, and she was looking straight up at me. Its giant bill came straight out of the water like a missile bringing its massive head and everything else behind it at full speed. As a final act of desperation, the fish had again decided it was going to take flight. Jumping boat side is a common play in the black marlin playbook. It's a move that makes them a worthy adversary, and it's also a play that has led to lots of heartbreak.

I refused to let this be another heartbreak story. Just before she was about to go completely airborne, I drove down that tag pole into that leviathan with everything I had. All the pain, all the hurt, the heartbreak of every last bit of it I shoved into that thrust. I gave that tag shot everything I had, mostly because I knew this was a once-in-a-lifetime moment. I leaned into that tag pole like I was slaying a mystical creature in a fairy tale. A tag only needs to penetrate the thick skin in order for it to anchor. When the fish pulled off the tag pole midair, the pole was missing the last six inches of fiberglass. I had hit that fish so hard with the reality of my life that I shattered the end into pieces. I yelled, "Tags in!" letting everyone on board know the catch was official. But that yell was probably heard back in Cairns. Wuzza took double wraps and locked in under the cover boards to crack the beast off so we wouldn't get involved in another time-consuming battle with a fish that was already technically caught. Wuzza was able to pop the leader after landing the jump.

The fish darted approximately fifty feet before doing a glorious freedom jump, showcasing its awesomeness one last time unchained from man's desires. There was something very satisfying in watching a fish I so badly wished to hold instead happily swim away. Truly at that moment, I realized at home I was trying to hold on to a fish that was better off swimming free and that I needed to go back to sea to be truly home.

We didn't win the tournament, but you wouldn't know that by the excitement on board. Ultimately, a team with four tags won the tournament. We ended with three tags. One other boat had three tags as well, and they wound up winning the runner up award because they edged us out on time. They may have gotten the metal, wood, and plastic trophies, but we had caught the real McCoy. They won money as well, but we didn't feel like losers as we had caught the true Cairns gold—a grander.

Even more important to my soul was that I found the Kenton I was looking for in that fish's final jump. I realized that letting go didn't mean failure. It simply meant that some of the most beautiful things in life are meant to be set free. That big beautiful fish summed up in one splash what a hundred self-help articles and a hundred bottles of whiskey couldn't. I was going to be okay. The sun was warm, and the *Viking Two's* spray felt like a light tropical rain as Wuzza and I sat on the back-covering boards drinking a cold beer on our steam into Cairns on the final day. It was good to be a fisherman again.

# CHAPTER 7

# THE JOY OF DROPPING A BIG LOAD

A woman's word is one of the most powerful weapons in this world. Nothing can bring more devastation than the betrayal of the male's ego. On the rare occasion that the male truly drops his guard and lets a woman in, he then exposes all of his vulnerabilities to the outside world. These vulnerabilities are the cornerstones of his foundation—his background, his upbringing, his family life, his pain, and his weaknesses. When he drops these walls, he then gives an all-access pass to his woman to the sacred places no one else is allowed to go, a place where dreams are both broken and still alive. Together, they live in close proximity to one another. It is an area of the mind that works on a fragile balance of both self-doubt and hope. Often unbeknownst to the man at the time he grants permission to his woman to walk through this gate, she is often handed the strings to become that man's puppeteer.

A man exposes himself to the razor-sharp words of a scorned woman when he takes down his guard and reveals his vulnerability. A woman has perfected the art of stabbing at the core of a man with little more than the utterance of a few choice words. A woman has a better memory than an elephant, never forgetting a word. She stores them in a vault just in case she someday needs them during the art of war. A woman will rip you to shreds with just her words faster than Bruce Lee's fists. A woman's cut is so precise, so deep, and so fast that you often won't know what happened until you are lying on the ground gasping for oxygen from the veritable force of the strike.

You may have left the house with your chest puffed out, thinking you have won an argument, but it's just a mere matter of time before you find yourself bleeding to death in the car or, in a fisherman's case, the boat. In the same sense that a woman's first kiss will invigorate the soul, making one revisit that moment time and time again, a woman's jagged words will saw at your core like a recurring nightmare.

Hate in its purest form derives from a formula not that much different than love. So, as we thin the line between love and hate, we often don't know whether to cry or to scream. This agonizing gray area keeps us from moving forward or going back, an area of treachery and space of limbo best described as a living hell. Hate crosses into talks of love as quickly as love slips into arguments of hate. Breakups are battlefields of our past and present, surrounded by a moat of depression. We quickly expose the crosses we bear and the monkeys we carry. For who a more worthy opponent than the one who knows you best? The one you gave your heart to now possesses the power to rip it out.

You're on day five. You've broken your hard-and-fast rule of never heading out on the big moon with a time limit. You were in such a rush to go back out fishing that you even forgot to pay your mortgage. You now sit in your helm chair, shaking your head. What the fuck were you thinking? You know that the big moon is the hero or zero play. She's either going to be wide open, or she's going to be a miserable bitch. She's definitely not wide open. In fact, she's fucking terrible. It's looking like she might have finally gotten old Captain K. It's looking like it's going to be the first time you haven't covered at least expenses since the time the humpback whale got entangled in your sea anchor in 2011, taking you for a Nantucket sleigh ride that ended with a violent thump that thankfully parted just the 1.5" main line off your bow. The whale took your $3,500 parachute and any chance of you and the crew making any money on that voyage. Unfortunately, it was a night bite at the time that required you to have a sea anchor to catch fish. The trade winds howled, making the vessel skate downwind. Despite your best efforts, you couldn't get the boat to move slow enough or cast your lines deep enough to tend properly. In short, you were fucked. Or so you thought . . .

This time was something different. The current unreliable. The birds untrustworthy. The fish you did find, unwilling to bite. You begin questioning everything. Is the fish machine broken? Perhaps the sonar? Then you play with every wire in the engine room, thinking you must be running hot. There must be a bad ground. But in the end your search comes up as empty as your fish boxes. We know this as the full moon fist. Not even your luckiest shirt could help you out on this one.

Here you find yourself on the final evening, staring at the blank screen of the fish recorder. The sixteen crushed Red Bull cans on your console reveal you lied to yourself; you're back to your terrible offshore habits. Your promise to sleep every day broken, you're somewhere around fifty hours without sleeping. Every painful word your ex ever said to you haunts you to your core. The words "You're going to die a lonely old man" play on an endless loop. Why were you out here? Was it the money? Was it for the fish? Was it for ego? Was it for the kids? Is this best for the kids? What about the kids? *Why? Why? Fucking why?* For nearly a year and a half after your boat sank, all you have thought about while feeling trapped on land is being back out here. Now out here, you feel trapped inside your mind.

This was your chance to find that missing piece. You now question whether there was a missing piece at all. Maybe you are just totally broken. This was supposed to be your happy place. This is where you supposedly found success. Maybe you're incapable of happiness and were never successful in the first place. Out here tonight, back at the helm of the ole *Makana*, you're now more divided than the political parties. Your divorce and the words of that woman consume you. My God did you love her. You loved her with every ounce of you that didn't belong to the sea. You now see hell in the seas and hell in her eyes. You finally pass out somewhere on the emotional roller coaster. Even the 50/50 mix of Red Bull coursing through your veins has failed you yet again.

When you awake in your helm chair, you see it on the chart plotter. It's a memory, though distant. You remember seeing this strange occurrence on the plotter once before. You've drifted in a perfect circle and perfectly reversed in the same circle. You say to yourself, "No fucking way."

Your former business partner and one of your best friends, Brett, had found the fish out in Zion once upon a time while the rest of the fleet and you were catching cock on the normal fishing grounds. It was on the same moon phase that you witnessed the same crazy current on your plotter. Brett's discovery aboard our second boat, the *Malicious Intent*, resulted in a wonderful ika shibi bite that lasted in that area for two weeks and proved to be very profitable for you. But you soon realized this was an ocean anomaly. The fish located in that area faded away, but clearly not its memory. The previously fish-rich area was well away from the traditional night fishing grounds you frequent. Could lightning strike twice? *But, that was years ago,* you remind yourself. *What are the chances the same kind of anomaly could again exist?*

You try to remember the numbers of that location. You know you wrote them down somewhere, but where? You rummage through your old backpack that still has a permanent smell of rice from when an Asian woman decided to vomit in it instead of making it to the head down below on a charter years ago. Despite it spending a week in an OxiClean bath, her legacy lives on through the smell in your faded worn-out sea bag.

One logbook, two logbooks, three. Nope. Nothing. *Where the fuck are those numbers?* You find the page in logbook four, ironically earmarked by a photo your ex-wife's pickle-smooching buddy Sean took. The photo is of a much younger version of your ex attempting her best star of *The Blue Lagoon* impersonation. You immediately give the photo the float test. Its buoyancy characteristics are weak at best. Looks like it won't be of much use on this mission.

You've punched the numbers in; it's a big play. It's a sixteen-mile move from where your first miscalculated bait drift has landed you. The clock is ticking, and before you know it, the sun will rise, bringing your 138-mile drive of shame home with it. You look at your hollowed eyes staring back at you in the reflection of the turned off sonar, yet what you see are the eyes of the thirteen-year-old whose only dream was to be a fishing boat captain and own his own boat someday. He wouldn't give up; no fucking way. That kid was the most painfully optimistic kid on the planet when it came to fishing.

You take off your war-tattered lucky hat and scratch your unbathed scalp. When you put your hand in front for inspection, you realize your nails are full of what could only be best described as what your grandfather called every strange substance—the "Chinese Crud"—some type of dandruff, saltwater, ahi blood concatenation percolating under your "will dance for poke" hat. It's a hat someone designed to have both ahi and pole dancing strippers in perfect symmetry. Disappointed you weren't there to witness the night that led to the creation of such a hat, you let out a slight sigh. You take note you should ask your beloved hairdresser, Ishael, about that funk going on up there when you return to land.

You're sure she's going to tell you that showering every week will cut down on that problem. Despite the shower being twelve feet away, you're paralyzed to grasp it until you have a full boat. However, much worse than the crud, your hand contains a healthy portion of gray hairs. Your beard had already betrayed you two years ago, now it's happening up top too. For fuck's sake, is anything loyal?

For the thirtieth time, you nervously check your wristwatch. You tell your crew to pull the parachute. *Fuck it. Go big or go home*, you tell yourself. Are you still that kid? Or are you this nappy-haired tired old man. As you run full tilt, a blistering eight knots through the darkness, you can't help but wonder if you're chasing a ghost. You have no satellite charts, no other intel to go on. You are literally and figuratively in the dark. You only have history and a set of lat and long numbers you scribbled down in your logbook between a drawing of a heart that says "Briana and Kenton forever" and the phone number for a Great Dane breeder in Oahu who ultimately refused to sell you a dog because she said fishermen were gone too long for a dog to understand. Years later, you now strangely agree.

You've been steaming almost two hours. You're getting close now; your heart is literally sore. Is it the stress? Is it that damn logbook page? Or is it the millionth Red Bull? Self-doubt begins to enter your mind . . . what were you thinking? Why take such a gamble in the bottom of the ninth? You threw the Hail Mary when you built your career on being relentless with the fundamentals. You pound and pound and pound some more until the fish ultimately submit. Your stomach also starts to pain you. Again, is it a Red Bull overdose or stress? You half-heartedly attempt to relax, saying "Namaste" over and over in about the same fashion George's father on *Seinfeld* would say, "Serenity now."

As you pull back the throttles to throw the parachute, Daft Punk's "Get Lucky" comes more and more in the foreground of your ears as the roar of the Caterpillar 3208 diesel engine subsides. You don't need to wake the crew. The change in the engine pitch has already got them stirring. They've donned their orange Grundens rain pants and put on hats that look like they belong to a solider in the French Foreign Legion. They smoke clove cigarettes and pound canned coffee.

As you idle down sea, lining up the wind to throw your sea anchor, the words "Well fuck me dead" instinctively come out of your mouth as you no sooner arrive at the waypoint and start marking fish. At first, it's just a couple scratches. Then it's hard red boomerangs. You can't help but think how nice those marks appear. The old Penn Senator reels start screaming, no sign of their standard sticky drags for which they've become so well known. These weren't rats. These were the nice ones. The reels sang as the line poured out.

Before the boys could even reach the reels, the twelve-inch rubber squid hanging (dangling) from the six stainless steel pipes you have on board, known as danglers, start exploding. The boat is shaking like it's in the midst of an earthquake. Your heart pounds in the same fashion. Fifty-plus-pound bigeyes are going off like hand grenades around the boat, and you haven't even thrown one bit of bait. The back deck of the boat looks like the fountains in front of the Bellagio Hotel in Las Vegas. Complete with the light show, the ahi blood turns the turbulent white water a bright red Kool-Aid color as it shimmers in brightly illuminated deck lit sky.

*Ohhhhhh yeahhhhhh*, you think in your best Kool-Aid man impersonation as you fire another slap gaff into a sixty-pounder that's absolutely losing its shit as you attempt to horse fuck it over the rail. Your forearms flare as your skull drags one fish after another over the rail. It's beautiful and savage. These fish are absolutely committing suicide on the danglers. You almost can't believe what you're witnessing. You can't help but think that this doesn't happen at this time of night. Don't say it; don't jinx it. The screen that remained blank for days is now covered with the hardest red mass you've ever seen. *Ohh baby. It's fucking on.*

You take the boat out of gear and play it safe. You don't want to lose this school in your desire to get the job done quickly. You know hooking and ripping off one of the dominate larger fish in the school could result in the whole school getting driven down into the abyss, never to be seen again and taking your newfound joy, hope, and paycheck along with it. You throw whole anchovies over the rail as the surface boils with smaller fish. As normal, the larger fish have gone deeper, aside from a random rogue stray that appears once in a while on the surface that makes your heart race. At first you catch more than you should at one crack to maintain good processing policies out of fear the pile may leave any second. You've gone from a broker trip to a small paycheck in a matter of just minutes. You pray it doesn't end. "Just one more box," you plead with whomever it is that listens in the universe when you make these types of bargains.

It's time to start cleaning fish, a task you've put off. But you know it must be done. The smaller fish continue to dangle, even with the engine out of gear and no chum to be found. You're forced to hide all the hooks inside the boat because of the small ahis' unrelenting attack on your squid. These are your favorite kind of fish, very hungry ones. You and the crew process fish as fast as you can. Once gill and gutted, they are rinsed and systematically packed in an icy seawater brine. Your first mate, Waridin, has mastered the art of piecing these ahi in the boxes like a jigsaw puzzle. You don't have to worry; you know he'll get as much weight in there as humanly possible without compromising quality.

You've completed the first round. Now, it's time for the jigs on the handline spools to try to focus on catching larger fish below. This is a task easier said than done, as the little ones above grab your jig on the sink. You eventually crack enemy lines, and your jig reaches roughly twenty fathoms. You take a single wrap of the 400-pound monofilament fishing line. With your right double-gloved hand, you start rhythmically pulling your jig through the water column with your left hand pulling the slack up behind as you dance your lure through the water. You are the rod; you are the reel. You are directly connected to the lure's action.

Positive thoughts and energy produce the best action. Stay away from the negative and angry thoughts. "They don't bite," you remind yourself. Be that thirteen-year-old; do it because you love it and not because you have to. You take a deep breath of the salty Pacific air and admire the large moon rising. You note that you are smiling. The line comes tight and you pull back on it, feeling its weight and power. You can tell it's a nice one that hasn't done anything yet. It's swimming in a large circle. The line throbs as it shakes its head back and forth. Just then it decides to run, and you use your right hand as a drag system that regulates the amount of pressure that goes on the line. Too much pressure and you break her off, not enough pressure and she dumps the spool, which then increases the fight time and the likelihood of losing a fish. The line is burning around your gloves. It's a nice one; this fish has cut your outer orange snot glove in half and burned through your rubber glove below on its first run, another line blister to accompany the large callous that is now your palm.

You wrap and pull with your right hand, but with your left

hand you can only painfully grasp and pitch. You know you've broken something in your hand five trips ago, but you're trying the denial health care technique. Unfortunately, it's not working. Up until this trip, fishing has been too good to take a break. And you reconfirm this with yourself to rationalize this decision. As you pull limp wristed on your left hand, you can't help but laugh as you hear your best friend Dan Maloney's impersonation of Chris Elliot in *Scary Movie* saying, "Grab my good hand" as the deranged butler offers his one gimp hand down to a person hanging from a building. The fish makes its final characteristic tuna death circle. As it nears the boat, you instinctively wrap up with your left hand, a mistake that sends pain coursing throughout your whole body and brings tears to your eyes. This will not be the last time you do this this evening.

As you watch this beautifully colored fish glistening in the brightly lit-up water, you can't help but find it amazing how much you still love what you do. It takes it final paddles with its magnificently crafted tail just seconds before your gaff strokes it with the vinegar shot. She's done. You pull this beautiful fish over the covering board on the end of your steal. You remark how much you love these things. However, you can't help but think about your high school science teacher Paul Lacourse asking you if you can really love something if you kill it—a conversation that arose after you spoke about your love for fishing. A question that has both troubled you and perplexed you since your days at Winnacunnet High School, you're now whaling on the fish's head with a Louisville Slugger bat. Quite the irony, or hypocrisy, you think. You bleed the fish, cutting the collars behind the gills and artery located behind its pectoral fin. Along with your crew, you will repeat this process many times tonight. The clang of bats echoes throughout the night sky.

The grade of fish generally declines throughout the evening, aside from an occasional nice one here or there. A few big yellows blast off at sunrise to say farewell. The screen again goes blank after boating the yellows. The ghost school's disappearance was as sudden as its arrival. You don't catch another fish after the yellowfin blast off. Probably just as well, for you were stretched on ice and time when you got done packing.

As you sit contentedly on the covering boards staring out at the storm petrels, shearwaters, and albatross gliding effortlessly through the early morning sky, you think about how ironic it is that you're about to head for home when you already feel like you are there. The only place in your life that has any type of normalcy is this place of never-ending changing conditions and uncertainty.

Kenny Rogers's "The Gambler" played as you took first watch. Your big Maui Jim's hide your tired eyes but not your smile. *Life is good*, you think as you daydream about playing with your children the following day and traveling abroad with them this summer. You pick scales and scrape blood off every inch of exposed skin you have. Your thoughts are again clear. Nothing straightens out the mind of a man faster than the hard pull of a fish. For today, you are happy.

# CHAPTER 8

# THE LIES WE TELL

We spend a lifetime building up artificial barriers around us without even realizing we've created our own prisons. A man can easily build more walls with his mind than with his hands. If you have ever lied because you believe that is what is expected of you, then you will understand my love affair with the ocean, how often I've muttered, "It's a hard life," trying to appease the general acceptance of what is pain, what is comfortable, and what is normal. We often say one thing about a situation and yet feel another. Is it fear? The fear of uncertainty? The fear that others will scrutinize our true feelings? The reality of a situation and the narrative we create about that same situation are often so dissimilar that we lose track of which one is reality and which one is crafted just to meet an agenda. We sometimes tell the story so many times that we actually believe the story ourselves, forgetting that we wrote the narrative just to appease the world around us. The truth is that a real fisherman never really intends to fully leave the sea, no matter what he may tell his significant other.

This was true of me. I repeatedly told my ex that I would go fishing less or I would stop offshore fishing all together someday. But I knew deep down inside that both were a complete lie. I absolutely loved fishing, but I also loved her more than anyone else in the world. So I perpetuated this lie so that I might hold on to both. Perhaps it was selfish, but I couldn't picture a life without either one. I didn't know how else to hold on to her and yet still wake up with the ocean. I figured that if she loved me like I loved her, then my affair with the ocean would be an acceptable part of our relationship. However, the truth is that very few relationships of any type survive an affair of any nature.

The problem with being in love with someone at a distance is that while you can call them as much as you want or send endless letters or texts, they can't truly feel your presence. They can't touch you. They can't experience the energy created by your love for them. A laugh enjoyed over the phone often pales in comparison to laughter enjoyed with the simple touch of a significant other's hand on your forearm.

That slight caress of the cheek that fills the body with warmth. The return kisses that raise the hairs on the back of your neck. Sadly, even those odd looks you give each other that result in breakdown hysteria can't be appropriately experienced any other way than in the flesh. Often, even attempting communication with land from offshore is difficult at the best of times. Rough seas and cloudy skies make expensive satellite phone calls and text communication spotty at best. Text messages from tired hands and fatigued minds are often misunderstood or lack emotion. The language of love is lost on archaic satellite phones that require one to hit a button three times to get the desired letter for a text. Character limits make a lover seem uninterested and more distant than their mileage out at sea. Delayed responses and a lack of service don't keep up with the speed of life upon land.

A fisherman remembers the world a certain way when he heads to sea. But the truth is that life on land doesn't live in the still frame one's mind remembers it as. So you live life at sea with a snapshot of your last glimpse of her. In reality, that snapshot faded the moment you chose the sea over her. A fisherman always remembers life as he last saw land, but life for the most part forgets about fishermen when the boat traverses past the horizon. Land has lots of moving parts, lots of things outside of your control. A lot of good things and a lot of tragic things. Life on land keeps moving at warp speed, despite the fact you're just moving seven knots at sea.

I have come to find that, despite a fisherman's best efforts, he will rarely not disappoint the woman he cares about the most in the end. Though fishermen are lots of fun to be around and exciting to chase, holding one's heart for any significant amount of time is more difficult than navigating straight into a hurricane. Attempting to conform to the standards of land-dwelling relationships often proves to be more slippery than his own foul weather gear. Generally, a woman longs to possess that which she cannot have—the heart of the fisherman.

Depressingly, in the face of her best attempts, she cannot possibly take it from the ocean's grasp. She may be able to grab a piece of it and even tear at it from time to time, perhaps even faithfully holding on in hopes this will someday change in her favor. However, this lie she tells herself will only prove to be a coping mechanism for the reality of the situation in the end. She will try and try again, but she will never hold the whole thing, despite her best efforts. This inability to obtain the heart is what stokes the fires of desire and discontent. It's so often what initially attracted them in the first place that ultimately drives them away.

A fisherman has had his heart taken so long ago by the sea that he doesn't even realize it's missing. A fisherman's devotion to her is so strong that somewhere in the change of tide he unknowingly became part of her. He breathes her, he feels her, he needs her. She calls to him via the wind and visits him when he sleeps. Since a fisherman spends most of his time staring at the distance looking for what the sea offers, he is unable to witness that he is in fact part of what she gives.

A fisherman commits to a woman with the best of attentions, falsely believing that both the woman and the ocean can live in the same bed. A fisherman can allot all that remains of his heart to a woman without ever realizing part of it was missing in the first place. This missing piece seems to cause all the problems. For although a man might spend all his time at sea thinking about the woman, when he is upon the shore he spends all his time thinking about the sea. The fisherman's lust for the ocean unintentionally ruins what should otherwise be quality time together. Despite the fact he spends the majority of his time at sea, when he walks upon the land he speaks not of land but of her. A woman can tolerate a fishing story or two. However, jealousy grows when they start to consume the day.

It's not the fisherman's fault. The ocean is the ultimate queen of seduction. Not only does she provide joy and pride in harvesting her bounty, but she also reminds us that she possesses the power to provide the means to fulfill all of man's egotistical wants and desires. She rarely does so, more often than not just flashing a glimpse of what could be versus what truly is. It's this power she holds over the hopeless fisherman.

A true fisherman will always be late to land but never to the ocean. A fisherman will always struggle to find time for a woman but never for the sea. Although the ocean's needs are complicated, they pale in comparison to the complexities of the opposite sex. The "ocean's rules" for a successful relationship are basic and simple:

Stay devoted.

Pay attention.

Work hard.

Never turn your back on her.

Always believe.

It wouldn't be a stretch to say that at times I took my wife for granted, despite continually singing her praises. In my heart, I believed I had signed on for forever and believed she had as well. It's also fair to say I may have gotten a little too comfortable because I thought love saw past the errors, mistakes, gray areas, and the few extra pounds. When you're of the understanding that you'll never have to be back on the dating scene, it's easy to round a few corners on the strong foundations of a relationship. It was an inherent flaw to presume that a marriage worked like a self-cleaning oven. That ended up turning my life into a three-alarm structure fire.

My bride always appeared steadfast and reliable, like a heavy-duty deck. Perhaps that's why I was unable to see the stress cracks forming under the paint. She was a mover and a shaker. She always appeared bulletproof. It was this strength and hustle that I instantly admired about her when we first met. When we were married, I actually appreciated her bull-like stubbornness. She was instantly put in charge of dealing with the confrontations in our home and business life that my Virgo nature shunned.

However, I would quickly come to hate this attribute in our divorce. Those lioness words that once broke other cages tore away at me with deadly accuracy. There will always be a danger when someone knows too much about you; that knowledge was used to claw each other's hearts out. Most of what I believed I knew about married life proved to be totally wrong—not just mine, but others that surrounded me as well. The moment I changed my relationship status online, otherwise happily married women on Facebook and Instagram started sending me messages. What at first appeared to be true general concern for my well-being following the divorce almost always ended up being a pass. These women were married and miserable, or at least married and not in love with their husbands.

Although my practice wife didn't value me as being worth a fuck, somehow these women considered me an upgrade or at least a distraction from their current situation. Several referred to themselves as living in "a marriage of convenience." The term "marriage of convenience" always made me scoff from behind my keypad. No marriage was convenient as far as I could tell. They all seemed to take a lot of work. Marriage of complacency would be a more accurate term. How often we call laziness and fear "convenience."

Relationship issues are often hard and potentially hurtful to address. That's why so many of them get put on the backburner. Not addressing them starts to build resentment. Eventually, the resentment begins festering into a boil that inevitably pops, and it's too late to recover when it does. The damage is done. The cuts are too deep. The moment to save the relationship has already passed.

I often wondered how many of the online women's husbands

were just as blind as I had been. I wondered how many of their husbands were listening but not hearing. I wondered how many of their husbands worked their fingers to the bone only to have their wives sending me nude photos and videos on Facebook Messenger. I wonder how many made the same crucial mistake and confused money for happiness. How many of these men had put aside their true dreams to focus on being the financial provider or had given up who they truly were to appease Mrs. Happiness? All the while she sent Snapchats of her finger blasting herself to the far-off corners of the Internet behind their back.

I didn't particularly trust women immediately following the breakup, even though I still longed for them. I tried to use their bodies lying beside me to fill a void that was actually deep inside. Date after date was the same. Every one of these women had the same exact story. Ultimately, all of their exes were fucking crazy— the "bipolar" call was the crowd favorite. In their medical opinions, they all really needed to get help. Some exes were lazy while others worked way too much. Either way, they couldn't get the work/family/life balance correct. Being a deadbeat dad was pretty much a given. The same yadda yadda over and over again.

I wondered if they were handing out a handbook to "dating after divorce" to these women as they left the courthouse or if they had to order it online. At one point, I could have just played a recording with a different woman sitting across the dinner table and saved us both the effort of talking. I could picture my ex telling the same well-constructed story to some other poor dinner date, who like me was just trying to get his rocks off. I wonder if they all rehearsed their lines together or if there was a jaded woman's group chat to which they all subscribed.

Regardless of their realities, the truth was that I shouldn't have been trying to date right off the bat. My heart wasn't truly open. I was so hurt and felt so lonely. The smell of a fresh kill lying beside me momentarily patched my broken ego, but it didn't heal my heart. It was so confusing; women came easily, yet the only one I wanted didn't want anything to do with me.

Women spoiled me, yet I had never felt like less of a man. I was in a committed relationship for almost ten years, and in that time a lot had changed in the dating scene. Dating apps came around somewhere along the line, a wickedly superficial and terribly effective way to get laid.

Profiles claiming "not looking to hook up" mean the same thing as a woman who tells you at a bar that she's not going to fuck you. Which of course means she's going to fuck you. Who is their subconscious trying to lie to anyway? It's certainly not the male mind. Is this again another chapter from the handbook they give out? The final chapter of course is the "I Never Do This" or "There's Just Something Different about You" chronicles. Ironically, the jaded woman handbook seems to end on the same chapter as the *How to Be a Barfly Handbook* they had in their late teens and early twenties.

What started off as a true desire to find a significant other and a happily ever after quickly became the opposite. The dating apps and the women they brought were addictive. I pounded dating apps like I pounded the offshore fishing grounds. I was relentless. I right-swiped like it was my job. I got to the point where I only swiped right for the sake of time. A little further down the road I got to the point where I didn't even look at the pictures. I just right-swiped as fast as I could and waited to see if I matched with anyone. The idea, of course, was that a woman, by her very nature, was going to put a lot more research into her mate than a male. I figured that rather than once again getting disappointed when a woman I was interested in didn't match, I would just throw all my ammunition against the wall and wait to see what stuck. I would then investigate the profile once I matched. Fittingly, one time I looked over at a large mirror in an airport as I was vigorously right-swiping and realized it looked just like I was masturbating with my phone between my legs. Ironic but not far off.

You wouldn't know this if you've never been lucky enough to never have to enter the terrible world of online dating. But for those of us who have given up enough on ourselves and society as a whole, we find ourselves shifting through as much bullshit as one can handle. You can find as many losers as you'll find at even the raunchiest bar on the Internet. Arguably worse. Online dating also has undesirable byproducts, which come at you in many different forms. An accepted part of the nondiscriminative right-swiping process includes scams and fake accounts wanting you to view their webcams. It is commonplace to match with a few trannies and a few queers once in a while—worse than the army of shemales, which are easy to recognize and avoid. You'll certainly find yourself matching with an army of undesirable women like vegans, redheads, and hairdressers. These are all just considered collateral damage in the time-saving process I came to call a "whole lot of love."

For the most part, it becomes painfully obvious which accounts are fake and which are real. Immediately after my divorce, I started dating a woman who was so beautiful that when she sent me a message on Match.com I thought she was a robot. Initially, I didn't pay her messages much attention, but I eventually realized she was a real person. We quickly met, and she was wildly out of place in our small town, a tall, extremely well-proportioned blonde from the Midwest. She had found herself on the online dating scene after a brutal divorce with the father of her only child. We immediately hit it off, but I came to find we brought out the absolute worst in each other.

It's fair to say that we both probably shouldn't have been dating yet. We were both still so angry at our exes. We enjoyed each other's company, but it almost became a game of one-upmanship of whose ex was worst. Our conversations often ruined my day. They reopened wounds I was trying actively to sew shut. Despite her immaculate exterior and crowd-stopping looks, I had to space myself from the recurring can of worms she would open. She may have been one of the prettiest places I've ever been in my life, but her dark alleys kept mugging me of any forward progress. I would leave her house well fucked, mentally and physically. But long after pulling out the painful conversations she brought up, they refused to leave my mind. She fit perfectly in my arms and would have been an upgrade for the family photos, but the crosses we both bared intertwined on a daily basis. We never once fought, but I would leave our meetings absolutely drained. I would kiss this beauty and tell her how much I couldn't wait to see her again, but at the same time my heart was so physically sore it felt like she had just hit it with a hammer. She was an incredible woman, but I don't think we could have met at a more inappropriate time in our lives.

We could have perhaps been a life vest for each other in a different time. When we were seeing each other, we both refused to let go of the anchors of the past. I couldn't keep drowning week after week, so I distanced myself so far offshore that even my own demons had a hard time finding me. The fisherman in me could easily justify in my mind for letting this trophy go. Some bullshit about if you truly love something let it go . . . blah, blah, blah. However, my heart would be lying if I said I didn't miss her even now.

Then there was the tooth fairy, an Airbnb guest, who quickly became a lover and even more quickly became a resident at my house. She was another bombshell blonde, a self-proclaimed unicorn. I call her the "tooth fairy" because it was like she lived in a whole different world than the rest of us. We rarely looked at something and saw the same thing. Her world didn't seem to have any negativity or sharp angles despite a history of hardship. She lived only in positive vibrations and perfected the art of speaking in inspirational memes. She always seemed to know the right thing to say. She was bubbly, beautiful, and equal parts confusing. No better lay have I ever had. Her pillow talk would make a man walk barefoot across town for anything she requested.

Over and over again, things just didn't seem to add up. She would be constantly late or not show up at all when she said she would. I tried not to look, but the holes kept showing up in the story. It was hard for me not to suspect the worse with my recent divorce. We had an on-again, off-again relationship. The last time we were together, she confessed she had told me a little white lie. She indicated there had in fact been another man in the interim after she had told me in fact she hadn't had one. This certainly didn't add to my trust level, and I struggled with this insight.

We just couldn't seem to get on the same page. She moved in and she moved out a few times. She said she was pregnant when she moved out the last time. To be honest, I didn't particularly believe her. I questioned whether it could be my child if she was pregnant, considering the inception date the doctor gave her put me on the Cross-Sea Mountain. I appreciated the gravity of the situation, but I also understandably had my doubts. Months and months passed, and I heard absolutely nothing from her, so I assumed it was a false alarm or someone else's child.

Still in pursuit of that missing piece, the only radar I was paying attention to was Tinder as soon as I got into cell service on my trek back from offshore. With every new load I came to drop off on the island came a new batch of potential matches that had gathered on the dating apps like squid in the offshore light. Not to say I didn't meet a lot of wonderful women, because I most certainly did. In no way do I mean to cheapen what we had. For even though our time together was often short, each encounter took a little piece of my heart, eventually leaving no parts for me.

Dating apps were fun and the distraction I may or may not have needed at one point. But they eventually became a full-time job and left me feeling heartless. Despite the company of a lot of beautiful women, I was left even more dead inside every time one of them stepped back on a plane and out of my life. Hawaii's constant supply of tourists is a great thing for a quick fix. But it doesn't mend the heart who wants a happily ever after. I watched one broken dream after another blow me a kiss goodbye from that Kona airport. Those big birds who brought in potential new love daily took them away just as quickly.

I loved the idea that my next true love could be at my fingertips, but often the reality of how quickly a girl from a dating app was riding my fingertips backfired on what I truly desired in a woman. Dating apps brought the chase to your living room. The women who take up the most space in a man's mind are just like timeless fish; they aren't the ones who just roll over and give it up. It's the ones you have to work for. It's the ones you have to chase. It's the ones who know they are something special and carry themselves in that manner. It's the ones who let you so close you can almost touch them and then rip off 500-yards of line and leave you standing alone at the front door. It's the ones where you find yourself after the most incredible night standing alone in the porch light. It's that humbling luminescent while your face wears a slight look of confusion that says, "Wow. Oh wow." Those are the fish (and the women) we truly want.

Women, nor beast, are truly appreciated when either are a foregone conclusion. This kind of a woman's absence makes you appreciate a sad song and in the same right, whistle along to a joyful melody. It's love and pain, seen in the opening and closing of her eyes. It's the ocean within those loving eyes that churns our emotions inside out. It's the love found in respect and not purely in lust.

A close mutual friend introduced me to Kristen. She was on vacation when I met her, and I was completely burned out on meaningless dating apps. She was extremely attractive and blessed with a rock-hard body. She possessed that nonchalant Californian attitude, mixed with a savory blend of sarcasm and the general air of not giving a shit. She made me work for it like no woman had since my divorce. I liked her immediately.

Timing will always be an intricate part of any fishing trip or relationship. Come across a large marlin too early and it may not bite. Come across a beautiful woman too early and she may not be interested. However, when either is attracted to what you're trolling, your heart will begin to race. Nothing excites the soul like the first time a unicorn comes into your spread.

Kristen's timing couldn't have been more welcomed. I was looking for something different, and she seemed to possess it. I met her on day eighty-nine of a 100-day yoga challenge I had committed to. My friend had put us in phone contact, and we had been texting back and forth. The plan was to take her out one night for manta ray diving on my buddy Ulua Matt's boat, which worked out swimmingly, so to speak. The Kona coast is blessed with a large inshore species of manta rays conditioned to come right up to people and their lights, eating the phytoplankton that gathers within the glow. Years of hotels projecting large lights into the water has created a dive industry that has capitalized on this natural attraction to the lights. Swimming with the manta rays is one tourist attraction I've never grown tired of. I love how these large, elegant creatures will do tight barrel rolls just inches from you.

The manta rays did not disappoint that evening. Sometimes, they don't show up at all, which is a real potential when dealing with Mother Nature. Manta rays, just like any other ocean creature, are not guaranteed. The mantas were breathtaking as always, but on this evening I found them overshadowed by Kristen's grace. Kristen had been a Division I collegiate champion and had race times that would have qualified her for the Olympics had she wished to stay the course. Where most humans look clumsy in a thick black wetsuit at night, she wore it well, gliding through the water like a seal. My eyes spent more time affixed to her than the mighty wings of the manta rays surrounding us.

She had extended her vacation right after we met and was staying at my home despite the fact I was already back offshore. I fell head over heels for this woman in short order. I excitedly worked in the knowledge that she waited for me in my bed. Within just a couple of weeks of knowing her, she was on her way to come stay with me down in Cairns.

I had flown down ahead of her to go fishing with another one of my fishing fathers, Brad Craft, an absolute legend of a man. I again excitedly worked away knowing she was on her way. This was an unusual and new feeling for me in Cairns. By almost all standards, bringing a girl to Cairns is a lot like bringing sand to the Sahara. Cairns is about as target rich of an area for women as you will ever find anywhere in the world. The gateway to the Great Barrier Reef brings women of all wonderful shapes and varieties from the farthest corners of the globe. The idea of importing would seem silly if one was just doing a simple surface comparison. The subsurface comparison is where Kristen heavily won out. The world is filled with beautiful women, but only a few will really grab a hold of your heart. She had me all twisted up from our first date. She was something different all together. I missed her from the first moment she stepped out of sight after our first meeting. She was exotic yet tangible. I longed for her from before our first kiss.

She arrived in Australia on my favorite national holiday, Melbourne Cup Day, a day devoted to dressing in the finest attire, gambling on horse racing, and heavy drinking. A holiday that finds the streets littered with beautiful women dressed in horse racing attire falling out of even the dingiest back alley pub. A holiday whose focus is well-dressed women slamming cocktails and gambling all day was just the icing on the cake for a country I already held in the utmost regard. Unfortunately, Melbourne Cup Day turned out to be anything but how I had envisioned it. Kristen traveled halfway around the world only to witness my broken marriage with alcoholism resurface.

One day, one fucking day in the country, and I made a complete cunt of myself. She might argue it was the mere offer of a pretty girl offering to get a drink that brought captain happy hands to the surface. But, I ironically knew it was something much deeper, the same curse that had plagued me in the past. I not only drank because of depression, but I also drank when I was happy. I was so happy she was here. I was so happy I didn't feel lonely. So happy she made me feel whole. The same feeling I felt from the moment I met her. The problem was that I was drinking far too much and getting far too happy and far, far too much attention from my good friend Cameron's cousin.

Cam's cousin was all kinds of trouble. The kind of trouble normally referenced as the best kind of trouble. The kind of trouble most sober men can't deflect on their best days and certainly not the kind an intoxicated man has any chance of avoiding. I did my best, but Cam's little cousin was as equally hot as she was devilish.

Somewhere during the umpteenth tequila shot, a little bit of slap and tickle came about in the far reaches of the bar away from our table; far away but not out of sight of Kristen.

Kristen was rightfully not impressed. I was completely hammered drunk. We immediately caught a cab back to Brad's. I'm pretty sure we didn't say our goodbyes or pay our tab. I can't remember much after the tequila challenge. I'm not sure what I said to right my wrong, but somehow in my drunken stupor I did a decent enough job of fixing things with Kristen, so much so that we started having sex. In proper drunk asshole fashion, I immediately destroyed all the ground I had made up. My level of intoxication even managed to fuck up fucking. Apparently unbeknownst to me, we had unprotected sex and I did completely the opposite of my drunken promise to pull out.

So when I came to the following day all chipper, I found my bedmate was anything but. Kristen wasn't even close to chipper. She was straight-up pissed off and stressed out. The idea of being impregnated by the drunkard lying beside her was superlow on her list of priorities. Kristen was not happy with me at all. I understood the severity of my fuckup once she explained the circumstances. I tried to console her by mentioning how many times I didn't get women pregnant having unprotected sex. This wasn't easing the stress or winning me any points.

Despite Kristen being extremely unhappy with me, she continued on with our prearranged plans to enjoy a marlin fishing tournament out of Port Douglas with my good friend Cameron and his family. We had an uneventful ride from Yorkeys Knob to Port Douglas. The weather was beautiful, the company was great, and the beers were ice cold. The only thing colder than the beer were Kristen's looks of distain. We arrived in port late in the afternoon. The tournament briefing was short and unmemorable.

Back on the boat, I routinely caught myself looking at Kristen. She was much bigger than her petite frame in so many ways. She was beautiful and vast. She would only let you in so far, yet what she gave you was more than most people could hope to get out of the deepest secret mines of Eden. She had lived a lot, but the wear was very low. She made me feel young. She made my scars fade. Cuts once so deep, shallowed. A river of pain ended when I held her. Dreams once thought dead, reborn. What she lacked in openness she made up for in wild mystery.

As I lay next to her nestled up in the tightest of crew bunks aboard the forty-foot Black Watch the *Black Magic*, I couldn't help but feel like a failure again. My mind raced and my heart was off beat. *How could I have possibly fucked this up so badly? How could I have acted so inappropriately?* Just two short days before, your friends had looked in disbelief as you informed them you wouldn't be heading out with them in town because you had someone really special coming. *Not this time*, you thought; *Drinking isn't going to take me down.* But it did. The strangest thing of all is the very thing you desired most in the world you had again washed away with one $180 bottle of champagne after another and a frenzy of cheap tequila shots.

Why did you self-destruct? Was it your ego? Was it the foolish bravado proudly displaying this goddess off your arm for all the world to see? Are you that small of a man? Using her breath-taking looks as credit of your worthiness and masculinity? Or was it that she was so incredible that she brought you to a place where you didn't feel worthy? Was she perhaps out of your league? Too beautiful, too strong? Or perhaps you were truly just a bad drunk.

The bed so tight, yet even at an arm's reach, she now seemed so distant. Days before and 3,000 miles away, she couldn't have felt any closer. Multiple times you sneak in for a kiss. Her body rejects you as do your own thoughts. At one point, she missed you, something no one had done in years. Now, her body language speaks a story of wishing she'd never met you. She was better than this, and we both knew it. When a woman can possess the world in her palm, she need not accept her stag having less.

I was paying for my Melbourne Cup behavior. It appeared I had finally hit rock bottom; the cost was finally too great. *You swore to yourself nothing like that would ever happen again. You vowed to the seemingly lifeless body beside you that you'd never fail her again. Though your two futures together were uncertain, you knew with full certainty your life was better for having met her. You closed your eyes and said "I love you" to your children and loved ones, finalizing this nightly tradition with the new addition of her name. With a huge inhale you took her in, and with an equally as large sigh that ultimately concluded with a kiss on the back of her head, you settled into a form of sleep for at least the time being.*

I found myself scouring the streets of Port Douglas looking for a chemist to purchase a morning after pill from. So as the boats prepared for fishing, I literally ran from chemist to chemist with no luck. Of the three chemists in town, the first two were out of the morning after pill. One chemist informed me it was hard to keep the stuff on the shelf. This didn't surprise me at all with the severity of drinking in this beautiful country and all the backpackers. I was excited to learn they had the pill at pharmacy three . . . but then they refused to sell it to me. Apparently, the woman had to come in. I asked why, and they told me it was to make sure someone wasn't trying to commit an unwanted abortion on someone. That did made sense, but I didn't have time for that answer. The boats were forming up for the boat parade that marked the start of the tournament, and my phone was absolutely erupting from the rest of the crew telling me to get my ass back to the boat. We'd start fishing the second the parade ended. I kept stacking money on the counter until I got to a thousand dollars in attempts to sway the chemist. Unfortunately, he refused to change his professional morals.

With the die-hard professional behind the counter and our lack of time, the placebo effect it would have to be. I looked frantically around the chemist and amazingly saw that his shop sold the same containers they put prescription medicine in. *Okay! Awesome!* I then looked for the largest aspirin pills I could find. I found a bottle of giant ibuprofen pills, something I'd never seen in the United States and that I was sure Kristen hadn't seen since she got to Australia. I purchased the empty container and the bottle of ibuprofen, then went straight to an outside trash can in front of the shop and used its rim like it was a secret laboratory. Hunched over and laughing like a mad scientist, I quickly put two large pills in the empty medicine container remembering I had read online it was a two-pill treatment. I threw out the rest of the pills and the receipt to dispose of any evidence. I tore down the empty streets of Port Douglas with the medicine bottle like an Olympic relay runner carries a baton in the most import race of their life. The two pills flew about inside the container like Mexican jumping beans.

As I hoofed it toward the town pier, my timing couldn't have been any better for intercepting the boat. I reached the pier just as the *Black Magic* was to pass by in the parade. A slight change of Captain Cameron's course and I was quickly on board. The placebo baton was passed, and we went fishing. The baton had its desired effect for the trip. Thankfully, no one questioned the lack of directions or labeling. It was an awesome multiday tournament, and we had the time of our lives. We drank and partied, ate amazing food, and karaoked our asses off, routinely using marlin lures as fake microphones. We bellowed out Cameron's and my personal favorite, "My Girl," as a duet with a large marlin lure in hand. We dove the pristine waters of the Great Barrier Reef and caught fish, including one black marlin over 800 pounds, on my favorite microphone, the Aloha Lure Xl beauty. We even won one of the tournament dailies when we tagged two marlins in one day. But, like many boat marriages, they are only good for the duration of the voyage. The damage was done for me and Kristen. I had lost her trust, and it didn't look like I would be getting it back.

We still traveled around Australia together for about a week after the tournament, but it was heartbreakingly clear to me that although she walked beside me she was already gone. At night, her eyes were neither definable nor reachable, often slipping from my gaze like ice off a spoon. She avoided eye contact at all costs. The truth was that she was leaving. And she would take my heart with her, whether I liked it or not. As she stepped out of the car and down to the hot concrete slabs of the Cairns International Airport, I wondered if she was being overprotective or if she was just playing it safe. Did she stop caring, or did she just lose interest? I watched as she bit her lip and contemplated her decisions.

The day was young but not for her. She noticeably stopped and breathed in the thick Australian air. I watched her and wondered if she was younger for being guarded or older for being wiser. Would I ever know the answer? All I could do was watch her walk away. She wasn't just another girl to me. She was my equal; she had humbled me. That hadn't happened in a long time. She brought my respect back not just for her but for all women. She was more beautiful than even her gorgeous complexion. She made me laugh, she made me smile, and more importantly, she made me feel whole again. I longed for her to stay, yet accepted she must leave.

I made my slow retreat to the parking lot after a final hug. I found comfort in knowing that wild animals like her are not supposed to be kept in confinement. She was a rogue wave, and rogue waves need a lot of space. I could only hope that one day when the sun rose, my dreams and her reality could be one and the same. I was alone in the physical sense but not in soul. I took a deep breath that would prove to be one of the clearest breaths of my life. I looked to the heavens and thanked the universe that my life was now bigger because of her.

When I got to my car, I did not start it. I didn't even enter it. I jumped up on the hood of my white rented Mitsubishi SUV. Using the windshield as a lounge chair, I stared at the sky cupping my eyes like blinders on a racehorse. I waited and waited until her plane finally ascended to the heavens. Despite every single part of me grasping for even the slightest piece of her, I found a strange comfort in knowing my angel was returning to where she came from. I tipped my hat to the big bird that took away my heart, and I slid off the hood. After taking one more seemingly endless stare at the dissipating vapor trail from her departed plane, I murmured, "Fly, angel, fly."

It's rarely the amount of time we spend with someone that brings value to our lives but the value that person brings to us in that given time we have with them. It's not the distance we travel but the adversity we overcome upon the road that ultimately determines the worthiness of the journey. Long miles traveled smoothly hold no memory of recognition compared to short yards that are battled for inch by inch.

The easiest days fall out of our memory as easily as they passed. But the most torturous paths guide us for the remainder of our years. Those who are burned by the stove rarely rest their hands upon the cooktop again without hesitation.

I again put the top on the bottle about a week after Kristen left. She was gone in every sense of the word. It was time for me to again dry out and really figure out what the hell I wanted out of life. At the same time Kristen was leaving, unbeknownst to me halfway around the world back in Hawaii, the tooth fairy delivered my third child, a large handsome boy. It turned out she was telling the truth. Although life seemed more confusing than ever, I wasn't confused about one thing. No matter what, I wanted to be the best father I possibly could be to our son. I was excited to get back to the United States and meet my new son as soon as possible.

Often it's the characteristics we admire most in the opposite sex that ultimately lead us to heartbreak. Unchained souls and free spirits don't live on the leashes of society's norms. The rushing river we wish to hold can only by its very nature slip through our fingers. You can feel its temperature, you can see its direction, you can vividly feel its energy. But, heartbreakingly, you cannot stop it or even hold it. Frustratingly, the harder you squeeze to hold on, the faster you ultimately push away what you so badly wish to contain.

All any one of us can really do is appreciate it for the beauty of the moments we share in its presence. It is better to be fully submerged in the water for even the briefest of moments and risk drowning than to watch and wonder from the safe distance of the shoreline. We struggle to hold on and try to contain the rapids for our own. Knowing damming these waters would only kill the very thing you desire the most, we begrudgingly must watch it flow on, taking and washing away pieces of our heart as it goes; eroding deep lines in our soul that one cannot see, but one can feel. However, at night, your eyes grow heavy and your body noticeably ages. Once again alone, you can take solitude in knowing that when your eyes finally close you can revisit the water just as you last saw it. Timeless, perfect, sparkling, and crystal clear.

It is in the lies we tell ourselves that we often find our deepest truths. It might take longer than expected to break through the concrete falsities, but something special happens when we do. In short, we realize the lies were our truth and the perceived truth was nothing more than lies. Then, and only then, can we find meaning, purpose, and our soul.

# CHAPTER 9

# A SHAMELESS LOVE LETTER

My United Airlines flight landed in Las Vegas, Nevada, in the middle of the afternoon on a blasé spring day in the desert. It wasn't particularly nice or lousy out either. It was the type of day where Mother Nature just didn't seem to care to perform one way or another, and at that moment I could completely appreciate the sentiment. I was mentally and physically drained, unable to sleep on any of the multiple flights over the last eighteen hours on my return from the Galápagos Islands. A master of procrastination and last-minute trip planning had found me on the least direct flights imaginable to and from my home in Kona, Hawaii, to San Cristóbal, Ecuador.

My taxi driver, having seen my Hawaiian Airlines bag tags, rambled on about wanting to go to Hawaii someday and the book he was writing. Trying to tune him out, I couldn't help but think that if even a quarter of all the taxi drivers whom I'd ever spoken with had published the books they were allegedly writing about their adventures, then all of Barnes and Noble would be yellow and black.

Though I had been fully aware and committed to a boys' trip to go sportfishing for leisure in the Galápagos for close to a year, I had booked my tickets only five days in advance. My amazing preplanning had found me practically circumnavigating the world to get from point A to point B. Normally, this wouldn't have bothered me much, as I've slept months of my life away up in the friendly skies. However, my leisurely boys' trip had come to a nightmare conclusion, and the worst kinds of thoughts were crossing my mind when my eyes were closed.

My time in the Galápagos had been awesome until my final

day. The accommodations were wonderful, the company fantastic and fishing amazing. I ate an obscene amount of ceviche and sank ice cold beers with one of my oldest dory mates, Willy Goldsmith. Willy and I have been fishing together since Willy was fourteen years old. At age fifteen, Willy caught the Junior World Record Atlantic Codfish with me at the helm of the first boat I captained called the *Bunny Clark* out of Ogunquit in Maine. Sixteen years later, as I heckled Willy about a recent embarrassing sexual experience he had with an NFL cheerleader, the record still stood.

I bonded quickly with Willy's two other friends Anthony and Daniel as we shared the common interest of fishing and picking endlessly on our buddy. Willy is one of the brightest, Harvard-educated socially awkward fish nerds you will ever meet. He is wildly successful and respected in his chosen field of science. His passion for fishing is admirable and continuous. He's handsome, though his handling of women and social situations is generally laughable and somewhat mind-blowing. All these factors make him one of my favorite people to pick on and one of my best friends. Though he puts me in my place more than most, the abuse is heavily lopsided in the other direction. It's not often that you find friends who you can lovingly bust each other's balls for nearly two decades.

The striped marlin fishing was very good. So good in fact that we even broke the boat record in only a half-day of fishing. We caught twenty-two striped marlin ranging from ninety to 200 pounds in three and half hours aboard the *Vertigo Two* operated by Pete Santini. Pete had employed Willy for many years back in his tackle shop in Massachusetts. Pete had countless stories to rib Willy about as well. Pete started abusing Willy the minute he arrived in the Galápagos. Pete and I got along instantly.

Despite a near-perfect fishing trip, Willy's complete mishandling of a young woman we met one evening only brought further abuse. This young woman may or may not have been overweight depending on one's point of view. Willy was leaning toward the

heavier side. This cute though arguably plump girl was so infatuated with our fishing buddy that the following evening when I
ran into her solo at a bar, Willy was all she could talk about.

Being the friend that I am, I decided to hand-deliver this stocky
beauty to his hotel door, but I didn't know what room he was in.
To find him, I started yelling his name at the top of my lungs over
and over all while knocking door to door. I woke up nearly the
whole hotel before finding a half-asleep Willy. Turns out his room
was one of the first ones I had walked by. Unfortunately, our
portly lady friend was not received in the fashion we had envisioned. Despite all our smooth-talking, she didn't make it past the
front door. Willy just wasn't having it. I felt sad for my new plum-
shaped friend as she was publicly denied in front of the other recently awakened hotel guests. She was cute enough and seemed
nice. However, in the same breath as Willy held his ground on a
few extra pounds, he also just forged at least another decade of
abuse from the boys.

Breakfast the next morning did not disappoint. Willy was under fire before he even reached the table, his masculinity questioned and his sexual preference under heavy scrutiny. Willy was
a great sport about the whole ordeal, and we went on to have a
fantastic last day of fishing together. Though most boat marriages
are short, most boat friendships are forever. Friends who fish together seem forever connected by a bond stronger than even the
toughest monofilament. Friends can go years without seeing one
another yet pick right up where the last cast ended without the
slightest of backlash.

Fishing is one of the rare occupations where someone who
works in the field enjoys doing it in their free time as well. I have
always loved fishing and for me, turning the handle gets no better
than when it's alongside a lifelong friend. I sat alone in a small
Internet cafe in San Cristóbal drinking Jack Daniels and gorging
myself on ceviche as I contemplated this very thought. The last-
minute booking of my plane tickets to Ecuador meant my stay
was going to be a couple of days longer than the others because

earlier departing flights were unavailable. I used this additional time to respond to emails, take pictures, meditate, do yoga, relax, and heavily drink.

On my last day in the Galápagos, the heavenly skies we had been experiencing turned a repugnant black. The rain hit the cobblestone streets so hard it was nearly impossible to tell which direction the water came from, whether it be up or down. The previous bone-dry streets quickly became riverbeds. Water cascaded from everything and everywhere. The awning that covered the Hotel Miconia sign and front patio looked like Niagara Falls as I stared groggily out from the covered seating area awaiting my transport to the airport.

Despite the relentless tropical rain, the air was still unusually sticky, or at least I was. I had found myself awake to the gray light hours with the hotel receptionist I had been shamelessly flirting with all week. My efforts had finally paid off although at the cost of any and all sleep. Though I had taken a ridiculously long shower, especially for an environmentalist haven where "Please conserve the water" is more of a lifestyle than just a mantra, La Fiesta de Todos Pilsener escaped my pores and pooled alongside its American cousin Jack Daniels. Despite it being early in the morning, I had already changed my heavily starched alcohol sweat-drenched shirts twice.

I killed my final minutes at the hotel looking through my phone. I immediately regretted that decision. Upon connecting to the world's slowest Wi-Fi, I was surprised to find my inbox overflowing with messages slowly and steadily coming in one or two at a time. Most messages said "call me" or "call when you can," but one of the messages cut right to the chase and cut me right in half in the process.

My friend Scott Davidson had killed himself. I couldn't breathe. My heart raced. I just kept saying, "Why didn't he call me? Why didn't he call me?" Eventually, that turned into, "Maybe he did call me. Maybe he did call me." I hadn't had phone service besides this slowass Wi-Fi for nearly two weeks. My tears now matched the heavy rain. I wiped at the emotional river my eyes had created, but this only redirected the flow and didn't help to stop it. When I thought about how tough Scotty was and how he wouldn't want me to cry for him, this only made me cry that much harder. I tried to toughen up for his sake, but my face sided with my heart and refused to lie on behalf of my brain. The tears rolled on.

My friend Scotty was grouchy and irritable, opinionated and stubborn. He smoked cigarettes more passionately than any other person I've ever met. Each inhale and exhale told a distant story as far away as his pensive stare. He only let so many people truly into his inner circle. His hard exterior was a false wall for the beautiful soul he kept within. Scotty would break me down with harsh words and just as quickly build me back up with encouragement. He was extremely knowledgeable and talented, gifted and skilled.

Scotty showed up when he said he would no matter how hard the night before might have been. He would grumble, "If you're going to be dumb, you've got to be tough" as he patted me on the shoulder with his rock-hard hands. We went to war together, we fished together, and found ourselves in the most uncomfortable engine rooms together time and time again. Scotty killed granders and caught world records as a sportfisherman. As a commercial longline captain, he caught the largest trip ever landed at United Fishing Agency at one point, a record that stood for many years.

Scotty helped me out so many times in my early years of fishing the sea mountain that I wouldn't even know where to begin to thank him. He donated his experience, his knowledge, and even his time when I first started. He fronted me top quality work on a handshake when I didn't have a dollar to my name. He had a soft spot for younger fishermen. Scotty was a beloved uncle to many more people than just those connected by his DNA. He bet on me when few others would, and I'll never forget that.

Scotty still called me kid right up to the day I left for the Galápagos although I'd known him for sixteen years. He told me he wanted to hear all about my Galápagos trip when I returned.

Scotty started most sentences with the word "Okay" followed by a smoker's hack and finished most sentences with an infectious smile. His laugh was contagious. He drank Coors Lights like water and had all the time in the world for me. No phone calls unanswered, no questions too hard.

One of those answered phone calls saved my life and possibly several others. Scotty always had an eerie way of knowing when to call and when to pick up. I did not talk to Scotty daily or even weekly, yet I considered him a close friend. Like Willy, regardless of how much time had passed between fishing or working together, lines started where we last trolled them, and wrenches turned on new projects as we had never wiped them off from the last. I loved working with Scotty and highly respected him. It was, for this reason, that I called him in my absolute darkest hour. He was a man who seemed to be able to fix anything, and I was broken.

I found myself surrounded by empty whiskey bottles and tanked up on a toxic concoction of prescribed antidepressants and Adderall. At one moment, I angrily ran my hands back and forth over my boat gun like a man clutches an ax before delivering a stubborn tree its final death blow. At another moment, I sadly caressed the rifle in my arms like I was holding my child. Despite my best efforts, I insistently ground at my teeth like a cow chews its cud. I wore my back molars flat, nonreversible damage I live with today.

My hands shivered from anger and then quivered from fear. Who was this terrible person holding this gun? I would close my eyes trying to shut off either the rage or the sadness. Regrettably, when I closed my eyes the other emotion would take over. So, if I shut my eyes in anger I would open them in sadness and if I closed them in sadness I would open them in anger. Several times, I put the gun down on my plywood workbench in my man cave and walked back upstairs to my bedroom. I tried to go to sleep repeatedly only to find myself pacing back and forth holding this same firearm wondering if I was capable of doing the worst kind of action possible of man.

Despite having lost my mind, a part of me still knew this wasn't the real me. Mentally, I was aware I had gone crazy. Physically, my stomach ached grotesquely, an unhealthy reaction to the medication. Heavily diluting the pills in whiskey probably wasn't making my decision-making process any easier. I'd put the gun down from time to time and pick up a bullet. I'd rotate the bullet in my fingers and hold it up to the light like a jeweler stares at a diamond.

This drove me nuts as I thought about all the hours I spent researching and locating the perfect engagement ring. It was easy to put a bullet in the gun on this thought. I opened and closed the chamber over and over. It was almost pornographic. I watched the perfect machining effortlessly make the bullet disappear and reappear. I liked the thought of making the bullet disappear into the woman who caused me so much pain. I liked the thought of making bullets disappear into all of her family members on her mother's side, who had recently caused me so many problems. I contemplated the idea of just killing her family, excluding our children. I wanted to take something away from her that meant as much as the boat she took away from me. I contemplated every murder scenario right down to the shootout that would conclude the ordeal. I had no intention of getting away with murder. I was completely insane. I wasn't naive. I wasn't going to jail either. I was going out with a firefight. I was fully planning on killing as many of the local police officers as I could who had recently illegally served me a restraining order at the police station within ten feet of my ex. I had violated the order the second I signed it.

When I simply asked, "Are you fucking serious? Can we talk about this?" I was manhandled and pounced on by the type of cop who beats off to Rambo movies. He tackled me all while going off about some nonsense he had been fed about me abusing women.

You like beating women? Huh, tough guy? Not so tough now, are you? I just said, What the hell are you talking about? I've never laid a hand on a woman. Ever, period. Full stop. I just shook my head in disgust. I had been arrested within twenty seconds of being served the restraining order in the police station lobby.

As I sat there waiting to be processed and have my mugshot taken, the darkness completely overwhelmed me. This was the first time I had seen the evil cloud that filled my mind since before my eldest child was born. Once my son was born, I felt like I finally had a real purpose on land. I knew I had to be there for my child. This beautiful child was going to need my help along the way. I had to be around for the long run. Suicidal thoughts weren't allowed to enter everyday thoughts. Stepping away from the pain wasn't an option. Entertaining thoughts about what bullets tasted like and how it would feel to fly from a building would no longer be an acceptable train of thought.

I had to be tougher than anything life on land threw at me for his sake. He would be counting on me, and I had no intention of letting him down. I was handed him within a minute of his first breath while his mother was getting stitched up from an emergency C-section. He was pliable and soft. He was fragile and beautiful. Out of all the things I had ever held in my war-torn hands, nothing I have ever possessed made me feel more like a man than holding my child. I knew in that instant that the title *Dad* was an even more powerful title than *fisherman*. It was a monumental realization. I excitedly spoke to him in a low tone expected in a hospital. I told him about all the fish we would catch together and all the places we would go, the things we would see, and all the stuff we would do. I stared into those baby crystal-blues and promised him I would never let anyone harm him. I promised I would always love him no matter what, and lastly I promised I would kill anyone if they ever tried to take him from me. A scorned woman and a judge's signature had just taken away the child I swore to always protect and daddy's little girl as well. The darkness was back, and it appeared it was planning on collecting past due rent along with interest.

I buried my face deep into my right hand, which was still free opposed to my left, which was cuffed painfully to a stainless steel bench. My wrist was sore, and my tailbone ached. Despite my discomfort, I refused to give the arresting officer the satisfaction of mentioning it. I deeply sighed, half-fueled with depression, half-fueled with my first taste ever of pure hate. How the fuck did it ever get to this?

I wasn't served a restraining order because I ever hurt someone. I was served a restraining order because I was furious over allegations of my children being abused at the hands of their mother's friends. I was pissed, and I made that verbally clear in person and via text message.

That was the huge mistake that landed me here instead of just going and getting a restraining order. I foolishly had threatened to get a restraining order against the person in question. In response, my ex turned the tables and got a restraining order against me. The allegations were fabricated aside from the encyclopedia of vulgarity that I did use to express my displeasure about our children's current situation. The packet of lies was padded with about thirty pages of me calling her and her buddy a "fucking cunt" via text. That part was definitely true. I was not impressed with her handling of the ordeal whatsoever. Verbal abuse aside, the crux of the order was a large blanket of lies about me being abusive, dangerous, and, ironically, bipolar. The order claimed I was a bad father and that it wasn't in the children's best interest to be around me. My former mother-in-law and sister-in-law signed off on the fictitious order ensuring that we would never have a healthy family dynamic again. My ex got me served on a complete foundation of bullshit, yet I found myself surrounded by a very real foundation of concrete and steel bars. Now locked behind bars, the false accusations felt very much real. In that cell, I unquestionably displayed traits that could be bipolar. In one moment, I felt like I could have killed someone. In another moment, I felt like I could have suffocated from depression kneeling on my chest.

My cellmate proclaimed himself to be the good lord Jesus despite the guard calling him David whenever it was necessary to again remind him to shut the fuck up, which was pretty constant. He annoyed the living fuck out of everyone in the surrounding cells and holding block before our bars. He offered unsolicited advice on repenting from sin to avoid the fiery hell we would otherwise succumb to if we didn't change our demonic ways.

Our savior was no foreigner to drugs, drinking, and spending time in the slammer. Until my stint, I was unaware that Jesus didn't look anything like the image of the long-haired skinny man nailed to the crucifix, different than what I was told to believe back at St. Michael's Church. I was surprised to find out that he was a short, skinny, redheaded man with medium-length hair and freckles. Jesus surprisingly also possessed the gnarliest peeling skin and face and neck sores I'd ever seen. He scratched at his sores endlessly, a gross visual I cannot get out of my mind.

Every time he inspected his dead-skin-filled fingernails, I would think, *Don't do it. Don't do it.* Then he would do it. He would put it in his mouth and eat it. *Ahh, so fucking gross.* The joys associated with smoking meth. *How lovely*, I thought.

The Kona jail was so overcrowded that they didn't have a bunk for me and several others. In a cell designed to contain one occupant, the lucky second occupant got a worn-out blue gym mat less than a half-inch thick lying on the filthy cement floor. Based on the markings, it appeared that the physical education department from the local elementary school had thrown it away the previous decade. Due to my height and the small cell, my head hit the bars and my feet had to either touch or straddle around a repulsive metal toilet. The previous tenants had no bowel control and also suffered from some serious food poisoning. The metal toilet was so fucking repulsive. Jesus being abbreviated struggled with his aim and I was fortunate enough to be blessed with his Holy Water. The good Lord pissed on my legs three times. I wasn't just losing my mind, I was losing my patience as well.

While I honestly never threatened any physical harm to anyone before being put into this cell, I threatened physical harm to my cellmate, David, once inside the cell. He was driving me fucking nuts between repeatedly pissing on me and then preaching to me in slurred words about worshiping him and his father.

The final straw came when he told me to "calm down" as I was rocking back and forth, legs crossed, on my mat talking to myself. I couldn't get comfortable in any position no matter what I tried, and I was losing my mind with the whole situation in general. I was too big to be on that floor, and I had just been fucked over by my ex and her family. My back severely ached, and I was getting claustrophobic. A man who thrives in the openness of the ocean dies every second in a jail cell.

David (Jesus) asked, "Why do you keep rocking back and forth?" Then he stated that I was acting like a crazy person. He continued, "It makes you seem strange. Maybe even nuts." My blood was boiling. Through clenched teeth and tightened fists, I notified him that my rocking and muttering was the only thing stopping me from murdering him. So, I could either put all my energy into rocking back and forth and continue talking to myself or I could it put all into attempting to kill him and he could take his chances on whether he would rise back from the dead a second time.

"Ohh, that's cool, man. Rock away," he said with a completely different tone. He now sounded like Tommy Chong, not the tele-vangelist I had been trapped with over the last few hours. He had a wide-eyed startled look as I gave him an unworldly death stare. Even this fake god could see the true devil was in my eyes. I don't actually know if I could have killed him, but at that specific moment, I was willing to give it a try.

Those were my final words with David and the last words I ever exchanged with any Jesus for that matter. He rolled over in his bunk, his ass now facing me. He ripped the loudest, wettest fart I'd ever heard. I was pretty certain he just shit himself, or at minimum sharted. *Jesus fucking Christ*, was all I could think.

I had the hardest time getting anyone to come to bail me out because I didn't know anyone's phone number off the top of my head and the overloaded police weren't particularly interested in helping me get numbers off my cell phone they now possessed. I spent most of the night in that miserable jail cell, forced to smell and appreciate Jesus's bodily functions as he detoxed.

My real father was the best chance of getting bailed out since he lived in town and had one of the few numbers I knew. The problem was that my father, just like myself, didn't pick up phone calls from numbers he didn't recognize. I sat there on an emotional roller coaster going from depressed to unbelievably angry. The legal system was cultivating and making the alleged anger real. I had never been so pissed off.

After spending that night in jail, I do not doubt that if I ever faced serious jail time for anything I would disappear from this country, never to be heard from again. It was obvious to me if forced to stay in a cell for any amount of time, I would unquestionably find a way to kill myself in short order. For a person who at times felt their personal space was violated when another boat parked within a quarter-mile of his, this was an absolute living hell.

The legal system will take your pain and use it against you as a weapon. Scumbag lawyers have perfected the art of grooming people to say and do things to damage the ex-partner's reputation. To have emotions is viewed as unstable. A person can steal your life's work, run away with your money, embarrass you, cheat on you, let your children get abused, and even hide your children from you. Yet, when you finally snap and call them a cunt, or push back and threaten the same actions they've been doing to you, you're suddenly the bad person. When so many negative things are happening to you all at once, you're made to look like the crazy person. They make accusations about your mental state, freely throwing around diagnoses they have no degree or credentials to make. People love to loosely throw around the term "bipolar" like it's the common cold. To this day I've never seen a fisherman, a woman, or even a body of water one couldn't claim possesses at least some bipolar tendencies.

Our perception and the following reactions to events ultimately determine the outcome of a situation regardless of the facts. Often the information we are provided is cut and dry. How we process and view that information determines the severity of the chain of events that follow. I didn't understand how the legal system worked, and I had no idea how unfavorably biased the cards are stacked against fathers until I experienced it firsthand.

Generations of losers who have hit women and children have

ruined what should be a completely unbiased arena. The family court system is a chain of old stereotypes a man is shackled to before even entering the room. A man is considered guilty before being proven innocent instead of the other way around. This chain is perpetually pulled along by an army of men-hating women, defeated social workers, and money-hungry lawyers. The chain is tugged even a little further down the line by those who make a living from being foster parents, from anger management programs, and from uninterested therapists.

The irony is that the false restraining order was in fact what now made me the most dangerous person I'd ever been. I'd never been a violent person in my whole life. I was so distraught following the restraining order that I went to two doctors in search of help. The physician I saw loaded me up with pharmaceuticals for stress, depression, anxiety, and my lack of focus. The other was a therapist who told me to stop taking medication altogether. The medical opinions were as conflicted as my thoughts. The antidepressants made me feel lethargic and gross. They put me in a state of slow-motion that only increased my feelings of melancholy. The Adderall he prescribed me made me so jittery the only thing I could focus on was how badly I was shaking and my depression. Sweat was omnipresent from either feeling sick from coming down on the antidepressants or from going up on the Adderall. The antidepressants ensured I was sick to my stomach, and the Adderall ensured I couldn't sleep. I was an absolute mess. The physician told me I needed to give the pills more time to work. My gut told me I needed to get off of them immediately.

On the evening I called Scotty, I discovered that if I took the pills with mouthfuls of whiskey, everything just went black on occasion, then instantly turned back on. Time went missing and so did my mind. My body was on autopilot, for my mind had defiantly stepped out. Anger and depression came and went with each closing and opening of the eye.

Eventually, my normal nature took over and depression won the battle over the unlikely visitor of anger that had decided to possess my body. I didn't hurt people physically, just mentally. I could club a fish to death without a second thought, but I could never hurt another human. That just wasn't who I was. It never was and never could be. The fact that I even had those thoughts at all only made me that much more depressed.

Imagine what kind of person kills the person they once loved more than anyone in the world. That thought truly horrified me. However, more troubling than that was that I actually had considered killing the mother of my children. *What a selfish asshole*, I thought. My ego was in tatters, and I was going to attempt to rectify it in bloodshed. I just shook my head. *What the fuck happened? Who is this dreadful person? How did I become so weak and broken?*

I squeezed my eyes shut and aggressively rubbed my temples in a failed attempt to relax and get myself together, but no intelligible thoughts came to mind. I stared at my M1 30 carbine rifle that the former owner had claimed "killed more of the Yellow Man than the swine flu." I had purchased it for a mere fifty dollars, a carton of Marlboro Reds, and a thirty-pack of Bud heavies. The previous owner, a disheveled Vietnam veteran with heavy facial scarring, had warned me that the gun was cursed.

I asked him what he meant. He said, "You'll see."

"Does the gun jam or something?"

"No, no nothing like that, but that gun brings death to everything it touches."

"Isn't that what's supposed to happen when you shoot something?" I said sarcastically.

"Only to what you're shooting, not the person pulling the trigger," he said.

He slammed the tailgate of his tired old truck and said, "You be careful with that thing."

"I will. Don't worry!"

He let out a bizarre laugh and the final words, "You'll see!"

Eerily, two nights later, I found out he died of a cocaine overdose nearly immediately after selling me the gun.

I had possessed the gun for over a year at this point and until this moment, it never looked like anything more than a tool of the trade to me. It was a firearm, and it was pretty cut and dry. It was metal and wood, nothing more. The rare occasion it came out of its Pelican Case while commercial fishing it performed its task of killing a large marlin boat side effortlessly and diligently. I just wrote off the strange experience as the guy being coked up and me not recognizing the fact that he was on the Peruvian marching powder.

However, staring at the gun tonight, it seemed to possess a personality. It wasn't just materials crafted by man's hand to perform a task. The stock was scratched and scarred, the metal tired and worn. It was as if I could see the old man's face who sold it to me looking back at me hollow-eyed. He held a death stare that said, *I told you it was cursed.*

When the black clouds subsided, the gray clouds muddled my thoughts with suicide. *Perhaps I should just use the gun on myself and rid the world of this loser.*

I again left my man cave, grabbing a box of ammunition and my cursed rifle. I placed the box of ammo and the rifle on my custom monkeypod kitchen table. So many good times at this table, I thought, but that was all over now, I concluded. I poured four fingers of warm Crown Royal in a frosted glass I had pulled from the freezer. The mist that came off the glass was reminiscent of the New England sea smoke of my youth. Those were simpler days I confirmed to myself with a nod and a heavy sigh.

My phone had automatically connected via Bluetooth to my speaker system when I had again reentered my house. The Chairmen of the Board song "Give Me Just a Little More Time" faintly played in the background as I swished and swallowed whiskey. I pulled my phone from my pocket to increase the volume. The clock on the home screen revealed it was two twenty-two a.m. I couldn't recall if it had been two or three days since I last went to sleep. I struggled to answer this question. Despite my best information, I couldn't even confirm it had been as recent as three days. Between stress and my new heart-pounding regimen of Adderall, sleep didn't seem important or necessary. I worked in grueling conditions offshore with little or no sleep all the time. I routinely worked forty-eight hours straight on a steady diet of caffeine and pride. A few extra hours of no sleep weren't going to be noticed when I was fueled up on anxiety and uppers.

The whiskey I mostly consumed for the flavor and less for its alcoholic properties. The good stuff seemed no more potent than water while I was jacked up on Adderall. The familiar smell more so filled my mind with memories than drunkenness. I started the same song on repeat and cranked up the volume on my speakers. The music echoed through my empty house that was once upon a time my home—four bedrooms, three baths, and nearly 3,000 square feet of loneliness. "This house was better as a home," I said matter-of-factly out loud as if the ghost of the past could talk back.

I could always tell when a happy memory of her was on its way. My eyes would jam shut in an instinctual effort to damn my watering eyes. Most of the time, this seemed to work, but tonight as I rolled a bullet back and forth across my table, hand to hand, it did not. I grabbed the bullet with my right hand and made a misguided attempt to wipe away the tears. The tip of the bullet slightly rubbed across my cheek, lightly touching my sideburn and tickling my ear. Something about the point of the bullet was soothing. It almost felt like a loving scratch of a woman's fingernail.

I grabbed two more bullets and along with the third stuck them in the crevices between the fingers of my clenched right hand. The three long bullets stuck out of my fist like The Wolverine's blades. I closed my eyes and ran the bullets through my hair like a lover scratches their partner's scalp. I awkwardly loaded up my left hand with ammunition as well. I put my hands before me, looking at my claws like appendages. My clumsy left hand could do little more than just hold the bullets between its fingers, but my stead-fast and reliable right hand possessed not only the strength to hold the bullets but the dexterity to grab my whiskey glass without dropping a round or spilling a sip. I aggressively drank the remainder of the whiskey, proudly wearing the bullets like an animal costume at a college Halloween party. I let out a satisfying roar to complete the transformation. I was an animal all right. A true fucking monster, according to the court paperwork. I closed my eyes again and ran the bullets all over my face.

My hands and bullets took many courses across my skin. I ran bullets across my neck and shoulders, eventually scratching both forearms back and forth before putting the bullets back down on the table.

What the fuck was I doing? I screamed as the chorus, "Give me just a little more time and our love will surely grow" echoed throughout the empty house. I angrily wiped all the bullets off the table, including the remaining ammunition in the box, like a poor sport flips a Monopoly board after a long game of losing. The bullets rolled in every direction across my hardwood floor. I flipped the lever-style safety of the gun in front of me back and forth like a child flips a light switch on and off. A quick survey of the ammo dump on the floor reminded me that one bullet remained in the chamber.

I wouldn't need to worry about filling the whole magazine if I was just going to use it on myself. I could pull the trigger, swallow this bullet, and it would all be over. The darkness, the clouds, the pain, the fighting, the courthouses . . . all of it would be gone. I opened the chamber again, tilted the gun, and took out the bullet with my left hand. With my right hand, I poured myself a glass of whiskey almost to the rim. Pinching the casing, I dipped the bullet in whiskey as if to sanitize it. The displacement of the bullet and my fingers caused the whiskey to slightly overflow. I pulled the bullet out of the whiskey and popped it into my mouth horizontally. The large bullet was awkward to keep in there.

I didn't notice an undesirable taste so much as an unwanted feel of metal against the backside of my teeth's enamel. Using my whiskey-numbed tongue, I positioned the uncomfortable metal to face out of the front of my teeth. I eventually moved the bullet to the front of my mouth, where it sat facing inward like a cigarette on my lips. The thought of a cigarette hanging off my lips made me think of my ole buddy Scotty. Scotty could perform any task with a smoke hanging out of his mouth. Seemingly, Scotty could fix anything, so I wondered if he could fix my problems. I felt so broken I questioned whether even a man who had solved impossible boat problems could help put me back together. Scotty and I had been in some dark engine rooms together, but this alley was darker than any I had ever stepped in before.

At three a.m., I decided I would kill myself at gray light, my favorite time of the day to fish. My final gray light blastoff would be my own. I would swallow the centerfire cigarette hanging from my mouth at full speed like a bigeye tuna swallows an anchovy at sunrise.

I got up from the table gathering a pen, a couple of pieces of printer paper, and an envelope. I sat back down and began to write my goodbye letter. On the first page, the only word that came to me was "because." On the second page, I wrote a heartfelt apology letter to the ocean, and on the third page I wrote a letter to her outlining my decision and why it was best for everyone if I wasn't around. The letter was short and concise. I wrote down my favorite memories of her and thanked her for making such beautiful children. A letter that started with her nickname ended with smudged ink from my tears. I closed the letter with the last "I love you" I would ever send her. I sealed the three pages inside the envelope and shakily addressed the letter to anyone who might give a fuck.

I went to the fridge for water and then thought, *Why? Dead people don't have hangovers.* I grabbed an ice-cold Coors Light instead. I decided to grab my photo albums one last time and see if I could figure out what this madness was all about. I flipped through the pages. I found no answers, just confusion. Some photos made me smile, although I was on the verge of taking my life. The hardest photos to look at were of her and my old boat. I loved them both at one time, and now they were both gone. I slammed the albums shut. *Fuck this shit. I'm not sure I can wait until gray light.* I looked at myself in the mirror drinking the cold Coors Light and thought, *Man, now I really do look like Scotty.*

I don't know what possessed me to call Scotty at four in the morning, whether it was purely the alcohol or because I knew he was a man who could fix things. Maybe it was just the fact that my fake cigarette reminded me of him delightfully inhaling and exhaling smoke as he told me another incredible tale from his life at sea. Maybe I just needed a lifeline and didn't have the phone number for anyone else I related to on that same level.

Startlingly, he picked up on the first ring. "What's up, kiddo? What's broken this time?"

"I am, Scotty. I am, Scotty."

We spoke for a while about everything that was going on. He never once complained about the time of day I called. His words that could be notoriously harsh were nothing but kind and understanding. I could almost hear his mind computing everything I was saying between heavy inhales and exhales of his favorite cigarettes. He said, "Hey, kid, promise me this . . . don't do anything stupid. I'm coming to get you, alright?" I agreed. I wouldn't break a promise to a man who never broke a promise to me.

So, at the moment I was supposed to be taking my life, I instead found myself in Scotty's truck drinking coffee and watching as the rising sun illuminated the Pacific Ocean before us. We talked for hours on the rocky point in front of the harbor, watching the nighttime fishermen return and the charter fishing boats going out for the day. We talked about boats and fishing for hours, and I forgot all about all my other problems. Scotty said one thing that stuck with me like glue.

"Kid, you don't need to load a gun to solve your problems. You need to load a boat."

He continued, "Kid, you're not a land person and that's okay. A lot of people aren't ocean people either. Don't take your life because you don't fit in where you are. Live where you fit in."

He was right. I was putting a lot of effort into living a way I didn't want to and it was literally killing me, or I was going to kill myself, I should say, because I was so miserable. Scotty told me it was time to get back out there offshore fishing again and when I got a new boat he would help me get it ready for free.

I didn't want free help, but I loved the idea of working again alongside Scotty. Scotty also told me to get off all the pills and fuck those doctors. He concluded that the only medicine I needed was the sea. Scotty dropped me off at home. I threw the pills in the trash and dumped the remainder of my whiskey down the sink. I picked up all the bullets from the floor and put my rifle and all the ammunition away except for one round. The one round I had in my mouth went into my fishing bag along with the goodbye letter. They would be coming along with me as a reminder and motivation.

I called up Rob, my former employer from the *Makana*, and explained that I again wanted to go offshore and inquired whether he had any work. Later that week, we sat down for lunch and ironed out the details. In the years that had followed my original employment and subsequent firing from the vessel, Rob and I had worked through any issues over my termination and had become really good friends. At this point, it was clear that we mutually respected each other as fishermen.

Two weeks after meeting for lunch, I was the captain of the *Makana* again. I was excited and nervous. The excitement almost went without saying, but the nervousness I couldn't understand. What was I nervous about? I'd never once been nervous about going offshore. Perhaps this is the same type of mental strain an athlete comes under after recovering from an accident. Perhaps I was worried I wasn't the same caliber of a fisherman I was before the accident. I'd proven I was incapable of working on land, so maybe part of me worried that if this didn't work out there would be nothing left for me besides reconsidering the bullet.

I left Hilo Harbor in light rain. Scattered showers visited us the entire commute around the island to get to the Cross Seamount, which was 138 miles from the opposite side of the island. I drove the final hours of the forty-hour commute in a pitch-black night as the crew slept.

I hadn't been back on my favorite fishing grounds for over a year and a half. My first course of business upon arriving was going straight to the lat and long numbers where the *Vicious Cycle's* emergency position indicating radio beacon went off on that fateful night it capsized. I pulled the boat out of gear and put on my Grundens brand rain pants in my ceremonious style, not that dissimilar to Nomar Garciaparra with his batting gloves back in his heyday. I had the boat drifting side to side as light trade winds slowly propelled us down the sea. The night air was strangely hot. I found myself staring aimlessly into the night sky not exactly sure what I was looking for.

I honestly can't say how much time passed before removing a handful of items I prepackaged from home with me from my backpack. Among them was that goodbye letter that thankfully never got delivered, my favorite *Vicious Cycle* T-shirt, the *Vicious Cycle's* tattered flag, an American flag, and my wedding ring. I laid Old Glory out on the fish box and wrapped all the items, including a lead from the boat, in a maki-dog-style fashion. I also pulled that damn bullet out from my bag. This time, I didn't attempt to sanitize it before putting it fully in my mouth. I deeply inhaled through my nose, taking what felt like the deepest breath of my life and with a huge sigh released my past failures to Davy Jones's locker. I spit the bullet as far as I could and tossed my flag of shame to the abyss. With a movielike timing, the most amazing shooting star illuminated the whole night sky right on cue. In that instant, I knew I was where I belonged. Despite the sign from the heavens, I went below decks and grabbed my cursed rifle for insurance. I gave the gun a final lookover, dry-fired it, and tossed it into the ocean. The three-foot gun, despite weighing less than six pounds, made a large splash. I watched it sink past sixty fathoms on the fish machine before saying, "See you in hell, old man. See you in hell." I got behind the helm, pushed the throttle up, and went fishing.

Everything was so natural and comfortable on the sea mountain. It was like a day hadn't passed. I loved being back on the mountain. I loved how putting on my Grundens rain pants each morning felt like I was putting on bulletproof armor. I loved my music blaring as I yanked on ahi tuna at three in the morning. I even smiled and laughed when an ika sprayed ink in my mouth. I loved being covered in tuna blood as shearwaters swooped around the boat. I was home again.

Scotty had gotten me back out fishing and saved my life, yet had taken his own life without the slightest sign of duress. I couldn't stop wondering if he had tried to call me when I was in Galápagos. I just kept thinking that maybe if I was back home it would have been my turn to return the favor. Maybe we would have been drinking coffee in my truck instead. I beat the fuck out of myself over these thoughts. Scotty was so strong it was almost inconceivable that the man who gave me all the right advice to save my life couldn't save his own. The last time I had this little sleep was the morning that Scotty had saved me.

I checked into my hotel and lay down. Despite my best attempts, I was still unable to sleep. I looked in the mirror and realized I looked like absolute shit. My hair was shaggy, and my face was clearly tired. The bags under my eyes looked like horse satchels. *God I look terrible*, I noted. I decided to go to a hotel salon and get a haircut. The obscene hotel pricing didn't actually seem unjustified as the large-breasted hairstylist bounced her huge jugs off my face repeatedly, accompanied by an included scalp, neck, and shoulder massage.

I left the salon feeling as rejuvenated as possible given the lack of sleep. I decided that food and something to drink was in order. My overcooked steak sucked, but the Jack Daniels tasted perfect. After a few drinks, the thought of doing some gambling seemed like a decent enough idea given the fact that I knew I wasn't going to sleep any time soon. I lost a thousand dollars fairly quickly at the craps table and backed that up with some substantial losses at the blackjack table. I just wasn't feeling it. I couldn't get any momentum going. Although I had allotted myself more money to lose, I retired early. I just couldn't find my mojo. I headed back to my hotel room, and once again attempted to fall asleep.

I stepped into an empty elevator and just before the doors were about to shut, an unforgettable voice said, "Please hold the door." I hit the button, and the doors opened up to an angeliclike blonde goddess. *Nah, it couldn't be.* I was so startled that I couldn't smile despite feeling that I should. This woman flashed me a quick smile and nothing more. Turning her back, she stood before me. She wore a sequin dress that shined in all the right places. Her fragrance was my favorite memory of them all.

Years of wondering and searching, countless steamed miles, hundreds of flights, pages of stamped passports, Google searches, scanned crowds, Facebook searches, wild goose chases, and even a hired detective—nothing, nothing at all. Not one single trace of her. She was a seemingly invisible person who took up more space in my mind than any other woman I had ever met. I had seen her in countless sunrises and as many sunsets, her words often lingering in the wind like a favorite song. She surrounded me, and I could feel her through my hair, coming from the east and just as quickly leaving me to the west. My head quickly snapped one way or another. I would stare over my shoulder like I'd seen a ghost. Her memory caused me goosebumps on a cold winter morning or during a comfortable warmth in a tropical evening.

She had traveled with me everywhere I had ever gone since the day I had met her. Long ago, I accepted that I would never see her again. Yet, here she was standing right before me. The cliché of a woman improving like a fine wine over time was a perfectly fitting description. However, it instantly sounded stupid inside my head, unworthy of expressing her beauty. Her looks were truly the definition of timelessness, and her elegant steps the definition of grace. Was my imagination getting the better of me? Was I truly seeing what I was seeing? How much had I had to drink? I immediately started counting the glasses, shots, and the pours inside my head, reconfirming this figure with my fingers. Was I caught living in a dream or memory of her? Or, was she truly present?

I had thought about this woman for over a decade now, and yet she finally stood here within arm's reach. All I could see was my reflection in the elevator mirror and couldn't help but think I had clearly aged and she seemingly had not. Right or wrong, I was confident this was the case. She was perfect in every single way, a dream amongst dreams.

Each unrelenting gray hair in my beard represented one of the mistakes I had made to arrive at this point in my life—hundreds of hairs for the nights I should have gone home, a hundred more for women I shouldn't have gone home with. Each wrinkle was a story as hard as my calloused hands. They had appeared like waves, small at first. In the far-off distance, I noticed the small lines, quickly moving in my direction. But as the tide of life turned, they had started to come in ever-increasing sets, recently looking like a winter swell on the north shore of Oahu. My weather-beaten skin spoke of the cross I have borne to both the ocean and the whiskey bottle.

I stared back into those same big brown eyes that had gotten me into so much trouble over the years. I couldn't help but again feel unworthy. Self-doubt had kicked in. I stood there frozen, paralyzed. *She won't remember me*, I thought. *I look so tired and run-down. I'm out of shape and old.* Here was a woman I had lamented about, much like a senior citizen speaks of their one true love at the nursing home. I was powerless to do anything. She didn't even recognize me. I was gutted.

As the elevator arrived at her floor and she began to step out, I was watching what would surely be my ultimate regret unfolding in slow motion. She again was walking out of my life just like the million times she had before in my mind. I closed my eyes and let out a heavy sigh. Once and for all, it appeared the doors were finally closed on that memory.

Within inches of that final closure, the unmistakable voice called out, "Didn't I teach you anything, Captain K? The third time is always the charm." I instinctively slammed my hands in the doors of an elevator like a mother who finds the power to lift a car off their child, tearing and crashing through them like a runaway elephant in a village. Slightly stumbling like Cosmo Kramer coming through Jerry's door, I recovered my composure to see a memory smiling at me like a moment hadn't passed. She looked down at her feet and then back up at me, her eyes just as hypnotic as the first time I fell under her spell. "Did you forget about the ocean?" she asked. I smirked. "I did not," I said and half-laughed.

"Well, why didn't you say anything then?" The girl in the green hat asked.

"I don't know. I really don't. I think I questioned if you could be real."

"You have that much drink, ahh mate?"

"Nah, it's not like that. It's a long story."

"Well, you want to come back to my room and talk about it?"

"Ha, there is literally nothing more in the world that I want more than that."

We went back to her room, and I quickly found my head lying on her lap. As I recalled my ordeal with Scotty, she ran her fingers through my hair like I had run the bullets across my scalp the day Scotty saved me. It was comforting and troubling in the same breath. Here was a woman I had looked the world over for, and when she ran her nails across my head I envisioned bullets. Her words were kind and soothing. Soon the thoughts of bullets dissipated, and for the first time in days I was falling asleep. She moved me from her lap, tucked me in like a baby, and kissed me on the forehead.

"Good night, Captain K."

"Good night, girl in the green hat."

She laughed. "I haven't had that hat for years."

"You've had it every day in my mind."

Upon hearing this, she kissed me on the lips. She snuggled up alongside me, and I had the most restful night of sleep I had in a year. When I woke, she was lying beside me just staring at me.

"Morning, K."

"Morning, Mrs. Geer." We both let out a good laugh at this.

"You are a mess, Kenton Geer," she said in a loving tone.

"I most certainly am," I replied.

"Your children are beautiful by the way."

"Thank you. Wait! How did you know I have children?"

She smiled at me. "I saw you on a plane once."

"You did?"

"I did. You had two little beauties sleeping on top of you, and you were sound asleep. I ran my fingers through your hair and just kept walking. I was happy to see you at peace."

I remember once feeling her during a plane ride. She described an experience I recall. I knew she was there.

"You sent the napkin. I knew it!" Her eyes lit up. My suspicions were confirmed.

While at the Seattle-Tacoma International Airport, both my children had to use the restroom. I waited outside, but when my son Kanyon called for me, I went into the bathroom to check on him. He couldn't figure out how to make the automatic sinks stay on to wash his hands. It was really quite funny seeing him trying to negotiate using the sink he could barely reach. I placed my hand in front of the sensor so it would stay on as he stood on his tippy-toes washing his hands. When I came out of the restroom, my daughter, Vera, was standing by the restroom door where we had prearranged to meet.

"Here, this is from auntie," Vera said, handing me a napkin.

"What auntie?"

"The pretty one. She said to give it to my daddy."

I stared at the napkin, which had a perfectly symmetrical set of lips imprinted on it in lipstick. Written in elegant cursive were just two words, "Stay Beautiful," followed by a drawing of a heart.

It was her. I could feel it. "Which way did she go, Vera?"

Vera just lifted her shoulders and said, "I don't know."

"Was she blonde?"

"Yes."

"Did she speak kinda funny like Daddy's friends in Australia?"

"Yes."

"It's her. I know it's her."

"Who, Dad?"

"The girl in the green hat."

"She didn't have a hat on, Dad."

"Yeah, but she did once upon a time."

I dragged the kids all over that damn airport looking for her on our layover. I never found her. Maybe it wasn't her at all. Maybe Vera was mistaken about the accent. Maybe it was someone I knew from Hawaii that I just didn't notice on the plane messing with me. Whatever the case, I never confirmed the source of the lipstick artistry until now.

There will always be that one fish and that one woman that got away. You will have other relationships and catch other fish, but you will never forget either. As I lay there staring at her, I wondered how she hadn't seemed to age but only ripen. She was absolutely gorgeous, arguably more beautiful in real life than in my dreams of the last decade. Unlike the big ones that had gotten away at sea, here I was holding her again.

"What is your deal anyway?" I asked. "What's your real name? Are you married? Are you a spy? Who are you? Why did you give me an alias?"

She put her index finger up to my lips, gesturing to shush. "All you need to know is you're beautiful."

"Ahh come on. I've spent a quarter of my life wondering who you really are, and that's all you're going to give me?"

She whispered a name in my ear.

"Thank you," I said.

"You're welcome."

"I'm still calling you the girl in the green hat though. It has a nicer ring to it."

She playfully slapped me. "Oh, go on, mate."

We spent the remainder of the day doing what adults do in a hotel room and talking about life in general. Perhaps we should go gamble, I offered.

"I think it's better we keep gambling with our hearts this go 'round," she said. And so we did right up to the moment I had to leave.

The shoe was now on the other foot as she said, "Don't go. Stay with me." She lovingly begged and teased.

"I wish I could. I really do. But I have my children this week, and I have to be there for them. I also have to go back for Scotty's memorial and fulfill a promise to him and myself. Come to Hawaii and stay with me."

"Maybe someday. But I'm heading to South Africa in two days."

"I understand. I really do."

I passionately kissed her, and she slapped me firmly on the rear end upon my exit.

"I thought you didn't do goodbyes?"

"It's a farewell. Don't miss your flight, or you'll be stuck here with me," she said with a wink.

She blew me a kiss, which I caught and stuck in my pocket for later, with a smile.

Diamond Dave picked me up from the Kona airport and drove me home. On the way, I received a message on WhatsApp: three emojis of bright red lips and the words *Never forget the third time is always the charm, Good luck today Capt K!!*

I walked inside my house to shower, grabbed a notepad, and headed straight to the commercial banking department of the Bank of Hawaii. When the loan officer called me into his office, I said to myself, "Wish me luck, Scotty." I had promised Scotty I would do everything in my power to own a boat again someday. Now, I was following up on that promise. I started the conversation with Steve, the loan officer, by saying I was going all in, it's all on the table. I offered the remainder of my life savings and my house up for collateral. The girl in the green hat's final words that *the third time is always the charm* ran through my head as I started the loan paperwork on my third boat that day.

# CHAPTER 10

# VICIOUS CYCLE: THE OVERWHELMING COMPLICATED STORY OF MY LIFE

You do not see what I see out at sea, and I do not see what you see on land. Life on land is often as distant and foreign to me as the ocean past the horizon is to you.

Your rocky terrain countered by mountainous waves; your plains mirrored by oil-slick calm mornings; your desert represented in fishing grounds of the past. The ocean is just as diverse and as wickedly cruel in her own right as life upon the land, her mood and temperament as fickle as the beautiful lady she is the day before, with no representation of tomorrow and tomorrow no representation of today.

Her consistent inconsistency makes her a wild roller coaster ride to attempt, her tempest ways always luring with her potential treasures hidden within. Glimpses of hope given with one hand often smack you with the reality of the other. Oh, she's the most beautiful lady of them all, but her treacheries are second to none. She plays with men's egos like a child plays with a toy. She will quickly take you to the top of the dollhouse, only to you throw to the carpet and forget you.

You ask, why would a man live in these conditions? Why does any man pursue what lives in the shadows of the unknown or search for what lies beyond the next hill? To dwell in the same old routine of normalcy is to count the number of days till you die versus counting the number of days you really lived. You are hopelessly drawn to her.

The ocean does not play favorites. Rather, it plays odds. The greater your worldly commitment to her, the greater her returns to you. What outsiders may wrongly perceive as luck, good or bad, is generally a dividend for sacrifices you were or were not willing to make for her. Some costs are easier to recognize than others. Some costs only the participants will ever know. Time at sea is clearly counted, but the time lost at land always seems more muddled. Where the hand of that stopwatch starts or ends seems unmeasurable. What pain weighs upon those shoulders when no land is in sight, when darkness turns to night and night again into day. Where saltwater becomes one with you and you one with it. Where you sweat the sea and the sea you sweat.

Body parts that ache on land like century-old farm equipment mysteriously work fluidly and rapidly at sea like decades gone past when called upon to do so. Weights that would otherwise be moved with large sighs and much resistance on land are repetitiously completed at sea without nearly a mention. The sea gives power to as many as it takes it from. Her justice system doesn't take sides. Her rulings are brutally cut and dry and certainly not always the verdict one desires. She demands respect in her courtroom, and failure to give it may ultimately be punishable by death.

The sea may be your lover, but she is not your friend. You cannot safely turn your back to her. Her loyalty is that of an ex-wife, her characteristics more of a new mistress; she will bring you to your highest peaks, but beware for on the other side of the high ground lie valleys of unspeakable misery. Her mind games are second to none. She will lead you down darker alleys of your mind than you ever knew existed within. She will make you question all that you are.

She loves to bare her bosom but will only fade away again and again when she's just within your grasp. She will be quick to point out the days you weren't good enough and refuse to mention the days you were. You will always love her more than she loves you. It will always be a one-sided relationship, no matter what you tell yourself. For as you age, she does not. You will die, and she will not. You will be replaced; she will not think of you. She does not possess the trait of jealousy, even if you do in return. She'll carry no fond memories of you, thinking little of you once you are dead and gone. Perhaps the only recognizable sign you were even there are the scars you gave her for future fishermen to bear witness. It is a broken relationship, but none other would you have or want.

She doesn't think of you when you're on land. She doesn't speak of stories of your adventures together when you're gone. It's a love of passion for her, and you're no more meaningful than the john to the hooker. You won't leave a lasting impression no matter how hard you try. You will give her your all, and she will have had better. She eats the most hardened men for breakfast and breaks the hearts of the most passionate. She will tease you and seduce you, but she will never fully surrender or submit to you. When your bravado is at its highest and your confidence coursing like a runaway train, she will humble you. She will break you.

She is not a giver; she is a taker. She may provide for your family monetarily, but this is her ruse. Mistake not the fact that she charges for all that you take from her. Her bounty comes at a cost often as confusing as life itself, her terms of agreement littered with backhanded traps and dealt-with fine print even the most unscrupulous lawyer would grin over and smile upon.

You cannot trust your heart when it comes to the ocean because nature itself has already dealt the cards in a way that you cannot win. To truly love the ocean is to accept that you're in love with something that cannot possibly love you back. You can long to be upon her your whole life, and one day she may take your boat. A lifetime of riding her waves may someday end in an unrelenting undertow. You can lust to do battle with her largest leviathans, and you may never see one. She will drive you absolutely mad. She will make you spend your entire lifetime trying to outthink creatures that don't think at all. Yet, knowing all this makes her no less gorgeous, no less desirable.

The heart always wants that which it cannot have, and you cannot have the ocean. She will not belong to you or any other man no matter what imaginary lines may be placed on a chart. She is enchanting, timeless, and forever not yours. I unquestionably was born with the derelict fishing genes. Today, I've come to accept and understand this for what it is. Many times in my life, I've wished it wasn't true. However, the fact is that the deeper I've delved into what really makes me tick, the god's honest truth is that I love the things that kill me and I'm completely okay with it. I love fishing. I love pounding into a head sea when others are safely tied up in the harbor. I love the roar of the ocean few will ever hear besides those who work the sea. I love when the music we play and the ocean collaborate on a perfectly harmonious dance; a dance where the boat becomes rhythm and the ocean the dance floor, leaving the souls aboard in perfect step with Mother Nature.

The ocean's abuse doesn't break me. It's what makes me alive. Whipping winds fill my lungs and my heart. Rogue waves at sea and upon land aren't to be feared but respected for what they are. Heavy seas teach a man more about himself than any standardized testing. No place on Earth is a man's worth more quickly recognized than in the teeth of a gale. Those who have been coddled and those who have earned the hard yards themselves are clearly separated in the darkest of nights. The way a man carries himself when the wind refuses to relent and the sea refuses to subside speaks volumes about who he truly is and who he will go on to be.

I love that cancerous tropical sun that beats on my skin and warms my soul. The wrinkles I once stared at in distain I now recognize and appreciate as the story of my life. You will find your smile when the ocean is flat enough and the sun is bright enough. It's no mistake that the human heart and planet Earth have almost exactly the same composition of water.

I believe we need to go no farther than any coastline at sunset to witness the groves of onlookers catching one last glimpse of the ocean's grandeur to know it's not a mere coincidence that she calls to us. It's a primal urge to come to her. Many stare out upon her waters unknowingly looking at the birthplace of their souls. Many people stare out to sea without realizing the ocean is within all of us.

The ocean is a creator and a healer. She is wildly temperamental and devastatingly beautiful. She is comforting yet horrifying. For this reason, the sea will always be referred to in the feminine, as will Mother Nature. Even the most chauvinistic male deep down realizes the feminine ultimately pulls all the strings for the puppet show that is life. Who more powerful than the most beautiful female of them all, the ocean?

I love long pours of whiskey in the bars and total sobriety with my children. I love the confidence alcohol gives me when I'm alone, and I love the way being with my children reminds me that I don't need to drink to be happy. I love when a large marlin inhales a trolling lure. The line they rip off the reel and the time it takes to reel it all back in doesn't feel like I'm losing any time but instead gaining it. Large marlin frantically tearing across the surface that bring complete chaos to the upper water column calms my soul.

I love how the schools of tuna that commit suicide boat side are ultimately consumed by the people of Hawaii, not only bringing sore backs and injuries but true purpose. I love catching fish for those who can't do it themselves. I love fishing on every level. I love taking others fishing. I especially love taking women and children fishing. A woman can brighten up even the most faded boat, and a child's first fish can be more invigorating to the soul than catching a thousand-pounder. Often, it's not truly what you are catching but the appreciation for what you are catching that truly matters.

I love beautiful women. I love how a woman's hair in the right light shines like new fishing line. I love how a set of eyes can say more than the most talkative mouth. I love how a gentle touch at the right time can describe a lifetime. I love how a woman's soft skin blends perfectly with the most calloused of hands. I love how a woman's fragrance can be your favorite story. I love how a woman can make you feel like a man and yet how her laughter, in the same right, makes you feel like a child.

I love when you write enough words you discover that it's completely impossible to tell if you're talking about the ocean or a woman. I love the epic highs, and I love the epic lows associated with both. I love the roll of the dice every time I take a boat off-shore and every time I put my heart on the line. I love being humbled by the ocean, and I love being humbled by women.

I love my children most of all. I love the fact that despite my love affair with my demons, they love me unconditionally. I love that no matter how rough the sea or dark the night, they are excited to see me. I love how they motivate me and make me continually strive to be better and do better.

My life certainly didn't turn out how I thought it would, but perhaps in the end it turned out the only way it could. Few things in life are truly perfect. The calmest days at sea generally have ripples. The most beautiful women have hidden scars. The best laid plans inherently have flaws, and love is a matter of timing. Dream women walk out of your life, and dream fish break your line. Despite knowing all this, we don't stop setting the lines and we don't stop loving. That's not because we don't understand the risk associated with putting our hearts and lures out on the line but because the reward will always outweigh the risk.

Tight Lines,

Capt. K

# CHAPTER 11

# YOGA FOR SAILORS

Back when we were married, I was one of the assholes who immediately put up a wall of resistance when my ex mentioned the idea of me taking yoga classes. My uneducated mind pictured yogi men as a bunch of guys who were light in the loafers and wearing tights. For some reason, I pictured yoga to be a cross of the aerobic classes my mother took when I was a child and a Jazzercise class I took once upon a time trying to get laid by my would-be sugar mama in Stuart, Florida, back when I was nineteen years old. I couldn't picture a less masculine thing in which to participate. The idea of stretching as some type of sport or exercise sounded totally gay. My ego immediately rejected the idea I envisioned of me wearing tights and a headband like Richard Simmons.

Like a lot of things I would soon discover about myself and life after divorce, I couldn't have been more wrong about yoga. Undoubtedly, yoga was the number one thing (besides fishing) that helped me get my life back together and regain focus. Yoga isn't a sport or even truly an exercise, at least depending on which direction you choose to take it. Yoga is so much more than just your physical body's health; yoga is truly about the strength and health of your mind. There are many, many forms of yoga, but the underlying message is about trying to align your thoughts to be true to yourself while respecting others. Yoga is about being okay with who you are and who you are not. Yoga is about controlling our reactions and accepting things that are outside of our control. Perhaps the greatest lesson yoga helps us with is truly appreciating and living in the present. Yoga is equally effective in helping us on not focusing our precious energy in areas undeserving of it.

Yoga also offers a wonderful physical aspect of conditioning if we choose to go that route. I highly recommend yoga to any and every one. I wish I had taken that recommendation years earlier. Yoga is a lot like fishing in that there are many different avenues and thought processes one can follow. One particular yoga practice might not be the right fit for you, whereas that same practice might be perfect for someone else. This is very similar to many fly fishermen I've come to know. Some people are strictly dry fly fishermen, and some people are religious wet fly fishermen. Then there are others who don't allow themselves to be boxed into either tackle box and enjoy doing both. Don't let one class or one style of fishing determine if yoga or fishing is right for you. Try multiple forms until you find what's best for you.

If you're going to your first class, remember that yoga is not a competition. Yoga is only about what's happening on your own mat. Don't worry about what's happening on a more experienced yogi's section of the floor. Although classes bring a form of unity to all the participants, every single individual is still on their own journey. Stay focused on your own path. Like all things, your yoga practice will improve in time. If you are anything like me, your first couple of weeks are going to kick your ass, but keep going. You'll be glad you did when you start to see the gains, not only for your physical being but for your mental health.

If I was in charge of the court system, I would require that all divorced parents attend mandatory yoga classes instead of those stupid coparenting classes. Parents would be far better off learning and working on real world tools for communicating and dealing with post-divorce hostilities than being shown some generic VHS tape from decades ago and being considered checked off by the state.

Though yoga is derived from an ancient Indian spiritual practice and an explicitly religious element of Hinduism, you do not need to be religious to practice it. You just need to have an open mind. I cannot fairly speak of the religious aspects of yoga, as my true religion is the ocean. It would be a stretch for me to have a commentary on the religious component of yoga. However, I can safely attest to the fact that yoga highlights what our true core inner values are versus the baggage we have picked up along the road of life. Yoga helps us decipher what parts of our present life and our actions are beneficial to us and what parts are holding us back.

I met my favorite yoga teacher, Saifon Woozley, at a Thanksgiving get-together. I am forever grateful that I did. Saifon is not only an awesome yoga teacher and person, but today I can proudly say she is one of my best friends. I'm confident I would not be in the better place I am today if I had never met her.

As my interest and participation grew in yoga, Saifon suggested that I attempt a 100-day yoga challenge. This challenge is exactly what it sounds like—I would practice yoga every day for 100 days straight without taking a day off. She suggested the experience would be transformative. After completing the challenge, I completely agree. I also highly recommend it to everyone who is feeling a bit lost or in need of some motivation. Since the practice of yoga is about what's happening on your mat and your mat alone, you can set whatever parameters you'd like for your own personal challenge.

The only rule that I made was that I had to perform a least fifty minutes of physical yoga a day. I'm not sure where I actually got that number from, but that's what I chose. On some days, fifty minutes felt like a lifetime, and on other days, it felt like a blink of an eye. Some days, the practice felt forced, and other days, it came with ease. Yoga reteaches us a lot about ourselves and reminds us about what is truly important.

The 100-day yoga challenge is a perfect physical example of the ebb and flow that is life. Some days are always going to be harder, and some days are always going to be easier. That's the cyclic nature of life. The important part is to always show up and attempt to give it what we have at that moment. Some days, you are just going to be completely run-down and reluctant to perform the tasks at hand. Other days, you are going to be very well rested and highly motivated. That isn't a question. That is just life. The key is to approach the mat and life head-on even when you know it would be easier to sit on the couch.

I kept a yoga log during the 100-day challenge in the same way I've kept fishing logs for over two decades. The yoga log kept me accountable and focused. I actually went on to surpass the 100-day mark, finally ending on day 108 when my body requested a break, partially because I was fatigued and mostly because I was hungover as fuck. I am human after all and a fisherman. So, by my very nature, I'm beautifully flawed.

Although I was sort of bummed I didn't keep the streak alive longer, yoga had taught me not to be overly hard on myself, which is a hugely important lesson that most people could use work on. We will almost always be overly critical of ourselves. We routinely judge ourselves unfairly, using unrealistic measuring sticks found by watching television and perusing social media. These unfair comparisons make us routinely our hardest critics. I continue to work on this lesson daily as I still notoriously beat myself up over things that truly shouldn't affect me as much as they do.

Here is a great litmus test for whether something that is currently troubling you is worth stressing over: Will what's bothering you right now really matter in five years? If the answer is "no," then it's a burden unworthy of stressing out over today. I've also found that repeatedly reminding myself that life is a constant work in progress and not a finished masterpiece keeps daily problems in perspective.

Today, I try to do yoga three to five times a week to help maintain perspective. Before you start making excuses about why you can't do yoga 100 days in a row, I would like to point out that I performed a large number of my days in my yoga challenge in the small confines of an offshore tuna boat in grueling conditions, traveling or working as a deckhand on a big game sportfishing boat anchored up behind the Great Barrier Reef. I truly believe that if I was able find the time and space to pull it off, anyone who's committed to change can do so too.

*Yoga Challenge Log*

    Day 1 Colleen Hilo

    Days 2, 3, 4, 5, 6 Fishing vessel Makana

    Day 7 So fucking rough in the channel

    Day 8 Yoga center in Hilo Michelle

    Day 9 Saifon yoga Hale

    Days 10, 11, 12, 13, 14 @ home with kiddos

    Day 15 Tika yoga Hale

    Day 16 Melissa yoga Hale

    Day 17 Yoga Hale

    Day 18 Worked out with Saifon Kona 3 people in class

    Day 19 Restorative with Danielle

    Day 20 Danielle 2 classes did slow flow but then got crushed by her in sculpt class

    Day 21 My niece Celia, 3 classes Aleah, Tika, Saifon

    Day 22 Ex in class lol and Celia with Tika

    Day 23 Honolulu Tara @ corepower

    Day 24 Fishing boat Makana southbound from Honolulu

    Day 25 Early morning Makana

    Day 26 Cross Seamount to Hilo traveling, south wind

    Day 27 Suisan dock had more cockroaches running around than India

    Day 28 Yoga center - Amanda 2nd class and Colleen

    Day 29 Yoga center - Amy

    Day 30 Sportfishing boat Benchmark caught my dad's first marlin

    Day 31 Benchmark Kanyon on board lost a $100,000 plus 600lb fish

    Day 32 Benchmark caught Dad second marlin

    Day 33 3 Classes, Melissa, Saifon, Danielle

    Day 34 Ariel yoga Chantel then hot vin 1-2, With Saifon kids did cirque

    Day 35 Went to the Bikram studio in Kona with Melissa as instructor, not my favorite style, studio was really stuffy, floor felt like a greasy Brillo pad

Day 36 Saifon, 530 vin 1 vin 2 kids did "yoga" with Chantel

Day 37 Hannah from New Jersey at yoga Hale

Day 38 Sat. morning with Saifon, wicked hangover, thought I was going to have to leave to throw up

Day 39 Morning class with Hannah, evening restorative with Emily, next to Kerstin

Day 40 Flow with Melissa at media center in Hilo, next to Cari

Day 41 Fishing vessel Makana southbound, caught an ahi outside lava flow

Day 42 Fishing vessel Makana westbound 1:22 down sea run

Day 43 Sunrise on Makana Cross Seamount

Day 44 Great night of ika shibi mat covered with bloody footprints from blood that went down the inside of my rain gear

Day 45 Two classes Melissa followed by Saifon's class

Day 46 At home in Ohana, struggled

Day 47 Buti yoga with Saifon woah!!! Kicked my butt!

Day 48 Saifon, Vera waited in green room

Day 49 Hannah taught Saifon's class yoga Hale

Day 50 My living room in home sweet home

Day 51 Beach yoga, Vera played with friends in sand

Day 52 Saifon

Day 53 Saifon and Maria booty yoga

Day 54 Saifon vin flow and then Danielle for private

Day 55 Danielle (held Crow today!!!)

Day 56 Ride offshore Camela taught me how to play cribbage

Day 57 Cross Seamount 66 ahi ika shibi

Day 58 Cross Seamount 65 ahi ika shibi

Day 59 Ride in from Seamount 89 ahi ika shibi

Day 60 Danielle got (charged twice)

Day 61 Saifon 90 min.

Day 62 Tika then Danielle (2 classes)

Day 63 On Washington Seamount

Day 64 Cross Seamount 4 am

Day 65 Cross Seamount long session

Day 66 Cross Seamount midday mix up lost pile of fish

Day 67 2 am yoga session, felt good nice change up

Day 68 Hot vin one and two Saifon

Day 69 Hot vin Tika and Buti with Saifon and the girls

Day 70 Slow flow morning wake up with Emily then vin with Saifon at 530

Day 71 Kim back yoga

Day 72 Saifon hot vin

Day 73 Yoga tiki hut with Heather

Day 74 Core and restore with Danielle

Day 75 Hot vin 1 and 2 with Saifon

Day 76 With Danielle

Day 77 Hot vin with Saifon

Day 78 Yoga at Ohana

Day 79 Yoga at house

Day 80 Yoga at house

Day 81 Yoga at house and Buti yoga hurt my back going full wheel. Had to move. Back on mat to not hit girls next to me with my monkey arms. Doing so put my sweaty hands on the hardwood floor, and I slipped. The first time I ever had to end a practice early

Day 82 Danielle core and restore then Saifon hot vin

Day 83 Hot vin with Tika

Day 84 Makana absolutely gorgeous sea conditions

Day 85 Surprisingly great session after 65 ahi morning rush, beautiful sunrise with visit from a large leatherback turtle next to boat (very cool!), felt fluid and flexible

Day 86 Another good night of ika shibi rainbow filled the sky as performed practice, epic weather day

Day 87 1,200 lb morning rush weather remains absolutely gorgeous

Day 88 Steaming home trades, 15 kts, sea state choppy as heading straight into it

Day 89 Yoga at home after unloading, felt a little rushed as I had to really watch time to go on a manta ray dive

Day 90 Hot vin with Tiki, my energy was really down, but successfully sweated my ass off

Day 91 244-degrees heading south of Ellis Seamount, down sea slight sea breeze, the best kind of delay has you in this location

Day 92 1 a.m. while the boys had a slow pic on squid

Day 93 Morning session, all though the practice was great, the fishing was terrible

Day 94 Did yoga with Kristen, Emily was teaching

Day 95 Did yoga with Kristen, hot vin Saifon teaching

Day 96 Yoga at home before flight to Australia

Day 97 Yoga at Crafty's house in the rainforest

Day 98 Yoga at Crafty's house, 5:30 a.m. amazing

Day 99 Yoga at Crafty's

Day 100 Great Barrier Reef!!! North Opal Reef

Day 101 Great Barrier Reef ribbon reef number 3, caught a 300lber, 400lber, and 800lber

Days 102, 103, 104, 105, 106, 107, 108 Too many fish and too many drinks to remember details besides my sweat smelled like Bundaberg Rum

Day 109 Rest

These are the lessons 100 days of yoga in a row taught me or reminded me about life and myself:

- Yoga reminds us of the difference between pain and discomfort. Pain requires healing, whereas discomfort creates growth.
- The first step is always the hardest.

- Flexibility requires learning how to bend. Don't be too close-minded to look at things in a different light.
- You don't lose when you bet on yourself.
- You can run, but you can't run from yourself, so you better learn to enjoy your own company on this journey.
- We are all beautiful.
- You only get one body. Take care of it.
- We all wish life was as beautiful as the first photo on someone's Tinder profile, however, the reality lies somewhere around photo number four. Learn to appreciate the perfection in your imperfections.
- We all make mistakes!!!
- We are not our mistakes!!!
- Filtered photos filter our true beauty. Embrace those scars, gray hairs, and wrinkles. They are a testimony to where you've been and who you are. Plus avoiding filtered photos will help you avoid the "what the fuck moment" on a first date.
- It's better to show up and do your best than to forever wonder what could have been.
- Love is beautiful, but nothing is more beautiful than watching a fish take hundreds of yards of line off a reel in seconds.
- People almost always tell you what they think you want to hear; the reality is that you need to listen to what they are afraid to say.
- What other people think of you is their problem, not yours.
- In your travels, the moment is the greatest place you'll ever visit. Live there!
- Living in the past isn't living at all.
- When given the chance to try something new and possibly embarrass yourself, always take the chance.

You might just end up impressing yourself. Worst case, you'll get a good laugh out of it.

- The craziest stories that come out of limousines are all true.
- Sarcasm is an art. Not everyone appreciates art.
- You will always more vividly remember the ones that got away than the ones you caught. Love the memories, and learn from your mistakes.
- Money comes easy when you're happy. When you're unhappy, no amount of money is enough to justify what you are doing. Make sure you're doing something that makes you happy.
- The happiest people aren't those with the most possessions to appreciate but the people who appreciate what they do have the most.
- The fastest way to help yourself is to help others.
- Fish and life are always better fresh. Invite people over, and share both. Don't freeze either for later. Later is uncertain and never as good as now!
- Dance everywhere, anywhere, and with anyone.
- If the definition of a friend blurs when they have alcohol on their breath, they aren't really your friend.
- Goals too broadly defined feel unrewarding when achieved, and goals too narrowly defined can make success feel like failure. Be careful when setting goals for what you truly hope to accomplish.
- Dream big, however be realistic about what you want and are willing to do to achieve it.
- Every dollar you make at sea costs you something on land, and every dollar made on land costs you something at sea.
- Balancing is hard. Like anything, it will improve with practice.

- Don't be so hard on yourself. We are always our hardest critics.
- Practice, practice, practice!!!
- Don't fuck women who claim to be separated!
- Relationship goals should never have a timeline or a loose ending. A goal for a relationship shouldn't have a completion date. It should have a series of ongoing goals.
- We all have of our niche. Embrace it.
- Every day we are given the choice to be happy. Do whatever it takes to make the happy choice a reality.
- There are girls, and there are girls with hats. But there will always be just one girl in the green hat.
- Kindness is always the preferred option. When given the chance, always try to use it.
- If you can touch them, then they are real. End of story.
- You most likely won't truly know how many people can fit into your bathtub until after you're divorced.
- Drink lots of water.
- If you're stressed, get out of the house, get off your ass, go for a walk, a jog, a run, a yoga class, whatever. Just go do something now! (Fishing and yoga are always my number one recommendations.)
- When you don't get what you want out of a situation, what you get is experience.
- The world will not wait for you. Saddle up and ride.
- The difference between can and can't is one letter. Are you going to let Mr. T stop you?
- Most things are easier to achieve once you shed other people's opinions and perceptions of what's possible and not possible. Don't let others hold

you back from your dreams. Everything was impossible until someone did it.

- Other people will often tell you how you are supposed to feel or how they think you should feel. The truth is that only you and you alone can know how you feel about a situation. Don't let other people's perceptions of how you are supposed to feel or act become your reality. Be proud of who you are.
- It's okay to hurt, and it's okay to bleed. Bleed out all the pain so it doesn't bring unnecessary hurt into your next relationship.
- Most importantly of all, BREATHE!

# CHAPTER 12

# THE TRAGIC CAPSIZING OF MY ONLY LOVE: PART I

The farther we distance ourselves from the shoreline, the further we distance ourselves from the normalcies of society. The more we become one with the ocean, the further we draw our attention away from the glimmering lights and noise that lives upon the land. Those things that once distracted us no longer catch our eye. Material possessions hold less weight, except, of course, items like fishing rods and surfboards. Impractical items such as three-piece suits and ties become obsolete, whereas board shorts and slippers are essential.

The more time we spend on top of the water or submerged within it, the greater we understand that a lot of things that happen on land just don't make any sense at all. Society often places the strangest things high upon the priority list. Somehow, people reference heavily mortgaged houses and large vehicle payments as signs of success. People often care so much about what other people think that they forget to think for themselves. People routinely get themselves into financial trouble trying to live a meaningless and materialistic life they can't afford. People spend what should be the best years of their lives working at jobs they hate to impress people who don't care. Just how ridiculous everyday life on land can be is somehow made so much clearer from behind saltwater-covered sunglasses.

Social media makes people feel grossly inadequate while trying to match apples with oranges. News feeds of six-pack abs make healthy people feel fat. Lamborghini-filled driveways of the rich make honest-working people feel poor. Botoxed and liposucked women make beautiful women feel ugly. Social media influencers falsely showcase the world as perfect. Instagram pages of perfectly lit photos hashtagged #nobaddays skew reality.

When one paddles out to a surf break or steps upon their boat, the ocean begins to wash away all the craziness found back on shore. A surfboard or a boat becomes our own tiny island. Although potentially deadly water surrounds us, we find ourselves safely comforted by the distance the ocean creates for us from the absurd happenings upon the shore.

When one spends enough time floating around on their own personal island, they become different. They find a certain freedom in less. Less distractions, less needs, less wants, and less nonsense. Magically, when living in less, we actually gain much more. More space just to think and more time just to be. In these times, we really learn the most about ourselves. Something beautiful happens when others' opinions don't affect our decisions. What wave to catch, what compass heading to take, what to believe and think—all these things just come easier without the barking of society.

One can become so in love with this freedom that it totally disconnects us from society all together. But, in its own right, this isn't necessarily a terrible thing. However, this freedom will be routinely under heavy scrutiny when you are married or have children. What is often viewed as a selfish life is anything but selfish. It's self-care and routine maintenance for those who weren't built to live in the confines of everyday society upon the land. Water is to our soul what oil is to an engine. It's our lifeblood. It's what keeps up going. It's a terribly difficult balance to live this life of freedom and to keep a foot in everyday society.

I immensely struggled with being in love with my wife and being in love with the ocean. When I was at sea, every part of me wanted to have a fairy-tale marriage. When I walked upon the land, every part of me wanted to be out fishing. The same clouds I saw at sea reminded me of closely holding my wife, while on land showed me holding giant marlin bills and tuna.

The more time I spent on my boat, the more it truly became its own island. It was truly a different world than that which I lived in back at home. On my boat, I almost always knew the right thing to say and do. At home, I almost never had the right answer and rarely made a decision that satisfied.

The question wasn't whether I loved my wife. The question was this: Could I ever be home enough for the feeling to remain mutual? Our distance from each other grew, not only in nautical miles but in the love we shared. Our conversations became a list of things for me to do instead of talking about places for us to see. It was obvious that our marriage was heading for the rocks if we didn't change our course.

To save our marriage, I advertised the need for a relief captain. Together, my wife and I devised a plan to find a captain to run the boat part time or ideally on an every-other-trip basis. In theory, this would satisfy my lust for the ocean, the financial component to keep the family afloat, and allow me to be around more for my wife and children.

In theory, it penciled out well on paper. However, the reality is that it would be very difficult to replace the drive of an actual owner operator. Every time I took that boat out of the harbor, I looked at it as my name being on the line. The truth is that it was. Commercial fishing has a very thin margin for failure if you wish to be a success. At the easiest of times, the financial gains can be slim with the costs associated with properly maintaining a vessel. As every good captain will tell you, you're only as good as your last trip. Back-in-the-day stories don't pay the bills of today.

Previously, I had mixed results using relief captains. I was very fortunate to have some wonderful ones in the past. Nate Cary, otherwise known as Nate Dogg, and Gus Johnson, otherwise known as Gus Gus, my "brother from another mother," had consistently produced for me and treated the boat with the care and respect a boat owner wishes to see. However, they had both moved on to other things in their lives. Young Micah Tower, who came along after Gus and Nate, had done well fishing. Unfortunately, his timing in the marketplace couldn't have been any worse. Micah came aboard with us as the auction became a losing proposition for all the handliners and small boats. Low-grossing trips were nonreflective of the amount of fish he stocked aboard.

The brutality of a somewhat always volatile marketplace was absolutely savage.

The ups and downs of the market has always been the most difficult part of using a relief captain. Ahi fishing around Hawaii, like most commercial fishing, has to be looked at across a yearly average and not a week-to-week average, both in volume of catch and market value. It would be maddening to break the business down on a week-by-week basis, for some weeks would leave your thoughts totally unrealistic with what fortune there is to be made fishing, and other weeks would leave you suicidal at the realization that you committed to this line of work.

It is superhard to justify to spouses and loved ones why you were just gone for a week with little or nothing to show for it. This vicious cycle keeps a lot of good fishermen bound to land and jobs they hate. Their commitment to their love is both commendable and depressing in its own right. Great landlocked fishermen secretly text other fishermen about fishing like they are cheating on their wives, one eye constantly looking over their shoulders. Heaven forbid should the loved ones find out that, although he sits beside them on the couch, he's 100 nautical miles away in his mind.

Then there are the other captains, the ones who bring in more drama than pounds of fish. We had the nice man on land who became Captain Bligh out at sea, his screaming so relentless that the most hardened crew refused to ever go fishing with him again unless they were allowed to kill him. Then we had the captain who we didn't even let take the boat out after training him because he showed up to captain his first trip absolutely stinking drunk. Then we had the captains who couldn't pass a drug test or captains who just couldn't get the job done. None of these scenarios worked for me.

My boat was my island. My paradise wasn't going to have hypodermic needles and liquor bottles littering it. I certainly wasn't going to have someone screaming at my beloved crew. Crewmen are family, and you become very protective of the good ones. The undesirability of these captains was the reason I had given up on having someone else run my boat. However, I couldn't afford to just have the boat sitting around either and reach the family's financial goals. The bills didn't stop coming in even if we stopped going out.

So it was much to my delight that the first person who contacted me was a person whom I held in a very high regard when I posted an ad looking for a captain. Tommy was his name, and he was the first captain I ever caught a tuna with back when I was fourteen years old in New England. I always liked Tommy. He was funny and jovial. A man's man, if you will. He loved drinking Budweiser, NASCAR, country music, chasing women, and, I thought, fishing. I admired him as one often does through the rose-colored glasses of youth. I thought of Tommy as "the man" without really ever dissecting that viewpoint, partially because I had caught my first couple of giant bluefin tuna with him and because I thought he was my friend. What's more, I thought of him as one of my really good friends.

Quickly and excitedly, I bought Tommy a ticket to Hawaii. *What great fortune*, I thought, *an experienced seaman.* He was someone I really admired, and I thought he could run my boat. Tommy explained that he had hit a bit of hard luck back at home and could really use the money. He said he couldn't make a living fishing out of New England anymore because of all the new regulations. I remember thinking this could be a real win for both of us. I could have a trustworthy friend running my boat, and I could help my old buddy out of his slump. What could be better? It seemed like everything was perfectly falling into place. I couldn't wait for him to get to Hawaii. I was looking forward to fishing with my old dory mate.

The Tommy who arrived in Hawaii was not the man I remembered. He was considerably overweight and clearly out of shape. It looked like he hadn't been particularly kind to himself over the last ten years. He still possessed that big jovial grin, but his smile seemed forced. He was complaining from the second he got off the plane about how uncomfortable the airline seats were and how bad his back was aching.

We went back to my house and got Tommy settled in. We got caught up over a few ice cold Kona Brew Longboard Lagers. It was great to see Tommy again although also very strange. I was looking at the same man I remembered like a hero, but his tone and attitude about life seemed very dark and very different. We would laugh about one thing, and then he'd have something really negative to say about another. I had not been in close quarters with such a downer in a really, really long time. I had never seen him like this before; he was jaded and seemed obsessed about money or at least about other people's money.

He asked about the cost of just about everything I owned. He wanted to know what I paid for my house, my cars, my boat, and on and on. It made me really uncomfortable. I thought it was a particularly strange conversation, especially since I hadn't seen him in years. I did everything in my power to politely deflect these questions.

It became very apparent that somewhere along the line he felt like he was handed a raw deal. Seemingly every boss he ever worked for was a greedy prick. I asked about a mutual friend, Peter, and he responded back with "Fuck that rich prick." I asked about a man named Mike, who was a highliner when I was a kid. They called him Sea Bat, but Tommy said he was just another "rich cunt." I asked a bunch of questions about the fishery back at home, but apparently only the "rich fuckers" could make money now. What about my friend Jimmy working out of the Merrimack River? Or my friend Tim working out of Portsmouth? They seemed to be surviving, I suggested. His rebuttal was that one was illegally lining his net and the other was illegally fishing in closed areas. I really didn't know what to say. He had something really lousy to say about everyone I liked and inquired about. If it wasn't the boss who fucked him over it was the government's fault for making unreasonable regulations.

He talked proudly about stepping away from fishing to be back at home for his family. However, he almost seemed angry with people who still were going hard at it. I wasn't sure what to make of what he was saying. Perhaps he'd had a few too many drinks on his commute. Perhaps his inability to get comfortable in a comparably tiny airplane seat over the course of nearly eleven hours of flying had left him totally exhausted and bitter.

My wife took me aside and asked, "This is Tommy, like the Tommy you spoke so highly of?"

I shrugged and said, "I know."

"Do you even think he can do the job? He's been bitching about his back and health problems nonstop. Is he always so negative?"

"I've never seen him like this. I'm just hoping he's kinda tired and kinda drunk. Otherwise, I'm really not sure what to say about him."

His attitude seemed greatly improved the following day. So I just took it as he had been having an off day. Within a couple of days of him landing in Hawaii, we left to go fishing. I didn't have to cover most of the basics with Tommy, as he was literally the man who taught me them in the first place. We went over the safety equipment, safety checks, and our standard predeparture drills. Our first trip fishing together after all these years was pretty much unmemorable, aside from the feeling of nostalgia that comes in the presence of childhood heroes. The catching department wasn't anything extraordinary, but we did mostly fill the boat.

However, I was surprised at how physically weak Tommy had become. A man I once believed to possess Thorlike power was now huffing and puffing at even a simple task. I had personally witnessed Tommy singlehandedly pull over a 500-pound bluefin tuna on a gin pole with no mechanical advantage, yet he now moaned at pulling mere forty-pound fish over the rail.

Tommy constantly complained about his back, neck, and shoulders.

"Never get old!" was Tommy's unrelenting war cry. He repeated it over and over. Sometimes, he said it like it was a joke to laugh at. Other times, he would say it seriously, following up with, "I'm getting way too old for this shit." He looked remarkably tired. However, he told me not to worry and that his back wouldn't hurt so much once he shed the "winter weight" and he'd be fine. He said he was here for the loot and he was going to get it.

Overall, he did a very good job despite grumbling about the aches and pains of growing old. I was actually surprised by how well the big fella was getting around despite looking so out of shape and run-down. Tommy was no stranger to working on boats, and so it appeared that his muscle memory was carrying the weight his back couldn't.

He had apparently hurt his back, and it was just one of those things he said he had to deal with now. I didn't give it much thought as I know a lot of fishermen with chronic injuries. As I write this, my shoulder has been injured for over three years. Injuries are commonplace in a world where sometimes you go to bed in a bunk and wake up in the air before crashing on the deck. A constantly moving vessel and an ocean with a wickedly cruel side leaves constant opportunities for injuries. I also didn't give his injury much thought because, as a captain, he wouldn't be required to do anymore lifting than he wanted to. He literally could go out and run the boat as a captain and not touch a fish if that's what he desired.

He ran the second weeklong trip as the captain. I only supervised and made suggestions if I felt it was necessary. I also answered questions if he had them. He did a very good job, and although he had only trained with me for fourteen days at sea and an additional two weeks of working on the boat and learning while it was tied to the dock, I believed that he was fit to take the boat offshore without me, especially given his thirty-plus years of experience on the ocean. Tommy held a Coast Guard-issued captain's license as well, so he was well educated in what was expected of a captain and all the responsibilities that come with being in charge of a vessel and its crew. Tommy took the boat out as captain and put together a good trip, especially considering it was his first time captaining a vessel alone in Hawaiian waters.

I was happy things worked out. So was he; at least I thought he was. He thanked me profusely for the opportunity. He said he liked the feel of some real money in his pocket again. I loved that my boat was not only helping out my family but also my longtime friend's family as well. I was starting to see some of the old Tommy I knew and loved shining through again. Apparently, he connected more of his confidence and self-worth to money than I had ever realized. He was smiling and joking again. The man who flew into Hawaii with a black cloud following him around seemed to finally shake it off out at sea.

In short order, Tommy had a new wardrobe and a new pep in his step. He now endlessly conversed with multiple women, not just his girlfriend he had tired of back in New England. He said he only had a girlfriend when they were in the same area code. The zip code rule was being closely abided. Even old high school girlfriends had reemerged with naked selfies and video images I wish I could get out of my head now that Tommy was Mr. Adventurous living out his dreams in Hawaii.

Dealing with a single woman is often tiring. Dealing with multiple women is downright hard work. It seemed that nude shots of other women's privates were widening the hole in his already difficult relationship with his girlfriend. He went back and forth from constantly sexting to constantly arguing. He just couldn't put the phone down. He became wildly distracted. He said he couldn't wait to get offshore away from the phone. The multiple time zones he was dealing with left him with little time to sleep.

Since Tommy had a successful initial trip, I felt confident that he could run the boat in my absence. So my wife and I booked what was unknowingly our last vacation together. We flew to Whistler Blackcomb Resort on Vancouver Island in British Columbia for a kids' free skiing trip and to work on the cracked foundation of our struggling relationship. Meanwhile, Tommy waited back in Hawaii for a weather window he was confident in taking the boat out in.

The winds blew northerly and northeasterly about twenty-five knots with an occasional gust to thirty. This is not particularly rough, so much as just generally uncomfortable. We fish the better half of the year in winds in the twenty to twenty-five knot range offshore. I personally wouldn't have waited even a minute more than I needed to with those wind conditions; but I wasn't going to push the subject as the captain is ultimately in charge of the vessel and everyone's safety. Tommy kept asking me what I would do, and I told him I would go. I was very comfortable in that weather and had been through far worse on that boat countless times. Concerned about his injuries, he stayed lashed to the dock.

Although I personally would have charged straight out, at the end of the day I didn't want him to take the boat out in anything he wasn't comfortable in. I knew all too well that the last thing you ever want to do is add unnecessary additional pressure on a captain who already has a lot on his plate.

The wind came down to around twenty knots, and Tommy ultimately decided to go fishing, but he didn't particularly seem happy about it. I kept reminding him that he could wait until I got back, but this somehow seemed to upset him. It was as if he thought I was questioning his manliness or seaworthiness, which I certainly was not. Immediately following the departure, I spoke to him several times on the phone and he almost seemed angry with me. He made some comment about me being greedy and how it was easy for me to say I would go fishing when I was going on vacation. I really didn't understand why he was getting upset. Multiple times, I told him that if he didn't want to take the boat out he should just wait. Tommy said that he would make less money if I was on the boat, which may have been true if he hypothetically caught the same amount of fish without me as he would catch with me.

If I went fishing with him then his crew would share a smaller percentage of what we caught. However, he then wouldn't have been fully in charge of responsibilities that come with being a captain. Also, he would have another set of experienced hands and a seasoned captain on the boat with him. Ultimately, I hired Tommy to run the boat so I could spend more time with my loved ones. However, if he still needed more time getting used to the boat to confidently run it alone, then I could appreciate that as well. I personally had no hesitation with Tommy taking the boat out based on the strength of his resume alone. Tommy decided, after looking at the subsiding weather, he would take the boat out.

My wife and I enjoyed fine meals, mediocre ski conditions, and each other's company. We laughed and bonded like the good ole days. I saw that girl I fell in love with lying beside me. I ran my fingers through her beautiful blond hair as she lay asleep. I watched giant snowflakes slowly fall past our frosted window and couldn't help but think how we found the warmth that had gone missing in a cold mountain town.

Aside from Tommy's insistent grumbling about how the weather affected his sleep and back, things were going perfectly on his trip. Tommy was on the fish. He was quickly on his way to filling the boat with a nice class of tuna. He reported being knee-deep in fish, and we had reports of knee-deep powder coming our way. At dinner, we filled our glasses with expensive champagne. The feeling in town was electric. The whole town buzzed as the large snowstorm brought the promise of dreamlike conditions for the following day. The energy was contagious. My wife and I were rubbing our legs together below our dinner table, creating a fire I couldn't wait to take care of back at our hotel room. We looked into each other's eyes and promised that we would be better to each other from then on out. It all seemed too good to be true because it was. Our dreamlike conditions would prove to be a nightmare.

Upon arriving back at our dark hotel room, we were greeted by a green flashing light from my phone, which I had left behind to charge. The light indicated that I had received a message while we were away at dinner. As my wife went to the bathroom to freshen up, I went over to the phone to check the message. I opened my phone to discover it was not one message but multiple voice messages from the United States Coast Guard.

The emergency position indicating radio beacon—the EPIRB—aboard the *Vicious Cycle* had gone off. Although not the type of message you want to hear, initially I wasn't overly worried because over the years I had heard of multiple times that EPIRBs had been accidentally set off. This has become more commonplace now because many, like the one I had on board, are water activated. It only took a splash of water to set it off. I myself had already had an incident on board where a crewman accidentally set one off while cleaning. Looking at my watch, it was very possible the boys were already scrubbing the boat on their way home with the amount of fish Tommy was reportedly catching. So, I thought it was very probable that this was what had again occurred.

The weather was no greater than what we commonly fished in, and I had a well-seasoned captain aboard, so why should I worry? However, I became concerned that Tommy wasn't picking up my calls on the satellite phone or returning my messages on my Garmin. But even at that point, it was prime fishing time and he could have been easily on the back deck yanking on fish with the music blaring—common practice when you aren't expecting to talk to anyone.

Another possibility was that he was on the back deck scrubbing with the boys. Although many captains are rarely on the back deck scrubbing, I always helped clean, especially after a slammer, when excitement courses through you despite bodily fatigue. So maybe Tommy was out back scrubbing and laughing with the boys as they bathed the boat in bleach and bathed in the feeling of success knowing they were heading in with another full load of fish and a strong market price.

Then, of course, they could have been fighting one of the giant marlins that routinely harass us around the tuna piles. This has always been my absolute favorite reason to not pick up the phone. I could think of so many positive reasons why Tommy wasn't answering that my mind didn't immediately go to a terrible place.

So many of us fishermen go to sea to be away from a phone. In fact, with all his recent women drama, Tommy had said he couldn't wait to be out of phone range, so maybe he was just indulging in the freedom of being out of cell service.

The Indonesian crew members on the boat would never wake up a sleeping captain if it was his rotation to sleep unless they had a real emergency on board. A ringing phone would have not been a strong enough reason to wake a resting captain. But all of my false hope was destroyed when I got a phone call informing me that my second backup EPIRB had gone off as well. At that moment, I knew something had gone wrong. However, I didn't envision the boat capsized or sunk. I thought maybe they had somehow lost power. Perhaps the batteries had caught on fire, leaving them powerless or something along those lines. Over the years, I had helped tow in more than one boat, so I knew that firsthand accidents like this happen even to seasoned professionals.

But I would eventually field a phone call that started an epic and painful journey over the next three years. The Coast Guard dispatcher confirmed that my boat was in fact gone and my men were now in a life raft. A United States Coast Guard C-130 airplane circled above them in the dark of night like an ewa bird circles above a school of mahi mahi in the height of day. The airmen now kept a constant eye on my boys down below. They dropped flares, an extra life raft, and a handheld VHF radio. The flares hit their mark, illuminating the area surrounding the raft. However, the boys didn't attempt to grab the other raft and radio as they felt they were too far out of reach. Tommy fired off parachute flares, and the Coast Guard pilots maneuvered the giant bird to signal back that they in fact saw them.

Throughout the whole ordeal, I was constantly on the phone like a switchboard operator. I spoke with either the Coast Guard, Navy, friends who heard the news, or the loved ones of those involved. All I could think about was the safety of my crew. Now was not the time to deal with the condolences that had started to pour in as word of the accident spread across our small island chain. I had to again and again politely hang up on people so I could leave myself available for those working on rescuing my men.

I was in shock that the boat sank in only twenty-four knots of wind, as indicated by the Coast Guard buoys they had dropped on the scene of the accident. We lived in those types of conditions. I would stress profusely over the boat in the future, but right now all that mattered and all I cared about was the men's health. Boats are replaceable; men's lives are not.

Thankfully, the airplane's onboard thermal imaging equipment showed my full crew of three within the confines of the canopy-covered life raft. Though we could see inside the raft, we could not converse with them and find out if anyone was hurt. I prayed they were all uninjured.

The boat had sunk or, so I was told, had sunk on top of the Cross Seamount 138 miles southwest of Kona. The closest available Coast Guard ship was fifteen hours away. The closest fishing vessel willing to assist was about eleven hours away. The Coast Guard did not have a helicopter in Hawaii with a large enough fuel capacity or range to come to the rescue and still doesn't to this day.

As luck would have it, the Navy happened to have a helicopter in Oahu that could possibly just pull off the rescue. It was armed with a crew of young flyboys and rescue swimmers who were willing to give it a try. The helicopter would be returning back to Honolulu on fumes even if everything went perfectly. There would be zero margin available for error. I was told the helicopter crew would have approximately seven to fifteen minutes maximum of working time to get my boys safely in the helicopter. If not, they'd have to leave any or all of them behind who didn't make it in the basket and up into the helicopter. I worried the most about Tommy, with his new obesity and his known chronic back problems and injuries. Earlier in the trip, he had already been complaining on the phone that he was getting too old "for this shit" as he called it. Apparently, his back was bothering him again to the point that he was having difficulty sleeping. I prayed he could get into the basket in a timely manner despite his back issues.

Minutes felt like hours. Waiting for updates felt like days. My heart raced so madly my chest was sore. Approximately seven and a half hours after the men entered the life raft, they were now tearing wide open through the skies northbound to Honolulu in a United States naval helicopter. The Navy rescue had gone flawlessly. My boys were bundled in emergency blankets and reported no injuries. I sighed a giant breath of relief.

Up to that point, I hadn't had time to be emotional. The only thing that mattered and the only thing that I cared about was getting my crew safely home, and I had stayed 100 percent focused on that task; but now that I knew my men were in safe hands and again would live to see another day, the realization struck me: My beloved boat and income were both gone.

When that boat capsized, it flipped everything in my life completely upside down. As the gear of the *Vicious Cycle* sank to the bottom of the ocean, so did my childhood dreams. I had dreamed of owning my own boat since I was thirteen. The *Vicious Cycle* was it. She was my baby. I loved that boat like a first child.

Now my first child was gone.

# CHAPTER 13

# THE TRAGIC CAPSIZING OF MY ONLY LOVE: PART II

I wrote the words "I love you" with my finger on the frosty window of our hotel room. Though the window viewed the outside world, all I could see was the reflection of a world that had just drowned within. My wife walked into the room and saw the writing on the glass. "Ahhh, I love you too," she said, hugging me from behind. She was unaware that message was for my true love who once floated upon the sea and not the mistress I had married who walked upon the land. I was too tired to sleep and too sad to cry. I had so many questions. I was extremely happy to know that my crew was alive, but I now personally felt dead inside. I wanted to talk to my crew so badly. What the hell had gone wrong? I had so many unanswered questions that remain unanswered even to this day.

But more than wanting to know what had happened, I wanted to tell my crew how grateful I was that they were alive. The helicopter landed with only minutes of fuel left, and I finally received a call directly from Tommy on a government phone line. I'll never forget the first words out of his mouth, not only because they weren't what I expected but because they weren't true.

They weren't hello, sorry, or thank God we are alive, or anything along those lines like one would suspect. No, they were nothing like that at all. The very first thing Tommy said was "Don't worry. I won't sue you." I was taken aback; I certainly didn't expect that. I wasn't worried about Tommy suing me. Why would I be worried about Tommy suing me? He just sank my boat. Why would I be worried about him suing me? It was an accident. Accidents happen in the fishing industry every year.

I said, "Of course, Tommy, why would you sue me? Of course

you wouldn't sue me." Why would I worry about my friend suing me over an accident when I was not only not on the boat, but he was the captain? I was literally in tears telling him how glad I was he was alive. He again repeated those words: "Don't worry. I won't sue you."

It was so bizarre. I was pouring my heart out about how much I appreciated him and loved him like a brother, and he was coldly stating for me not to worry he wasn't going to sue me. I figured he must have just been taking it all in professional stride and just looking at it like any other nuts and bolts of the business end of being a professional captain.

I had an emotional attachment and love affair with that boat, so maybe I was being overly dramatic. To be fair, the crew was only in a life raft for a little over seven hours in eighty-degree water. While I'm sure it was uncomfortable, it wasn't horrific by any means. I suppose my mind had been fueled by passion, and I had lived on that boat for years. To Tommy it was just another one of the numerous boats he had worked on.

Our vacation was over in every sense of the word. We returned home to discover that the true shitstorm had only started. And it all started with those initial words that had come out of Tommy's mouth. When a person comes out of a life raft and tells you not to worry that he's not going to sue you, that in fact actually means to start worrying that he's going to sue you. I had never thought for a second that one day my friend would sue me for everything I own. If I had, I would have seen all the red flags. Things just didn't add up—the constructed story that changed multiple times depending on the audience or who was on the other end of the line. The original story where Tommy went from scurrying into a life raft as the crew tried to save the boat turned into Tommy swimming back to the boat and rescuing the men who were both accomplished watermen but miraculously scared of the water this particular day.

Tommy told me and everyone else that the two Indonesian crewmen's accounts of the story was incorrect. He told me they didn't know what the fuck they were talking about. Tommy was proud. But even then, I was surprised he got the Coast Guard inspector not to write down the crewmens' accounts for the incident report, claiming they didn't know what they were talking about and didn't "speak English too good."

The thing was that the crew members were well-seasoned fishermen and had over six more months experience on the boat than Tommy. In many ways, they knew the boat better than he did. He used the excuse of their broken English to take away their credibility. Had I known he was planning on suing me immediately from day one, I would have pointed out to the insurance company and insurance inspector all the holes in his story that kept popping up.

I did several things to try to help Tommy. I wish I hadn't included signing off on items he claimed to have on board when the boat sank to get the insurance to reimburse him. Knowing what I know now, I'm sure those unlikely expensive items he claimed to be with him on the trip and the large sum of alleged cash that disappeared were most likely just another part of a shameless money grab.

But I wasn't going to call my friend a liar. I wasn't going to point out the change in the narrative because as the days passed, Tommy had again reunited with that dark cloud he brought with him from New England. The cloud grew larger by the day and so did the darkness within Tommy. He again found that jaded person he arrived with at the airport, although the anger now seemed solely focused on me.

It was all very strange. Tommy was living at my house but routinely mentioned it would be his house if he decided to sue me. He kept telling me how lucky I was that he wasn't suing me. It made me very uncomfortable. He kept telling me I'd be just fine. That I had money. That I'd be getting insurance money and I already had plenty of money, so I didn't have anything to worry about.

The funny part was that the insurance money was for less than a third of what it would cost me to replace the boat I lost. Considering that and although I had some savings, I was still a blue-collar worker who needed to work for another three or four decades.

So I wouldn't really be just "fine" as he put it. I was starting over again, like an eighteen-year-old kid in many rights, except I had a mortgage, two car payments, and three additional mouths to feed.

The double stinger was that I had recently upgraded my onboard electronics with about $50,000 worth of new marine electronics. This included a large bird radar and a new side scan sonar. I had talked to my insurance agent twice previously about increasing my insurance coverage to protect these new investments. The agent I had worked with for years had told me to just send the receipts for the items in the meantime and not to worry. The receipts would suffice if there was any type of accident until I could get a new marine survey at my next yearly dry dock. The problem was that the next yearly dry dock never came and apparently our conversation never happened. The insurance agent, although acknowledging the conversation on my first call after the accident, would never again agree that conversation ever occurred.

If the loss of my boat was teaching me anything, it was just how cheap a person's word had gotten to be back on land. It also showed me how nobody took accountability for the things they said and did. Tommy crafted his shameful and gross negligence into a story where he was actually now a hero instead of the captain who made a series of grave missteps. It was easier to cast the owner of the boat as another greedy rich prick than it was to take total accountability for his mistakes.

Tommy would go on to tell people that I forced him to go fishing. Tommy would go on to tell people that my boat was a piece of shit and completely unseaworthy. Tommy would claim that the wind was much greater and the seas much larger than they were. As Tommy's tall tale grew, so did his appetite for alcohol and pills. Tommy diluted his pain with handfuls of Vicodins, sleeping pills, and Budweisers. Following the accident, everyone else in the *Vicious Cycle* family was apparently totally incompetent except for him.

Tommy talked poorly about me and my wife to anyone who would care to listen all while living in my house for free. He talked shit about me to my neighbors, friends, and family members. This was extremely awkward, to say the least. He would sit in my living room trash talking about me on the phone as I worked at my desk just ten feet away.

My crew was apparently worthless, and so was I. Every time he told the story, Tommy would become more and more of a hero and I became more and more of a villain. The crew became more helpless and his actions braver. I had grown into this slumlord type of boat owner who shoved him out to sea in some rinky-dink piece of shit boat without a chance in hell of surviving. Yet he beat all the odds despite my best attempts at killing him.

The most common account of the sinking that Tommy told totally countered what the crew said occurred, so it was hard for me to truly understand what happened that day. Initially, I believed Tommy's version of the accident because I'd known him for thirty years. The foreign crew, although extremely knowledgeable sailors and fishermen, did have difficulty speaking perfectly fluent English.

However, I clearly understood what the Indonesian crew was saying on this subject, but mentally, I couldn't get around the fact that it was nearly the complete opposite of Tommy's account. In my mind, their version made much more sense but also made Tommy incompetent and negligent. I couldn't bring myself to believe that Tommy would lie to me, the Coast Guard, the insurance people, and all of our mutual friends.

Though I found Tommy told several versions of the tale, the one he most commonly told put him traveling from the Cross Seamount with a full load of fish. This was completely the opposite of the first version he told me of the story. There, he claimed to be on the sea anchor getting a twenty-minute nap before he started heading home because he was so exhausted from the trip and dealing with all the bullshit with his girlfriends on the satellite phone. His back was killing him, and he just wanted to lie down. The phone records would back that he used more minutes on that one trip than I would usually use in two or three months.

I gave him a strange look and said, "You're kidding me, right?" I couldn't imagine anyone stopping to take a nap before driving home, and I couldn't imagine anyone fighting on a phone that cost nearly a dollar a minute over some nonsense he could do nothing about in the middle of the Pacific. He literally would have had nearly forty hours to rest before getting all the way to Hilo on the far side of the island and at least twenty hours of phone reception before hitting port. I only heard him mention the sea anchor one other time around my family. He adamantly denied that he even threw the sea anchor at all. It was all very strange and hard to understand. Tommy's go-to version of the story put him steaming northeasterly into a head sea and setting the course home as the boys packed the final fish securely for the bumpy ride home. They packed the boxes with ice and pumped off any excessive water that could possibly start to slosh, making the fish move about and get damaged.

According to Tommy, he had just taken off his rain gear and settled into the captain's chair for the long ride home when the engine room's high water alarm started to go off, indicating that sea water had gotten approximately eight inches deep in the engine room. This would be a lot of water since the engine room was not only regulated by one emergency bilge but three individually wired automatic bilge pumps, each on independent float switches and wiring. Any one of or all the pumps would have turned on when the water reached anywhere from approximately one to two inches deep.

As part of his job and standard operating procedure for my boat, Tommy had confirmed on a phone call to me that he had tested all three of the engine room pumps and float switches before he left the dock. So it was almost unfathomable to picture that much water had penetrated the engine room without some type of catastrophe unfolding.

The three pumps could pump approximately 108 gallons a minute from the engine room if they were all going at the same time. If, for some miraculous reason, he lost even one pump (or an unimaginable two pumps), the third pump would have carried almost any incident except a complete submerging. I could see no scenario where all three pumps could possibly fail at the same time unless the separate battery banks they were all connected to somehow caught on fire and the wires all melted. The batteries were located up forward under the main cabin, and Tommy reported nothing of the like happening.

When Tommy first told me and many others the story, he claimed that the dripless shaft packing had failed on the port engine, allowing water to flood in past the seal. I could see a lot of water coming in if the seal completely shattered but not by it just getting past the seal. Also, it's fairly easy to tighten up a dripless packing at sea. That left us scratching our heads and saying the same thing: that it didn't seem likely that a leaking seal would have caused enough water to come in at such a rate that the water would get above all the pumps.

When questioned on this several times, the story, interestingly, morphed into the exhaust pipe for the starboard engine's wet exhaust, which I had rebuilt three weeks prior, failing. Tommy said the fiberglass exhaust I had replaced had blown off and that was in fact what flooded the engine room. He said he couldn't plug the leak and save the boat because of how extremely rough it was.

Tommy said he didn't initially tell me this because he didn't want me to have that kind of guilt on my conscience. He said he couldn't imagine what it would feel like knowing that my shitty workmanship nearly killed his crew and sunk my boat. He said he was doing what friends do, looking out for me, not telling anyone the truth. He said he didn't want me to look bad.

Although I still questioned the extremity of the weather on scene, I believed Tommy about the exhaust I rebuilt imploding because I could definitely envision a six-and-a-half-inch diameter pipe allowing enough water to flood out an engine room if it was not quickly plugged. I actually had an emergency plug for the exhaust in the engine room, but Tommy said it all happened too quickly to do anything about it. That was probable enough, I supposed.

I didn't take the revelation that I was responsible for sinking my own boat very well at all. I could barely get out of bed the week after Tommy told me my poor repair job had compromised everything for which I had worked. I was so depressed at the idea that my workmanship had failed not only the test of time but everything and everyone in my immediate life.

Tommy stayed in Hawaii, and we tried to find him a new job working on a different boat, but no one seemed to want to touch him while he was being so negative. We went down and talked to my friends about work, but he self-sabotaged every job offer I got him. "Jeez, that guy is grumpy. I couldn't imagine being on a boat with him for a week" was the common response.

"You sure that guy is really your friend?"

That fucking dark cloud he brought with him was back in full force, and it was keeping him pinned down under my roof. One particular interaction at the harbor really set him off. I had brought him down behind Rob's boat, the guy who actually built the *Vicious Cycle*. Tommy told his heroic tale of woe, and Rob blatantly said, "No way." Rob said it was impossible for the boat to sink like that. Furthermore, he said there was no way the boat was even sunk at all. Rob had designed it with so much foam in its bow that it couldn't physically sink. He said it might have capsized some, but that was it. The boat was still out floating around somewhere, he said.

This really pissed Tommy off because an intricate part of his story was that he watched the boat sink directly below the life raft with all the lights still on. He spoke about how it was strangely beautiful to watch the lights of the boat sink farther and farther into the abyss below him illuminating the surrounding ocean like in the lights in the movie *Titanic*. He said he watched the boat sink to at least 100 feet below before the lights finally went dark in the crystal-clear water. That's when he claimed he saw God for the first time in his life. It was a tragically beautiful story but ultimately untrue. Rob calling out the hero and calling bullshit on him really upset Tommy. Tommy was angry and kept saying "Fuck that" for days following our meeting. He didn't like the fact that people were skeptical of his account.

The other problem was that all the Indonesian crew in Hawaii are not only like a giant family, but many of them are actually related. The Indonesians have the most admirable and tight-knit community you could ever imagine, and my crewmen's version of the accident had passed rapidly through the ranks and gone straight up to almost all the American captains. Their version of the story was so wildly different that it made you wonder if they were talking about the same boat.

The crew's version was one of an overly tired, lazy captain who sank the boat in his own greed. Their account and Tommy's really had just two similarities: They both agreed they had filled the boat with fish, and they both agreed they ended up in a life raft. Other than that, the stories had little commonality. Tommy's version had the boat safely underway toward home when the high-water alarm event off. The crew's version had the boat grossly overloaded with tuna. They claimed the final box was nearly full and the deck was completely loaded with more fish than they had room for. The crew claimed the boat dangerously squatted and listed with the excessive amount of tuna on the rear deck jamming the scuppers. With the scuppers being completely plugged with fish, the water had nowhere to go when and if water came over the lowered rails as she squatted. The crew claimed they told Tommy they were catching too many fish, but Tommy allegedly yelled back at them that they were there to make money and that was what he was going to do.

Now, here is the part where the stories differed the most: Whereas Tommy's revised version had them steaming for home, the crew's version had an extremely tired captain throwing the forty-foot across sea anchor parachute that would hold the bow of the boat directly into the wind like a traditional anchor would hold the boat, which allowed Tommy to sleep. This directly coincided with the first version of the story Tommy had told me but that he quickly retracted. The crew told me that the boat was still deck loaded while Tommy threw the sea anchor in the water from the bow so he could take a nap. Apparently, his plan was to sleep as the crew figured out how to put all the fish away that remained on the deck.

The problem was that as the vessel drifted down sea in the

trough of the waves waiting for the sea anchor to open up, a wave landed over the windward railing and the water had nowhere to go because all the scuppers were jammed with fish. The sea anchor started to come tight on the same side, creating an even greater list on the vessel. A series of small waves with nowhere to go now flooded the deck. Tommy panicked as the water filled the deck and put the vessel full throttle forward. Unfortunately, being on the sea anchor, the additional throttle only buried the listing side further under the water, completely submerging the listing starboard side until the rear end of the vessel was completely under water.

The water came so high into the boat with the force of the throttled-up engines that it was blasted up through the engine room breathing ports because the deck was stuffed with fish. The heavily listed boat was a sitting duck with no way to clear the water off the deck. Tommy opened the engine room hatch to assess the amount of water that came through the breathers. This would be the final kiss of death for the *Vicious Cycle*. When Tommy opened the engine room, he exposed its heart to the ocean. A series of waves washed over the listing boat, and the flooded decks completely flooded the engine room. They quickly went down stern first, eventually floating upside down. It didn't look I was going to get Tommy on another offshore boat. Everyone disliked his negative attitude, and everyone thought he caused the boat to sink. None of the captains and offshore fishermen we talked to thought the story added up.

Former crewmen and captains kept taking me aside and asked what the real deal was. Did I think he sank it on purpose? My boat was a legendary sea boat around Hawaii. It had been faithfully bringing men to sea and back home again since 1991. No one who had ever fished on her decks or alongside her pictured it sinking in any type of weather.

I stood up for my friend again and again. I said there was absolutely no way he would ever sink my boat on purpose. I agreed that it was tragic that the boat sank, but I also knew it was an accident. It also looked like—at least based on what Tommy was saying—the accident was falling heavily on my shoulders. That part was particularly devastating for me. The problem with all these conspiracy stories was that parts of them were plausible. Tommy was obsessed with money. Tommy did feel like he had been dealt an unfair hand in life and constantly talked about how much money he would get from me if he ever decided to sue me.

I tried to never let my mind drift in that direction for any period of time. I actually felt terrible for buying into any of the conspiracy stories for even a second. It's easy to not want the accountability for an accident on your shoulders, so every time I started to play the blame game in my head, I manned up and accepted what Tommy said as fact about the exhaust bursting. I accepted that the accident was all my fault.

Now, it would have been easy for Tommy to continue to shit talk me and have me just take the relentless abuse because I'm nonconfrontational to a fault and because I was completely emotionally drained about losing my love and my livelihood. However, something happened that Tommy never counted on and threw a major wrench into his credibility.

That piece of shit boat that Tommy had described in painstakingly vivid details sinking was not sunk at all, just like Rob had insisted. The same day that the *Vicious Cycle's* life raft and a debris field from the wreckage was found in front of my home on the Kona coast, the actual vessel herself was spotted eighty-four miles away south of Honolulu by the longline fishing vessel *Marie M* on her transit offshore. The boat hadn't sunk. This brought up all kinds of questions.

Tommy was quick to point out that it must have sunk, dumped its load, and come back up. That theory definitely didn't make sense. The hatches on the *Vicious Cycle* would have all dumped fish immediately when they hit the water. I didn't care about any of that though. All I cared about was that my boat was still floating. This meant maybe she could be saved. If we could save her, then we could again fish together.

The capsized boat brought me lots of excitement, but it brought Tommy a lot of anger. I excitedly told him that they had found the boat, and he responded, "Fuck that boat." Now, Tommy had already been acting strange around my house. But he was straight-up bizarre after the boat reappeared. He seemed really pissed that I was excited the boat had been seen floating offshore.

"That thing is a fucking piece of shit!"

I didn't know how to respond to the negativity, so I didn't. I fantasized about rescuing my beloved boat from the grasp of the ocean. The following day, it was seen off Maui. She was steadily moving more or less northbound despite the fact that the current was south where the boat sank. The giant counterclockwise ocean gyre had delivered the *Vicious Cycle's* dumped contents to my home waters off the Kona coast, and somehow, against all humanly possible odds, it was on track to deliver the boat right back to the very harbor I had bought her from, Kewalo Harbor Basin on the South Shore of Oahu. This old horse knew her way home.

The day after she was spotted off of Maui, she was then spotted twelve miles off of Barbers Point on the southwestern side of Oahu. Though she was a mere stone's throw from Pearl Harbor, at this point the vessel was considered a total constructive loss by the insurance company. In other words, she was already written off for the full insurance value of the hull. The insurance company had no interest in pursuing the vessel if they didn't have to because it would cost them additional money to deal with it. It was all about keeping the loss to as minimal of an expense as possible. The company didn't want to throw money at salvaging a vessel they didn't have to deal with.

They hoped that the boat would just drift away into the vastness of the Pacific Ocean. Out of sight and out of mind. This totally bummed me out, but I understood that from their point of view, they had already lost enough money on the ordeal. I absolutely loved the boat. I had pursued private salvage quotes, but they came back greater than the amount of money I would receive for her from the insurance company. So although I passionately cared for the boat, I also had to be realistic about what made sound financial sense for my business and my family. It was too cost prohibitive for me to salvage the vessel on my own.

The sun set on Hawaii and my hopes of recovering *Vicious Cycle*. I was superdisappointed. *So close yet so far away*, I thought. I was trying to be rational about the whole situation. I knew it didn't make sense to spend a fortune trying to recover her, but I did want her back. It looked like this was going to be just "another one that got away" story in the life of a fisherman. That was until the most peculiar Kona winds arrived late that night while I slept. The southerly winds and a strange easterly current pushed the old girl toward land at an angle I wouldn't have personally believed if I hadn't known for a fact it really happened.

Kona winds are a rare condition at any time but particularly at that time of year. As I slept, the unlikely winds pushed the *Vicious Cycle* within a mile of the famed Waikiki Beach and the harbor I first placed my eyes upon her. It almost seemed that the boat was on a purposeful mission, like a salmon that comes all the way back to the very stream it was born in after spending a life at sea, only to die after spawning for the betterment of future generations. Her return back to the Southern shores of Oahu was so wildly improbable, it seemed like she had at least one more story she needed to tell, and it turned out she did. When I awoke, I was told that the boat was threatening to wash up upon the most valuable piece of real estate in Hawaii and the insurance company changed its tune about rescuing the vessel. With the real possibility of an environmental disaster on Hawaii's fabled beach, the company sent out a salvage operation to tow the boat in.

When I arrived in Honolulu the following morning, the *Vicious Cycle* had already been towed in Ke'ehi Lagoon with apparently great difficulty. The strong Kona winds and the weight of the capsized boat made a formidable match for the towline, which parted three times in the course of the rough evening. The short tow took far longer than anyone could have ever anticipated and consumed most of the crew's night. The old steed was stubborn to the very end. Eighteen days after being lost to the sea, she was again back in port.

They would not right her again till the following day. The task, like almost all things commercial-fishing related, took far longer than expected and proved to be far more difficult than antici-pated. The first thing I noticed when she was righted in the water: The large sea anchor that would have lived in the bow anchor locker if the vessel had truly been underway was tangled astern on what remained of the shredded awning. The parachute was intertwined with a menagerie of different ropes and lines that now looked like Medusa's hair.

The wickedest of snakes was the parachute's trip line, which was still clearly cleated off to the side of the vessel. There was no way that boat had been steaming for home like I had been told with the sea anchor still cleared off. This was the first red flag that's Tommy's version of the story might have a few discrepancies. Regardless, it was still an awful accident and nothing was going to undo the vessel having capsized. I bit my tongue and simply observed the salvage operation. I supposed being on the parachute wouldn't matter anyway with the exhaust blown off and the shaft leaking.

It took almost the entire day to get the boat towed from the front of the lagoon to righted upward in the Ke'ehi Marina haul out slip. Many men, multiple boats, a tractor, and a giant travel lift also participated in the effort. Once they had the boat facing right side up in the giant slings of the travel lift, they pumped out all the water that remained in her. The fish boxes, engine room, and the cabin all had surprisingly little water in them. She was very quickly pumped out, and within thirty minutes she was again floating on her own bottom just like she had for the past twenty-five years. She looked haggard but certainly not totally defeated. You could still see her strong lines despite being covered in algae and fish scum.

The remainder of the 10,000-plus pounds she contained within her when she went down left an unforgettable stench of death and failure. It smelled like a combination of a marsh at low tide and a rotten dumpster. A thick white film of tuna residue covered eve-rything on the boat like vernix caseosa on a newborn baby's head.

Particularly bad was the inside of the cabin, which contained multiple carcasses and ahi skeletons. I even found an ahi jaw hanging from the VHF antenna wires.

The scene was surreal. It felt like a tuna apocalypse had happened on board. Looking at the items that remained in the cabin left no part of me believing the boat actually sank. I knew that it had merely capsized. Nonpressure-sealed plastic box items still remained untouched by water. A paper collection in an everyday Walmart storage bin remained bone dry. The very bow of the boat never went underwater. The romantic story of the boat sinking out of sight in the moonlight was a lovely story for girls Tommy told it to, but it definitely wasn't true.

I was somehow still okay with Tommy's story. It wasn't like fishermen didn't embellish tales from time to time, especially when trying to get laid. I myself have definitely used this story since the capsizing to get fucked, so I can understand that part. Also, the parachute being deployed didn't matter that much since my exhaust repair had failed. Tommy probably just didn't want to admit he was taking a nap before driving home, which when said out loud to any fisherman sounded ridiculous. Who would take a twenty-five-minute nap before a forty-hour ride home where they could get so much sleep they would have to worry more about getting bed sores than being sleep deprived?

The problem was that there was no blown-off exhaust when I was finally allowed to step foot on board the *Vicious Cycle* along with the two Coast Guard inspectors and the insurance investigator. Nor was there even a leaking packing. We all scoured the boat from head to toe, looking for not only a catastrophic leak but any leak at all. However, there was none. Not even a drip. The exhaust was fully intact, and the dripless packing remained dripless. The old girl again sat properly on the water, bone dry.

I knew in an instant that the crew's story of the deck being overloaded with fish and Tommy's original story of throwing the parachute to take a nap was true. It was the only possible way that much water could have risen high enough to pour into the engine room vents. I could see it all clearly in my head now. Tommy's seemingly insatiable appetite for money had gotten the better of him, and greed had in fact taken the boat down. It had nothing to do with my workmanship.

I was absolutely heartbroken that a friend would put that kind of guilt on me. For nearly three weeks, I had felt three inches tall thinking I had cost myself my boat and put my crew's life in jeopardy. None of that was true at all. Tommy made me feel terrible and constantly guilt-tripped me. My shitty workmanship nearly killed him, he said over and over. My workmanship proved to be 100 percent seaworthy after all. However, it was unfortunately not greed proof. Tommy's lust for the "loot," as he called it, had jeopardized his better judgment and he had overloaded the deck with fish. Now, the true weight of his decision rode on my shoulders.

I tried to talk to Tommy on the phone about what we had found, but he just continued with his slogan that my boat was a piece of shit and I was lucky I wasn't suing him. I didn't push the subject. He was still living with my family, and I didn't want to cause anymore unnecessary waves than the ones that had already come crashing through our lives lately.

Tommy's version of the story was already signed off on. My disputing it wouldn't change anything now. In fact, I wondered if his incompetence would actually jeopardize my insurance claim. Tommy was definitely at fault, but I wondered if that really mattered. An accident is an accident, and I'm sure he hadn't really wanted to sink the boat, although so many others believed he had. I never subscribed to him purposely sinking the *Vicious Cycle* like so many others suggested. I just believed that his strained female relationships back on land had caused him sleeplessness. That, accompanied by his bad back and desire for money caused him to make a series of bad decisions that ultimately capsized the boat.

I shifted through the aftermath of the disaster for the next two days. I did my best to salvage any items and gear that were salvageable. Most everything in the cabin outside of fishing lures was destroyed, aside from the few items that had remained dry in the storage containers. On top of what remained destroyed in the cabin, countless items had been dumped on the ocean floor or had floated away.

It was absolutely heartbreaking. My dreams lay in tatters. I threw out countless destroyed memories. Lucky this and lucky that items filled the dumpster located below the captain's window on the hard stands she now stood on in the Keehi Marina dry dock area. I threw $70,000 of ruined electronics out my window like one tosses a piece of paper in a wastebasket. I saved what I could, but more often than not most objects had succumbed to the effects of being in tuna slime and the ocean for eighteen days. The stench of failure was ever-present. It not only filled the cabin but my soul. I had been through some stuff in my life, but this was by far the hardest.

The insurance company only gave me twenty-four hours to decide whether I wanted to buy the boat back from them before it would go up for auction. Every part of me wanted to buy her back and rebuild her to her former glory, but my business partner, who was also my wife, didn't want anything to do with the boat. She considered it a possible blessing that it was gone. Now, I would be around home more and I could spend more time with the family. We could do more things together. I could get a normal job . . . whatever the hell that was. I was more emotionally wrecked than the boat. I wanted to save my boat, but I also wanted to save my marriage. I always wanted to be remembered as being a good fisherman, but more importantly I wanted to be remembered as being a good father. If not keeping the boat meant being a better husband and a better father, then I really didn't have a choice. I struggled with this decision more than any other I'd ever made. I loved that boat, but I also loved my wife.

Most of my life, I had notoriously made the wrong decisions when it came to women. So this time I decided to go against my gut and not buy the boat back. It was a painstakingly difficult decision to gamble on leaving the boat behind. However, it wasn't a difficult choice to put all my chips on the family and see where the cards would fall. I would need to figure a lot of stuff out, but right now I didn't have the time to do it. I had to get my stuff off my old boat so it could be auctioned to a new owner.

I had many visitors as I cleaned out my past. Some people came just to gawk, others just to talk. Some came to give sympathy, and others came to see if they wanted to bid on the boat. Then there were others who weren't really sure why they came at all. I watched some walk up to the boat like they had something they wanted to say to me, but then they walked away last minute. Perhaps those were the ones who understood my pain the most—the ones who knew no words could ever be fitting in a situation like this.

The most confused guest I had was also the saddest. My old comrade Shaky noisily banged his way up the rungs of the ladder, making a presence ten times larger than his paper-thin frame. At this point, more than a year had passed since I had last seen him. He looked worse than the boat. When Shaky climbed aboard, he was clearly high as fuck. He stared right through me like I was a ghost. His giant wired eyes surveyed the wreckage as his right hand scratched insistently at his left forearm. He was endlessly sniffling.

He stated, "I once used to work on this boat."

"I know, Shaky. I know you did."

Shaky just about fell over when I said his name. The fact that I knew it really troubled him. He clearly had no idea who I was despite years of us knowing each other and fishing together. He clambered for the ladder he had just climbed up on and frantically dove back over the side. He claimed he would be right back in a minute. That would be the last time I ever saw Shaky as he never returned to the boat.

However, the strangest guest I had wasn't Shaky. Rather, it was Tommy. Before the boat had reemerged, we had already organized a get-together at the Barbers Point Air Station to celebrate the rescue of my crew and give appreciation to the hardworking Coast Guard and Navy personnel that were involved in the rescue. Tommy walked around the boat kicking it all over the place like a frustrated driver kicks a flat tire. He kept saying, "Fuck this thing."

One incident happened upon his visit, which I would have never given a second thought to in my life if Tommy's lawyers hadn't, in fact, requested the items three years later. On the starboard rail of the boat, I was drying out my soaked maintenance logbook, safety equipment, and master logbooks. Tommy said, "Why are you saving that shit? You'll never need that stuff again." He tossed one of the logbooks in the dumpster below. I agreed with him that I was probably being overly sentimental. I was an emotional mess, and I threw the remaining logbooks in the trash as Tommy looked on.

I was in such a difficult spot. On one hand, Tommy was my friend. On the other, he wasn't taking any accountability and was showing no remorse. I was emotional dying, and he continued to stomp me emotionally and the boat physically.

He said, "Let's get off this piece of shit and get going."

It was perfect irony that we celebrated his and the crew's rescue on April Fool's Day because the version of the story he told was a total joke. The newspaper and local news station were there to capture Tommy in all his glory. The waves were greater than ever and so were his amazing death-defying feats. I had to just respectfully watch and applaud Tommy on his heroic tale of swimming back to the boat and individually rescuing each crew member there. He even received an award normally reserved for Coast Guard members for his incredible act of bravery that the crew claims never happened at all.

Why would men who swam like fish need him to come back and rescue them?

In fact, the crew's version had them trying to unplug the scuppers and bailing out the engine room as Tommy deployed and jumped in the life raft by himself. The crew believed they could have saved the boat if they had just unjammed the scuppers and had gotten the boat moving forward to dump the water off the deck, and they were probably right. Regardless of what really happened, the Coast Guard and Navy did an impeccable job and my boys were all alive. That's what really mattered.

However, I would be lying if I said it wasn't hard to look at Tommy the same way as I did before knowing he had lied about the pipe bursting. He was taking zero responsibility for the accident and zero accountability for the events that happened. He never apologized for his decisions. It didn't seem to matter to him that he blatantly lied to countless people about a faulty pipe bursting. What's more, he was shaping his failures into heroics. I suppose it was much easier to put the responsibility on someone else. Unfortunately, in this case it was me. What really bothered me was that he made it appear that he had saved the day rather than potentially almost killing everyone. But out of respect and professionalism, I just swallowed my pride and said nothing publicly. I just wanted Tommy to leave, and I wanted to get all this behind me.

I know Tommy never expected that boat to show back up by the way he went off the deep end when it did. He never thought his story would ever be crossed-checked. I'm sure it was way easier to contrive stories than just say, "Hey, I really fucked up. I got greedy, and I got lazy. I caught way too much fish and dropped my guard because I was overly fatigued."

I imagine the pressure of knowing that he put himself and the crew in the water that day was staggering. I know how terrible I felt when I was told my repair work failed. I can only imagine how terrible it must have really felt knowing he really was at fault for the accident. I'm sure that's why he had to get sleeping pills from a doctor. I wouldn't be able to sleep either knowing I cost my friend his livelihood and life's work.

The thing is that I always just wished he would have admitted it. Accidents happen, but it was no accident that he tried to shame me. That's what hurt the most out of everything that happened up to that point. Why would he put that on me? Why would he not take responsibility? Was he afraid I'd sue him for negligence? I'd never sue a friend over an accident. Why was he blaming me? The only mistake I ever made was putting my trust in him, a mistake that haunts me even today.

The last words Tommy and I ever shared face-to-face as I shook his hand goodbye before his flight back to New England were the same bizarre first words he said to me over the telephone when he got off the helicopter: "Don't worry. I'm not going to sue you." I went back to the boatyard and said my final goodbye to my beloved boat with a tear in my eye before flying back home to Kona. That was the last time I ever saw my old boat or Tommy in person.

Three and a half years after the boat sank, I was served with two lawsuits. I had already lost one without even knowing about it. Tommy won a default judgment against me. Tommy and his lawyers got a judge to believe it would be difficult to find me to serve me without knowing where I lived. So the judge allowed the lawyer to notify me by publication. Conveniently, not only did they misspell my name in the tiny advertisement, but it was also published in a local newspaper and not on my island. It was published in Oahu, 142 nautical miles from my home. Nobody I knew ever saw the ad for the court date. So when I didn't show up, Tommy won by default.

Tommy literally not only lived in my home for several months, but he was my "friend" on two social media sites. We exchanged messages from time to time. Tommy literally had just sent me a congratulatory message no less than three weeks before when I got a new boat. He said, "If anyone deserves it, you do buddy." Unbeknownst to me, he had already filed two lawsuits against me and won one in a superslimy way. Fortunately, we had enough supporting evidence to have the default judgment thrown out.

As I write this chapter, Tommy is still attempting to get 1.5 million dollars from me for the capsizing of the vessel. He claims the boat was unseaworthy and that his seven-plus-hour ordeal in the life raft has caused him back, neck, and shoulder problems, all not reported at the time of the incident. His biggest argument is that he can no longer fish because of the trauma caused by being in the raft despite the fact his Facebook page and Instagram page are covered with photos of his recent catches.

The whole thing is almost unbelievable to me. The man who literally caused the boat to capsize from greed, which inevitably destroyed my finances, is now suing me for everything I own. I would laugh if someone had told me that scenario if it wasn't really true. Some find themselves in the ocean, and others get terribly lost. I believe that Tommy was just terribly lost. I used to think he was a true fisherman, but I know now he truly never was. He went to sea not because he belonged but rather because he had nowhere else to go. It doesn't matter how many fishing tattoos you put on your skin. If your heart's not truly committed, you'll never be a real fisherman.

From the lawsuits, I discovered that Tommy had never held a job for any amount of time in his life. Even our mutual friend Peter, his longest-running employer, couldn't remember Tommy ever working more than a couple of months at a stretch without quitting at some point. I've come to find that those who don't really belong on the ocean will cut at you with words and gouge at your heart with lawyers. They will drown you with paperwork and attempt to discredit your entire being.

They will forcefully restrain you by a necktie, the choke collar of a fisherman. They will steal your most limited commodity—your time—and yet they will think nothing of it. They will make you burn money that hasn't even been earned yet from fish that haven't even been caught. They will chain you to land by court dates and tie you up like a derelict vessel. They will take and take until there is nearly nothing left to give financially, physically, and emotionally.

Often, those you tried to help up will, sadly by their very nature, find it easier to attempt to drag you down. What we the optimists blindly mistake as those falling on hard times often in reality are people living at their personal peak capacity. Those unaccomplished and unfulfilled are more often than not truly only a victim of themselves. Some spin tales of negligence and failures into false heroics and begin to believe the fairy tales. Accountability is such a foreign concept to them that it might as well be spoken in a foreign tongue.

However, there is a part of every true fisherman that no one can take away. It's that freedom that comes with no roads. It's the ability to chase that sunset and know some day you might just catch it. It's those breathtaking sunrises reserved for us select few. It's the salt air that fills your lungs as the sea breeze surrounds your sun-kissed skin.

It's the way a hot cup of coffee indulged in the company of shearwaters and flying fish feels like heaven on Earth. It's the way an albatross is as beloved as a family dog. It's the way you become one with your surroundings. It's the way you feel the ocean and how she seems to feel you. It's what the ocean gives and, most importantly, what it doesn't. It's the recurring lessons that are felt and not spoken. Someday, somewhere, somehow, someone might come along and try to take away all that a fisherman may have. However, they will never be able take away that part of you. It's that part that truly holds the most value.

# CHAPTER 14

# SECOND CHANCES AND LETTING GO

This chapter is dedicated to a fine fishing family that helped remind me that the next generation of fishermen will always be just as important as the current one. Thank you to Adam Modert, Lindsey Modert, Tyde Modert, Maverick Modert, Maximus Modert, and Isla Modert.

Initially, I wasn't going to include in this book the story that follows because of my own insecurities about people believing that it occurred. However, if I've learned anything from listening to a lifetime of fishing stories, the best ones are often somewhat unbelievable yet totally true. And in general, life has taught me what we at times leave behind is often more important than what we take with us. For those reasons, I decided to forge ahead and include this.

The size and type of fish you're trying to catch really has little do with the amount of enjoyment that comes from its capture. In fact, often the physical capture itself isn't nearly as important or as exciting as the journey that led you to that moment. The finest novelist couldn't describe most of the greatest moments of a fisherman's career, not because elegant enough words don't exist to paint the picture but rather because fishing in its purest form is a feeling and not an action. It's a feeling you cannot fake and one others cannot take away from you. It's an earthly and primal vibration stored deep inside the human spirit that revisits the surface when our hands touch a fishing rod at just the right moment.

True fishing is not an activity; it's a mindset and a way of life. It's a beautiful parallel world that exists before all human eyes but is rarely understood by others than the actual participants. Outsiders often confuse the term "fishing" to mean a "hobby." Rather, fishing is truly a lifestyle. An onlooker might view a cumbersome piece of equipment on a game boat bearing a winchlike reel or a long awkward wiggling stick one dances above a country stream as just objects. But in reality, these poles are truly extensions of who we are. A fishing rod is not simply a rod nor merely a piece of equipment. It's much more than that. It's a direct connection to nature and a direct line to our soul.

A fishing rod can be made from nearly anything; its material has far less to do with fishing than the feeling of the person standing behind it. A panfish captured on a stick and a piece of string can be as equally meaningful to a fisherman as capturing a thousand-pound marlin with a $2,500 state-of-the-art fishing rod.

Every fisherman has an individual journey, and every fisherman has individual goals to support that journey. Although we may enjoy parts of our journey with others by our sides, our most memorable moments are often shared alone. It's a fish of a lifetime we release back into a river despite knowing we will never see it again. It's the king of the pond we spend years trying to capture and in the moment when we finally do, we quickly let it go to continue its reign. People often confuse the size of a fish with the true meaning and significance of a fish. And that is how I found my entire life of fishing flashing before me.

I again took watch around noon as we approached the fishing grounds. I held the wheel through the night and slept away the early morning. The first thing I noticed when I awoke was that the boys still hadn't put lures in the water despite the sun being up for hours. I grumbled something about "What the fuck. What are you, guys, all rich now? Just out here yachting?" They looked at me with smiles and confusion; they had no idea I was taking a stab at them.

I grabbed a couple of the rigged chrome jets we normally run, but they all looked as haggard as the women I generally take home after last call—skirts tattered, beat up, covered in bite marks and blood. *Well, that's not going to work,* I thought. *I'm way too sober to be seen with these things hanging around the boat.*

A search of my bag brought up two pretty ladies. One was a brand-new jet that shined like the top of the Chrysler Building and the other a triple-skirted blackheaded bullet that Jonah Marks had gifted me before going to Australia; however, I had yet to run it. Cowering like a cat from the heavy spray, I ran out on the back deck barefooted in an attempt to avoid the cascading water on deck like a businessman avoids puddles in his fancy dress shoes.

I hurriedly set the lures. Disgustedly, I found myself soaked from head to toe running back into the cabin like a schoolgirl. Safely back in the cabin and toweled off, I went about my daily onboard yoga routine. Around twenty-five minutes into it, I found myself in a terribly formed downward facing dog while constantly staring at my lures between my legs.

*A marlin is going to eat that bullet*, I thought as it perfectly dish-ragged down the large swells. No sooner had the thought crossed my mind than did I witness the most mind-blowing head and shoulder marlin bite. It's the only one I've ever watched upside down. This fish was spectacular in every aspect, her overly com-mitted bite absolutely radical, her initial mind-blowing run leg-endary. The great fish's speed made the old Penn Senator reel scream like the siren of a fire truck. Salt that had accumulated on the line now made a six-foot cloud around the rod and reel like locust around a field. The fish's aerial display was breathtaking. Every time I thought she must be done jumping, she jumped again and again. It was incredible; she threw white water across the surface like a waterspout. Water exploded all around her like she was setting depth charges. She plowed through the heavy seas like a bulldozer does a forest.

At times, she thrusted her massive head out of the water, seem-ingly running on her giant pectoral fins. She threw a rooster tail behind her like a jet boat going sixty miles an hour. Even the tur-bulent seas seemed tranquil compared to her chaotic display. The old reel got so hot to touch that we threw buckets of sea water on it to cool it down. I cranked on the fish for as long as I could before it became obvious that if I didn't drive on this fish and drive hard, we were going to get spooled. The huge spool was emptying at an unprecedented rate.

At one point, we were in a seemingly endless standoff where, despite turning and chasing the fish with the boat, we were going full noise and we couldn't get an inch of string back on the reel. I stared at the monofilament to Dacron splice out my driver's side window for what seemed like forever without gaining. Later, the GoPro would reveal that forever was thirteen minutes of watching that splice not move despite the boat giving it everything she had. Smoke belched from the diesel engine, and the hull shook like a teacher on a caffeine overdose. This fish was hell-bent on swimming straight into the sea. My crew did an awesome job all around, from cranking like champions to wiring and handling the fish boat side. She was a big and absolutely gorgeous fish. She wasn't short, and she wasn't skinny. Although it's hard not to argue that her hooter would have looked awesome polished on my desk at home, I told the boys to put the gaffs away. They looked strangely at me.

"No gaff?"

"No gaff," I said.

"Shoot?"

"No shoot," I said.

"No kill?"

"No kill."

"1,000 pounds, captain . . ."

"Maybe bigger."

"No boys too big to keep," I said.

Their confused looks summed up my last two years. Waridin, my first mate, kept saying it was over a grander, and I kept denying that, not because I didn't agree but because I had a promise to fulfill. The universe has a funny way of testing us sometimes. I could only laugh that of course the next marlin I would catch would be this one. I grasped the leviathan's giant baseball-batlike bill as the engine of the *Makana* remained just in gear slowly moving forward. I struggled to hold on for dear life as its sheer weight alone pinned me to the covering boards. My ribs compressed, my diaphragm ached, and my breathing struggled. I sweated in what appeared to be two particular rivers; one dripped from my nose, the other puddled underneath my right eye after being dammed off by my Maui Jim sunglasses.

I attempted to wipe the cascades off my face on the shoulder of my shirt, which at that very moment officially joined the exclusive ranks of the lucky shirt drawer. I caught a glimpse of my now already scratched up Citizen watch peeking out from underneath my heavily seasoned gloves. I noted that a journey of nearly twenty years took two hours and fourteen minutes to complete. The chains that had bound me for so long could now be broken. I literally possessed my greatest dream in my hands. I had envisioned this moment countless times—in my dreams, while jogging, while standing in line at the bank, while staring out airplane windows, and even while making love.

However, none of my dreams prepared me for how it would feel to reach the climax of my marlin fishing career. None of my dreams contained conflict, sadness, or any remorse. There were never, ever any questions, not one single doubt about killing the beast before me. I lusted for it. I longed for it. I had worn her blood like Rambo. In my greatest fantasies, my children were even with me to celebrate the kill in a triballike ritual. I shared her flesh with all of my friends. I drank beers at the dock with her magnificent bill slung proudly over my shoulder like a big leaguer with a Louisville Slugger baseball bat. It was to be the greatest day of my career, but that's not how it felt at all.

I stared deeply into her breathtaking grapefruit-sized eyeball. I talked to her like a newborn baby. I told her how I'd been looking for her for a very long time. I told her how happy I was she had finally arrived. When you meet something so beautiful, it is only natural to share the highs and the lows and the ups and the many downs the journey has taken you on. I went on to jabber; I laughed. It was like the world's greatest first date.

As an outsider looking in, you would think I was totally insane.

Perhaps they might be right—what sane man would sacrifice everything in his life in the pursuit of a smelly old fish? But, I don't care what they think. I never have. I've always been different. I've never felt like I belonged or quite fit in. I've lived a life as a square peg in a world full of circular holes, often uncomfortable and socially awkward, overcompensating for my inability to fit in on land with over-the-top actions and heavy drinking. Historically, I'm my own worst enemy. More often than anything, I feel like I'm drowning on land.

However, she's not just a smelly old fish to me. She's gorgeous. She's beautifully proportioned. She's massively thick all the way to her tail. She's a proper one, all right. She's perfect. It's her. It's the biggest blue marlin I've ever caught on rod and reel. People have unquestionably caught bigger fish than the one within my death grip, but this is my personal biggest.

I have only witnessed one fish bigger with my own eyes, a fish that I came to name Scar Back, a blue marlin of unworldly proportions put on this earth to humble even the largest of man's egos. Scar Back took up a short residence on the Cross Seamount but a permanent residence in my mind.

I would witness her in all her glory for two trips in a row. This freak of nature was adorned with two giant scars on her back. It looked as if she had a run-in with a boat and the boat lost. Despite every ounce of my fisherman soul wanting to say otherwise, no part of me believes man has built a rod and reel to catch this wickedly awesome beast.

My first encounter with Scar Back was the most impressive I've ever had with a marlin and perhaps the most humbling of all my fishing experiences. We were working a huge pile of bigeye tuna that refused to bite. Despite the fact that the pile likely possessed around eighty tons of tuna, we couldn't get a single fish to bite. The school was huge, but lockjawed.

Now, it's not uncommon for fish not to bite, but it's extremely rare to find such a big pile that didn't even have one willing participant when you first found them. Such was the case with this pile. No matter how I drove on the pile and no matter what technique we used, the fish refused to bite. We could see tuna swimming all around the boat, but they just let the chum drift right on by untouched.

Eventually, I grew tired of catching nothing after a couple of hours of these charades. I decided to leave the pile and look for a different one despite how good it appeared. The funny part was that despite the fact I decided to leave them, they now refused to leave me. The school of fish now followed me everywhere. We call this floating or walking the pile, meaning the tuna get locked onto your boat like they naturally do flotsam, whales, or whale sharks as they move through the water. It's a natural desire and attraction to be around floating structure.

So, as I drove around looking for a new pile of birds in my binoculars, the huge school of tuna followed the boat like a loyal dog. Oftentimes, the pile would eventually bite or run under the boat into a new pile, causing competitive feeding that makes the fish go into an absolute feeding frenzy. I was looking and hoping for either scenario.

I didn't find another pile, but about an hour later, the fish under the boat decided to throw the switch. Just as I took the first bite of my lunch, the danglers absolutely started exploding with nice fish, which almost always seems to be the case. I can't even count the times I've had a sandwich interrupted by a biting fish. The universe definitely has a sense of humor when it comes to this. Amazing how you can go all day without a bite, but the second you take your guard down, whammo, you're on.

Sixty- to ninety-pound bigeye tuna committed to hanging themselves on the twelve-inch rubber squid hanging from the metal dangler bars with total disregard for anything but eating. The tuna battled for the boat side lures, none of which were more than four feet from the boat. We yanked the tuna frantically over the side. Another tuna would engulf it as fast as the dehooked rubber squid again hit the water. It was an awesome sight to see but nothing in comparison to what I was about to witness.

When I first saw the ominous black figure, I immediately said, "Fucking whales, here we go again. Just great." I thought they weren't biting because whales were around. I thought the large shadow was a full-grown false killer whale and that the whale was about to ruin the party. Once the false killer whales show up, they chase all the fish away and it often takes days for the area to re-cover. However, as the shadow grew, so did my disbelief at what I was looking at. "Holy mother of god, that's a marlin. Look, look, look!" I screamed, unable to compose anything more intelligible. The sea creature had everyone's attention as it effortlessly inhaled a ninety-pound tuna hanging on the back dangler inches from the boat. The marlin broke the 900-pound monofilament holding the tuna with little more than a slight ping sound. It was incredible to behold. Sixty to ninety-pound tuna skyrocketed all around the boat like minnows scatter from a bass in a lake.

The more panicked tuna met their end as they frantically col-lided with the spinning propellers. Large tuna bounced off the props with such furiousness that it felt like we were grounding on bottom. The tuna blender was claiming life faster than our hooks. Then a stillness settled upon us. A very awkward stillness. A blank fish machine and a blank look on each person's face. We still continued motoring slowly down sea. I just stood on the back deck trying to comprehend what the hell I had just seen. The fish was so radically big, I wouldn't even want to attach a number to it. I could dream big, but even in my wildest dreams I wouldn't have created such a giant fish.

Then I made a classic mistake by opening my mouth and tempting the ocean to humble me. I said, "Boys, you will never see that again. Never, ever, ever, ever!" At the same moment I was finishing that sentence, the danglers unexpectedly erupted again with the same class of fish. It seemed that the tuna had returned to feed. We again yanked sixty- to ninety-pound tuna as fast as we could over the side. No part of me expected the tuna to return, and no part of me thought I'd ever see that marlin again. But as I pulled a sixty-pound tuna over the rail, I watched that magnificent fish come up and grab an eighty-pounder so close in front of me that my only natural reaction was to reach out to try to touch its massive dorsal fin that protruded from the water like a submarine's conning tower. The vessel shook like an earthquake as tuna bounced off the propeller blades, and my heart shook twice as hard from the dream fish before me.

The second tuna the beast ate was completely different than the first. The first time she revealed herself from the depths, she allowed us to see her unbelievable power. On the second tuna, she allowed us to see how calculated she could be. Slowly and purposefully, she came from behind the frantically hanging tuna. Though the tuna was in a panic, she was anything but. With minimal effort, she stuck just enough of her enormous head out of the water to surround about half the tuna, her impossibly large bill shadowed over the tuna's head. With a slight flick of the head, the tuna was hers. She easily ripped the hooks out of that tuna's mouth like people tear junk mail in half. She gracefully swam off with that eighty-pound tuna head hanging out of her mouth like a dog runs with a bone.

As the biggest fish I've ever seen disappeared from my sight, I thought how strange it was that I was really happy knowing some fish just aren't meant to be caught or at least shouldn't be caught. She was one of those fish. Despite devoting my entire life to catching fish, somehow in my heart I just knew that one should be left alone. I wondered if even the most wildly optimistic dreamers had ever thought they might actually see one that big someday. I most certainly did not.

This was not the last time I would see that fish, but it was the most remarkable experience I would have with her. The other run-ins all got my heart pumping, but none of them were anything like the first time. She would come within ten feet of the boat again but never inches. So here I found myself with that same strange feeling that some fish weren't meant to be captured or at least not kept. This was supposed to be my time, my turn. This was my moment. I was supposed to take her life to fulfill my bloodlust, to fulfill my ego and desire. It was my time to join the others who came before me on that old dilapidated Grander Wall in downtown Kona.

Despite the fact that this was all I had wanted for nearly two decades, I couldn't take her. I couldn't kill her. I didn't know why, but I suddenly didn't want to kill her. Physically, it would have been very easy to take her tired body. She was a total layup in the gaff department. But, emotionally, I couldn't take her old soul. I felt strangely warm and fuzzy. The last twenty years flashed before me.

For most of my life, I had measured my self-worth by what the scale read—how many tons of tuna I put on the auction floor or how many pounds of marlin I strung up by its tail. My endless pursuit of fish affords me a lot of fun and at times lots of money. But I never went fishing for the money. I went for the indescribable feeling that is fishing. I went to connect to nature in the only way I knew how. I went to sea to fill a void that only seemed patchable with saltwater. I fished because no matter how hard things ever got onshore, I knew there was a place just past the horizon reserved just for me. Then there was that promise to fulfill. My eldest son, Kanyon, had told me just days prior that "you should let big marlin go, Dad, so I can catch them someday."

I said, "How about this, buddy? I'll let the next big marlin I catch go just for you."

He approvingly said, "Great idea, Dad!"

So, here I held a fish that took twenty years to catch and held a promise to my son on my back. Despite the fish being very heavy, the promise to my child weighed far heavier on my soul. Sometimes, there is something more powerful in knowing you can do something but then make the conscious decision to not do it. Sometimes, there's more power in not killing something and letting it be free. I patted this spectacular fish on her giant head and told her she better thank a little boy named Kanyon. Strangely, this old soul seemed to acknowledge this with a giant slap of her tail.

Cowboys find the same comfort on the open prairie that fishermen find in the open sea, so it's only fitting that country music played in the background as I held that giant fish. George Strait's "Troubadour" filled the air with an eerily relatable tale. I've often said you can easily replace the word "cowboy" with "fisherman" in just about any song.

I've heard bull riders say, "When it's the last one, make sure it's your best one. Tip your hat and walk away." With this sentiment in mind, I let go of the massive bill of the marlin with both hands, and she glided effortlessly away, upright, erect, and proud. God, she was beautiful. I pulled down on my lucky hat's tired visor like the iconic silhouette of the Marlboro Man. I kept my head tipped in a prolonged nod as if to say in a slow Southern drawl, "Well, thank you, ma'am."

Mostly excited, though partially in total disbelief, I 100 percent approvingly watched my twenties and early thirties swim away. Sure, she was a little worse for wear, but what creature isn't that spends their life roaming the sea? The important part, the part that truly mattered, was that she was healthy, free, and had another chance at life. Two of the most valuable things we possess in our time here on this planet are our health and our freedom.

Often, neither are appropriately appreciated and more commonly wildly neglected until either one or both are in jeopardy of being taken away from us. As for the third part and perhaps the most meaningful part of all, she again had another chance at life. In my dealings, since the time of losing my boat, family, and subsequently my mind, I had come to find that really all most of us ever truly need is a chance.

It's one thing to talk about letting go. It's another thing all together to open up our hands and hearts to do so. As a fisherman, I suppose releasing a fish you've devoted your whole life to catching and truly being happy about it requires having the same emotional capacity that is required to let your ex who left you live at peace on her own. It takes years of experience and vast amounts of pride-swallowing. But, when you finally grasp that these beloved creatures are truly more beautiful in their own environments, wild and free, doing what they were put on Earth to do, instead of sacrificing their beings to fulfill our own egos, that's the moment you truly discover the meaning of the word "love."

# CHAPTER 15

# LESSONS FROM THE *VICIOUS CYCLE*

Depression was beating on me again. The couch was magnetic and my breathing muffled. My heart seemed broken, erratically pounding, sometimes like a jackhammer, other times meekly like a scurrying mouse. I closed my eyes to darkness and indistinguishable white flashes. When I rubbed my eyelids, ships of failure sailed through my mind. I rubbed them harder and harder, eventually attacking my temples to relieve the pressure. When I opened my eyes, black dots traversed my vision from the ferocious rubbing caused by the storm I created in my best attempt to sink those ships. "Sink, fucking sink," I pleaded. *Why are these captains so well seasoned? Why are they so relentless? Why don't they fall off?*

I'd been exercising, eating right, and laying off the bottle. I was doing my best to stay healthy. But it only took one little stumble, one degree off course, and the armadas were right up behind me again. I worked hard for the gains, but failure came so easily. It took seemingly forever to get stronger or skinnier, but I lost it as easily as I cracked open that bottle. *Why am I on this path to hell again? Why do I drink when I know the joy is temporary and the pain seemingly forever? Why do I consume something that I ask the Lord above to forgive me for just seconds before it touches my lips?*

I held on to the glass that sweated like a triathlete, the melting tubular ice as hollow and empty as I felt. With a pair of small red straws, I chased ice around the rim. It reminded me of being a kid chasing snowballs around a frozen pond with a hockey stick. I hoped the pain would dissipate as quickly as the ice had. It smelled terrible, like a million bad decisions and countless nights of regret. *How can I be going down this road again? What is wrong with me? How can I be so broken? How can I justify the risk?* Despite knowing better, I again took that first sip down that road I said I would never travel again—just as the previous time and the time before and the time before that.

The vicious cycle continued. The first sip raised the hairs on my neck. It was like the zookeeper had just put a fresh kill in the lion's cage. The lion inside me hadn't seen it yet, but its aroma had just started to fill his sleeping nostrils. Upon the second slow and deliberate sip, I began to hear the low-lying rumble of the lion beginning to stir. The third pull off the drink was longer and deeper, bypassing my taste buds altogether and going directly to the place where all the trouble began. The lion was fully awake on the fourth and final inhale.

I satisfyingly put the glass firmly on the bar counter, like I achieved something worthwhile. I spun my glass with my right hand, sometimes slowly and sometimes fast like a top. My glass became an extension of my body. On the slow rotations, the precipitation on the outside of the glass pools around your fingers. On the fast spins, it shoots off like a wet dog drying off.

With my left hand, I tapped and banged the cardboard drink coaster that was supposed to be under my glass. I'd eventually bend it back and forth like a bow between my fingers. At some point, it would soften and I'd fold it roughly into four pieces. Sometimes, I firmly grasped this pile in my fist and slid it quickly out of sight due to embarrassment. Other times, I lightly tapped this origami I'd created on the bar until the bartender asked me if I'd like them to take that from me. Often, the remnants were closer to the pulp of papier-mâché after merging with the moisture of a working bar.

A fisherman can trust land no more than the drunk can trust gravity. I looked to the ocean from the seaside restaurant and could take no more. My patience with land was running extremely short. I'm not a land dweller. Although I love those who walk upon the land, I truly love life upon the sea. I can't help but imagine what time the fish will be biting as I gaze upon the moon. The fishing calendar that is my mind runs wild in the changing schedule of the seasons. The hair on the back of my neck stands up straight when I feel the wind shift to the conditions I've coined the "milk run" for the large harvest I've had in these same conditions.

I stared deeply into my glass of Jack Daniels and wondered what was happening with my loan paperwork for a new boat. I wondered if I would be approved. I wondered if I looked good enough on paper to get funding. I wished I could have put a picture of my soul on those applications. Surely, any banker could have seen that my heart was a sure bet even if my spreadsheets weren't.

I left the bar, went home, and pulled out every single logbook I had left. I laid out the library of Kenton Geer before me. I smiled, laughed, and reminisced as the ocean churned inside my living room. I studied them all and despite having written them, I found things that surprised me. I saw things I remembered and some things I wish I could forget. Some things were beautiful, some things beyond tragic, but all the things made me who I am.

When the sea settled, I again found myself in the lee of the island riding safely, captaining my La-Z-Boy recliner. I decided I would again be the owner of my own fishing boat regardless of what the bank might say. All the logbooks confirmed what my soul had already known. The ocean had never really changed, only my perception of what she offered had. I reconfirmed the pact I had made with myself and Scotty right then and there. I would do whatever it took to again own my own boat.

Now worried for some reason I might not get a loan, I poured a giant glass of whiskey and started an alternative game plan in case the financing didn't come through. I wrote and drank for hours. This reconfirmed something I learned long ago—a lot of problems in our lives are created by problems that don't actually exist at all. So, as I drank and wrote away the evening, I wasted not only my precious time but my brain cells as well. Liquor by any other name is still the worst kind of woman. She will seduce you; she will confuse you; she will fuck you, and she will leave you for dead.

Epic highs and epic lows live behind every whiskey bottle's label and behind every set of women's eyes. The same sugary sweet love that makes your heart beat will break it when either runs empty. The honeymoon phase with drinking and marriage is no different than the feel of the hangover they both have the potential to produce once they've run their course.

When I first met the hangover in my early thirties, I didn't personally know who she was. However, after about a hundred of these casual run-ins, I confirmed that I didn't particularly like her any more than I did a hungry shark around a pile of tuna I was trying to catch.

My worry and raging hangover were for naught. This is often the case in life. For when I painstakingly woke up, I discovered I had received an email in the early a.m. informing me that my boat loan was approved. I yelled in complete satisfaction like the overly competitive grandmother at bingo night. I was absolutely ecstatic. My hangover and worries were gone faster than a jet ski. Adrenaline and joy displaced the areas that had been filled with whiskey the previous evening.

The path was not always straight, and it certainly was not easy. Often, I was my own worst enemy when it came to battling the idea of what should have been with what in fact was. I broke promises I made to myself about getting sleep every night. More often than not, my helm was littered with Red Bull cans like a frat house lawn is covered with red Solo cups and beer cans.

I broke crew and blew off hatches that had faithfully withstood twenty years of loyal service. I missed dates and birthdays. I recklessly steamed into the darkest nights both on land and out at sea. I failed and failed again, and when I thought I couldn't withstand another failure, I failed twice as fucking hard. However, I kept getting up and pounding at that goddamn fucking wall I had built inside my mind, no matter how tired and no matter how much it hurt. I had to nearly lose everything to appreciate the value of anything.

I trudged through some terrible places to come out a much better person on the other side. I wasn't always proud of the awful places to which I traversed and the awful things I said. But I was really proud of the man who came out of the mud on the other side. I had been broken only to be rebuilt better than before. The truth is that the only things easily created are excuses. Anyone who tells you differently is selling you something. The glory is not always in winning any given event itself but in appreciating that winning or losing is simply temporary. When one masters the art of understanding this, they never really lose again.

Even divorce is ultimately a blessing, although it's often difficult to see it through your tears. Time and effort ensure that nothing remains the same. The more effort you put into anything, the more rewards will come out of it. Amazingly, the less we try to hold on to things we cannot control, the more things actually come our way that we can. When we spend all our time trying to reopen doors that have closed, we miss all the ones that have opened for us. It's an incredible thing, although not necessarily easily understood. The element of time and maturity help unlock these doors. Better days always come following a hurricane.

The new doors we don't unlock from letting go we will unlock with hard work and commitment. The truth is, in the world of fishing, luck is when preparation meets opportunity. Unbeknownst to many, this is exactly the same thing that occurs on land. Luck is often viewed as happenstance, but in reality most luck is a combination of the time you were willing to expend on an effort versus the amount others weren't.

Most luck is built in the shadows. It's built where the masses won't witness its creation. It's built in the early hours of the morning while others lie in bed. Luck is born in a chicken-scratched notepad in the deepest parts of the night. It's fine-tuned and crafted while the others long ago retired and rest at home. It's the weekends and holidays you didn't take. It's that relentless attention to details others don't see. It's a commitment to something that means the world to you even if others don't understand it at all. It's the repeated failings, but more importantly it's the endless recurring attempts. It's the never-ending questions and the constant pursuit of improving your craft.

Most people won't come along with you on this journey. Some won't come because they don't appreciate and value the details along the way. Others won't be coming because "good enough" is just that—good enough for them. The majority of the people won't be by your side on your luckiest of days because luck of that caliber is a lot more work than the majority are willing to put in.

I excitedly signed the loan paperwork for my third boat at the Bank of Hawaii, in Kona, on August 28, 2019. I put my house up as collateral without blinking an eye, taking on a pile of personal debt. It's not that I didn't appreciate the risk involved, it's just because over the last few years I had witnessed how much riskier my life was on land than at sea.

Unlike when I purchased my first boat, this time around many people volunteered to back me. Apparently, my hard work and commitment to my trade hadn't gone unnoticed over the last decade. Dave Meyer, an absolute genius in the realm of boat building, master craftsman, and all-around great guy, fronted me all of his amazing work on a handshake. He told me, "Worry about it later. Pay me as you catch fish."

Jim Black, a marine electronics guru, fronted me $50,000 worth of new electronics and installation just on my word. He said, "Just get back out fishing and pay me when you can." Nate Cary, one of my best friends and favorite fishing buddies, had magically reappeared in my life after venturing off to do different things over the past couple of years. The ocean had again come a-calling as it always does to true fishermen. Nate was fully committed to helping me in the yard and getting back out fishing. I was very happy about this on every level. I was glad Nate had found his way back to fishing, and I was twice as happy he would be doing it beside me. Nate is a great person, a great fisherman, and an even better friend.

Good ole reliable Diamond Dave was right there by my side

again with his checkbook in hand, betting bigger on me than anybody. He handed me an unbelievably generous loan from the money he had earned by captaining a boat and catching the largest marlin in the world on July 4th of the previous year. This catch won him and the crew the coveted Blue Marlin World Cup along with over a million dollars in prize money. Dave stuck the money in my hand, high-fived me, and said in his drawn-out California accent, "Alright, bro. Well, good luck with all that boat stuff. Time for some Panda." His tires squealed and the music blared out of his new white Tacoma as he tore out of the bank parking lot like a high school student borrowing Mom and Dad's car for the weekend.

I shook my head and laughed. It was déjà vu Diamond Dave who again made the difference in me getting a boat before heading to Panda Express. All just seemed right in the world. I said it the first time he bet on me, and it was only fitting the second time as he drove away. "Man, I love that fucking guy." It must be mentioned that none of this would have been a reality or possible if it wasn't for Mighty Whitey spotting me a few times along the path as I navigated the divorce process, allowing me to maintain my credit and sanity.

I owe a huge debt of gratitude to all these people and will be forever appreciative of the fact that they believed in me even when at moments I had my own doubts. I purchased a strong but well-worn boat named *Hoku*, whose history was as full of epic highs and epic lows as any of the best fishing tales. It had been captained by one of the best captains to ever ply the Hawaiian waters, but unfortunately he had succumbed to his own vicious cycle and demons.

Unlike the first boat I bought, this boat was no stranger to me when I went to look at her for purchase. Superficially, I knew this boat very well. I had fished around her for many years on the Cross Seamount. By many rights, she was once my nemesis. We had nicknamed her the *Death Star* because she killed anything she came around. This boat was also considerably bigger than a number of the other boats in the handline fleet. This vessel would often show up on a school of tuna we were working, armed with what appeared to be a million hooks and cause absolute devastation to the tuna. Often, she had stolen the pile or run the tuna off altogether if we were sitting on top of a pile diamond jigging on them.

The captain was very well seasoned and equally ruthless. In my earlier years as a captain on the *Sea Mountain*, he would pollute me with all kinds of bad information, which I would naively believe. In turn, this sent me on time-consuming wild goose chases for birds and tuna that didn't exist. One day when the captain had again relapsed on heroine, his drug of choice, he told me about the secret single side band radio channel he and his friend Mike talked on. I can guarantee he didn't remember telling me about that channel based on the conversations I would monitor over the next couple of years.

I never once chimed in on the conversations, despite all the terrible things I heard on that radio, because the fishing knowledge and secrets being revealed far outweighed all the racist comments. I learned a lot about fishing from just listening, and I learned a lot more about how people really are behind your back. He would speak friendly to me on the VHF radio then call me names on the secret side band channel.

Part of me took satisfaction in knowing I was getting his boat because of things I heard on that channel. But the other part of me just felt truly bad for him. I personally had experienced losing a boat and knew just how devastating that was. Eventually, his addiction became so bad he stopped fishing. He was forced to sign the boat over to his original business partner, Mike, when he stopped making his boat payments to him. The captain was to purchase the boat in its full entirety, but he became delinquent on his payments. Accompanied with unpaid mortgage bills in Honolulu Harbor, the captain got so badly behind to the point that the boat was in true jeopardy of being taken by the state and being put up for auction to settle the debt.

Despite my mixed feelings, the boat was for sale and someone was going to purchase it. I figured it might as well be me. She was a great boat that just needed someone to love her. I could relate to that. Not to say Mike didn't love the boat. He clearly did. I could truly see his reluctance to sell it in the way he constantly still checks up on her today. However, every fishing boat has a purpose, and this boat's purpose wasn't to rest at the dock. Mike gave me a very good deal on the boat with only one string attached— if I ever planned on selling her, he'd get first crack at purchasing her back. I understandably and happily agreed. Mike was nothing like his old business partner; he was extremely professional and had a very good full-time job along with a young family. He could have easily afforded to just keep the boat, but he didn't have time to take the boat fishing offshore. He treated me very well on all aspects of the sales agreement, and I greatly appreciated that.

The love of a boat and the love of a woman can be amazingly beautiful and complicated things. Sometimes, you just know either would be better off with someone else, but it's hard not to selfishly hold on. However, since we love these beings, it's even more difficult to not want the best for them. So, although it may pain us, we know in our hearts that we must smile as we watch them move on. Anyone who has ever witnessed an ex's radiant glow on a dinner date with someone else understands the confusion of watching your old boat unload a huge trip. Of course, we want the best for them, but a part of us will always wish we were still along for the ride.

It was an emotional goodbye for Mike. I could tell by the way he was choked up that he was really going to miss the boat. That's also the sign of a really good boat. You don't want a boat the previous owner can't wait to get rid of. You want a boat you can tell is worthy of love. I promised I would take care of her, and we parted ways. Mike looked on as we rolled out of sight.

I steamed the boat from its home in Hawaii Kai in Oahu to Kona with my friend and shipwright Pete Allison. The last time Pete and I had been on a boat together was when he helped me deliver my second boat, the *Malicious Intent*, to Oakland, California, from Honolulu after selling it. The *Malicious Intent* was a boat that

Mighty Whitey and I bought on an impulse within a year of buying our first boat. If we'd had a crystal ball, we certainly wouldn't have. The *Malicious Intent* had all the agony of the original *Vicious Cycle*, only it lacked any of the joy. We had more nightmares on that boat than they had on Elm Street.

The roughly 2,500-mile trip from hell that's worthy of its own book was a perfectly fitting end to a boat that took everything in our power to keep afloat, not just figuratively but literally. I've met some whores in my day, but she was the biggest of them all. I came to hate that boat despite landing the largest loads of fish I've ever caught on it. That boat seemed hell-bent on killing me, and more than once, it nearly did.

Our odyssey found us tangled in the Great Pacific Garbage Patch for three days. It ended with us pushing it so close on fuel because of a mishap with our spare fuel that the engine literally ran out of fuel as we tied the first line to the dock in California. I took the first watch on the *Hoku* as Pete got some shuteye. In practice, one takes watch of a vessel to ensure the safety of it and her crew. However, more often than not, you find yourself only truly faced with the task of surviving self-reflection.

"Watch" is one of those unique places where memories come to joyfully visit and to painfully haunt. Restrained by bulkheads and the surrounding sea, we are offered no way of physically engaging in the joy and no retreat to escape the pain. Sometimes, on the darkest nights, it's completely impossible to tell where the ocean ends and the heavens begin. Yet on other evenings, it's completely impossible to tell the difference between the horizon and a memory.

The toughest memories seem to have a tendency of barging in when the skies are the cloudiest and the seas the roughest. The preferred memories generally secretly arrive on the lyrics of a favorite melody played upon favorable seas. Not that there isn't any crossover; there most certainly is. The warmth of that distant smile that drives us eagerly into the teeth of the trade winds. The painful goodbye that gives us the shivers in the heat of the doldrums. Some watches pass in seemingly minutes whereas others feel like days. One may take watch on the same boat, on the same waters for many years, and never look out and see the same thing twice. One may be the optimist, the pessimist, the dreamer, the lover, the scorned, and even the completely broken with their head out of the same window.

The foreground may appear the same, however the distance is forever changing. We often spend a lifetime looking for something we've possessed or known inside all along, traveling countless miles only to discover that we had at hand the very thing we believed impossible to grasp. When we finally let go of the things that we cannot control, we in fact finally take control of that which had controlled us.

Staring out the cracked window of my newly acquired boat, I couldn't help but wonder if I was dreaming or if this was now my reality. The ocean was paper-flat, and the visibility was as endless as my newfound hope. The stars seemed close enough to touch, and the Milky Way was so well defined it was as if you could walk upon it. For the first time in years, the only thing clearer than the horizon were my thoughts. Three years of hell had ironically placed me at the gates of my own personal heaven. The autopilot held the course, and the sea teeming with green phosphorescence held my attention. The neon-green sea creatures danced below the water, so I decided to dance alone above it. A-ha's "Take on Me" played through my iPhone, taking me joyfully somewhere between dancing in my childhood living room with my sister and fishing countless nights under this same Pacific sky before me.

There is a comfort in dancing in any discreet setting, regardless if it's the back deck of a fishing boat or your very own living room that allows you to be totally free. In that freedom, we find our wings to travel to our favorite memories and we find our legs so that we may once again relive them. If song is the catalyst for remembrance, then dance is the fountain of youth for our souls.

A piece of every great moment comes out when you dance in

the confines of your safe place. Outside the view of judging eyes, our spirits interlock with our past and waltz right into the vault of our hearts. Memories, no matter how dim, once again shine as our bodies move and our minds take flight. It is not how the dancer looks but rather how the dancer feels that truly matters. So, as I danced alone on the back deck, I truly danced with all my favorite memories. I felt myself smiling so hard it almost hurt. Those muscles were clearly out of practice but fortunately still worked when given the right dance floor. My god did it feel good to have my own boat again.

A huge part of me that was lost in a capsizing out at sea and the remainder that went missing upon the land seemed to be re-discovered in that 145-mile transit. Another song played on my playlist entitled "Awesome." Each song was a memory, some beautiful, some tragic, yet all remarkably important to getting me to this moment. The irony of life is that you often have to know its pain to appreciate its joy. The playlist played on, and we fittingly moved forward. That is life; that is the vicious cycle. It's not that you won't experience storms and pain, for you most certainly will. Life is about holding the course long enough and true enough to come out the other side laughing.

Our transit to Kona was fortunately nothing like Pete's and my previous adventure. Our crossing was noneventful, aside from being as close to the heavens above as a man can be from sea level and being yet again hit in the face by a flying fish. I do not envy the flying fish. The flying fish, although arguably the most gifted of all fish, is also the most agonized creature in the ocean, its gifts both a blessing and equally a curse. God gave the flying fish the natural abilities that man envies: the capability to fly in the air and breathe underwater. Yet this skill set leaves it at a constant unre-lenting attack both above and below the waterline. When a flying fish isn't being chased by a larger predatory fish, it's generally be-ing chased by a predatory bird. This proves that sometimes the more God-gifted abilities we are given the more pressure we re-ceive from the outside.

I have never had a good personal relationship with the flying fish. Although I can appreciate their plight, their attraction to bright lights of the boat often leads them to the same demise the lights of the city leads sailors to. They recklessly come flying in often to never leave. Often, dead flying fish cover the bow of a boat like drunks cover Bourbon Street. Flying fish have broken my sunglasses straight off my face and have hit me so many times on deck I've lost count. They have violently awoken me in my bunk, having glided into the cabin at the most unlikely of angles. I've even had a giant flying fish hit the end of my penis so hard while I hung it over the side that I contemplated canceling the whole trip and taking the boat back to shore to get medical help for the swelling. I laughed at those flying fish hitting me in the face, extremely glad they hadn't hit me once again in the privates.

Our docking was flawless, and we had tons of fuel to spare. It was a good way to set the tone for the dry dock to come. The very first thing I did with the new boat was take it straight to the yard to modernize it and go through her top to bottom before again putting her back into service offshore. In dry dock, a man is given an opportunity to kill any remaining brain cells that the alcohol and drugs may have accidentally missed in the course of his lifetime. It's a place where toxins are indulged upon in copious amounts and in almost every format. The inhalation of caustic fumes is expected with the same probability that the sun will again rise. Paint thinner is the boatyard's morning dew. The stringent smell awakens the mind of a sailor as spring flowers awaken the mind of a poet.

The boatyard, a reflection of your life, reminds us that the least desirable jobs often prove to be the most important and fulfilling. The harder the task, the more one feels rewarded when accomplishing it. Paint erratically splatters on skin in the same fashion that the stars come to fill up the night sky, the constellations on your forearms telling of the most recent project. The boatyard is both heaven and hell. Dreams and reality violently pull apart your purse strings like a child opens a present on Christmas morning.

Time in dry dock is like working out. Although it may seem daunting and tiring, when you finally cross that finish line you're certainly glad you did it.

I was truly enjoying being a boat owner, steadily working away both day and night in the boatyard. The thing many people don't realize about owning a boat is that in reality the boat actually owns you. A boat demands your attention more than even the neediest women. This reality didn't go over well with my new extremely needy girlfriend, a woman who was excited I was getting a new boat until the reality set in of how much time I was devoting to the boat and not her.

Mother Nature had blessed her with the customary rear-end one expects of a Brazilian smokeshow. However, her chest was ornamented by a beautiful set of bolt-ons, arguably the only thing man has crafted better than the hand of God. Her ex-husband purchased this world-class rack, which, in my experience, is common in these transactions. It seems that more often than not, the true price tag for a breast augmentation in a relationship is the subsequent breakup that follows the operation. The set of titties that was supposed to spice up the relationship comes with a dose of artificial confidence larger than a J-cup. This newfound confidence and the additional attention received ironically makes a woman question the value of the purchaser himself. Mrs. Tig-O-Bittys now looks to upgrade her mate like her former partner looked to upgrade her chest. It's a cruel yet somehow fair system where the ultimate winner is the single brethren of the town.

I had been the recent winner of her ex's titties, and for the most part I couldn't be happier. Except the problem was that when I met her, I was taking the summer off from being offshore and I had nothing but time for her. When my new boat arrived, I had nothing but time for the boat. With the boat costing me thousands of dollars daily in the boatyard, I just wanted to get the boat done and out of there. She, like most women, had a hard time being second fiddle to the boat. I was working twelve- to fourteen-hour days minimum in the yard, then overtime at home trying to keep the relationship going. The hardest part of dry dock wasn't the unbearable heat or sanding fiberglass. Rather, it was the Brazilian's insatiable appetite for sex.

I would work all day in the yard only to really put in the overtime at home. When we first met, I thought the sex marathons were just the standard-lust filled beginnings of most relationships. I figured they would eventually subside, which is often the case. The Brazilian had other thoughts and no intentions of slowing down. Somewhere around the second week of dry dock, she introduced me to her "massager."

When I met her "massager," it became clear why this woman was never satisfied. I worked all day in the yard with sanders, grinders, power saws, and other high-powered equipment, and none of them took more out of me than this massager, which was roughly the size of a Sawzall saw. It plugged into the wall, went 3,000 RPMs, and took two hands to hold on to. Of all the grueling work I did during that time frame, nothing did more damage to my shoulder than the jack hammering of her massager. This occurred night after night. She would get her 120 volts of satisfaction, and I would get a blown-out shoulder. Something had to give, and most likely it would have been my rotator cuff. I told her I needed a night off, and she told me she needed more attention. She suggested it was either going to be her or the boat. She was very beautiful but certainly not as beautiful as my boat. The boat had claimed its first relationship, and we hadn't even been out fishing yet. I knew if she couldn't handle dry dock there was no way she was going to handle me being gone fishing.

So, the following day when she told me I had been away too much lately in the boatyard and it just wasn't going to work, I could almost feel my shoulder give out a giant sigh of relief. It was glad to know it wasn't going to have to pick up that fucking massager again. Relationships have to be mutually beneficial to be rewarding and fulfilling. One-sided relationships are like a misloaded boat. It only takes the slightest wave to capsize the whole thing. I could see the relationship with the Brazilian capsizing the minute she went head to head with my boat.

The dry dock went more or less as smoothly along as any dry dock goes. We updated the old girl and cleaned her up. We gave her new windows, new electronics, a new paint job, and a new life. The other thing we gave her was a new name. I just couldn't keep the name for too many years, as the name "Hoku" came with a dark cloud. When people in my circle heard the name, they thought of druggies who used to work on it. During the dry dock, I even found Shaky's long ago expired Costco card inside a small Ziploc sandwich bag behind a drawer I pulled out.

Thirteen dollar bills accompanied the card inside the bag rolled up tight like a straw. The bag still contained a drug that appeared to be meth. The same residue was on the edge of this card and lined the inside of the dollar straw. It was heartbreaking but only further reconfirmed the boat's legacy and need for a name change. When I heard the name "Hoku," I heard the old captain calling me a fucking *haole* over the single side band radio. I had no intentions of envisioning that the rest of my life every time I heard my boat's name called.

So, I renamed her the only name that seemed perfectly fitting—the *Vicious Cycle*. I did not name her the *Vicious Cycle Two*, or the *Vicious Cycle Forever*, both of which I heavily contemplated. On her stern you will simply find the name *Vicious Cycle* because the vicious cycle never really ever stopped from where I was standing. The original *Vicious Cycle* might have capsized, but the dream never truly drowned. Rather, it was merely held down for some time by the undertow of life.

Artwork designed by my father decorated her bow. It was a large coat of arms we called the Geer. It has a large shield with two gaffs crossed behind it like the bones of a Jolly Roger. The shield was broken into four quadrants. You will find three aces in one of its four quadrants, a homage to the girl in the green hat. In another quadrant, you will find a set of dice for the constant roll of the dice that is commercial fishing. In the third quadrant, you will find a full martini glass and a full beer mug for the vicious cycle that is drinking. The fourth quadrant is up for interpretation.

To some it may be a stripper with a dollar sign underneath her legs. However, when "someone" asked my daughter what it was, she said it was a ballerina. When asked what the dollar symbol was there for then, she said it was because ballet lessons are really expensive. You can bet your life that answer put a smile on my face and a frown on everyone else's. Regardless of your interpretation, a woman and a dollar symbol fill the fourth quadrant that represents man's struggles with both. The boat came out of dry dock looking amazing and ran equally as well aside from a few hiccups that one would expect of a boat that had been sitting for some time.

They say the two best days of boat ownership are the day you purchase a boat and the day you sell that same boat. I couldn't disagree more with this statement. I would argue that the best days of boat ownership are the days you truly get to know and learn your boat. It's the days in between when you learn what your boat can do and what it can't do. I would suggest that the most meaningful days on a boat are the ones you teach one another how one will react to the actions of another until you finally become one with the boat and the boat becomes one with you; a perfect complement and extension of one another. The best boats aren't merely objects; rather, they are loved ones interconnected so tightly with your soul that it becomes nearly impossible to know if you're talking about a piece of machinery or a lifelong love.

I fell in love with this new boat as quickly and deeply as one does with any woman. Like most of the things I desire, she wasn't the prettiest or the sleekest rig, but she went the hardest and could handle life at the roughest. She was a perfect complement to what I was looking for on land and out at sea.

As I come to the conclusion of this book, I type away on my iPhone wearing my lucky Red Sox hat. And although my lucky hat lost its shine and a better part of its material many years ago, it still has a strong core and protects me to the best of its abilities from the elements. Often, society gives up on things when they tire or fade, however more often than not, the ones with the most wear are the most loyal and resilient.

I've come to learn to never judge a man by his clothing or his circumstances. What we wear on the outside and our circumstances have little to do with determining who we are. It's what we carry around on the inside that reveals our identities. For this reason, those who often look the most downtrodden down are the ones with the most remarkable comebacks. The exterior never truly reveals the heart, unless it's in the form of never giving up on something that never gave up on you, like a lucky hat.

If you cannot fathom the power of a lucky hat or even a lucky shirt, it seems unlikely that you'll ever comprehend magic underwear, fish dances, fish whistles, and the bizarre routines that fishermen convince themselves are the competitive edge for harvesting fish. Although fishermen build their own luck by the energy they devote to the craft, a fisherman's confidence is reinforced by the items that have traveled along with them upon their journey. Like a faithful stead or a loyal dog, a lucky hat brings a certain amount of protection from self-doubt even if its remnants no longer can bring protection from the sun.

Fishing has an unexplainable magic that intertwines with all aspects of the participants' lives. Although the physical act of fishing may occur in the water, the life of fishing neither ends nor starts at the waterline. It begins when we wake up and excitedly prepare for our outing. It's seen in vivid daydreams that start with our morning coffee and haunt us in boring-ass meetings. It's all the moments in the day when we are on land but our spirits are out at sea. It's even found in those brutal days when all we want to do is go home and go to bed, for no place does a fisherman see more fish jumping than in their dreams.

My lucky hat has seen many countries, many oceans, and many fish. It has seen its share of first kisses and twice as many goodbye hugs. It has watched dream fish and dream women come and go. It has been wiped in blood and in tears. It has absorbed more whiskey than even the filthiest working bar towel. It has swum in the workout sweat of sobriety and has been drenched in hard work. It has seen the finest weather and the absolute worst.

If there is anything I've learned for certain in the twenty-three years it's sat upon my head, it's that you cannot make everyone happy no matter what you do. So you might as well make sure you're happy with what you are doing. So often we put our own personal happiness to the side to appease people who won't be happy with us no matter what we do anyway. If your best life lives past the horizon, so should you. I've learned to be unapologetically a fisherman, and I hope you may be unapologetically whoever you are.

Lessons are often learned through experiences, and I can say I have many experiences and learned many lessons along the way. Here are some that have stayed with me:

*In a jam, find a mentor or someone who has experience to help you.* One of my greatest mentors, Brad Craft, is a legendary Cairns skipper, shipwright, family man, and great friend. He is a man who can think like a fish and possesses a heart of gold. Brad was absolutely instrumental in helping me get my head out of my ass and get myself back on my feet following my divorce. My friendship with Brad is a perfect example that you just really never know what the future holds. If I never had lost my first boat, I would most likely have never connected with Brad, and that would have been a bigger shame than losing my boat. When you find yourself in a dark spot, try to find someone who has climbed out of that same dark hole. Their wisdom is invaluable and often comes for free. People who see a part of themselves in you often try to help you avoid unnecessary head-on collisions. Brad's commentary on communicating while coparenting has been worth its weight in gold.

*Lend a shoulder and an ear.* Scotty Davidson saved my life at my darkest moment by just showing up and being willing to listen and talk. Don't underestimate the power of presences and compassion. If you find yourself in a pit of despair scarier than you ever thought possible, don't be afraid to ask for or get professional help. Everyone needs help, and we sometimes need help outside of what our friends can provide for us. There is zero shame in that. Everyone has dark holes in their life. It's how we climb out of them that really matters.

*The first step is always the hardest.* It is always difficult to start over or start something new, but you'll be glad you did once you get some momentum going. It's better to show up and do your best than to forever wonder what could have been. You won't regret the things you tried, but you'll regret never taking a chance.

*There will always be more than one way to skin a cat.* Flexibility requires being able to learn to bend. Don't be too close-minded to look at things in a different light. It's amazing what we find when we examine things at different angles.

*You don't lose when you bet on yourself.* Sure, you might come up a little short sometimes, but nothing beats the feeling of achievement regarding something you or others initially thought impossible.

*You can run, but you can't run from yourself.* You better learn to enjoy your own company on this journey. This is probably one of the greatest lessons of living with a vicious cycle. It doesn't matter where you go or end up. If you're not okay with who you are, you won't be happy. Self-care is super important and highly understated, especially for men. Take care of yourself mentally and physically. You only get one body. Take care of it. I personally struggle with this even today, which leads perfectly to the next lesson.

*Life's a work in progress.* Life's a work in progress. It is a forever changing thing. Our wants and desires will constantly change, as will our circumstances. Life is not set in stone and nor should be our mindsets.

*The lessons of Tinder.* We all wish life was as beautiful as the first photo on someone's Tinder profile, however the reality lies somewhere around photo number four. Learn to appreciate the perfection in your imperfections.

*We all make mistakes!* We are not our mistakes. Don't let a mistake haunt you forever. Learn from it, correct it accordingly, and move on. We only get one life. Don't spend it living in the past.

*Love of a woman versus the love of a fish.* Love is beautiful, but nothing is more beautiful than watching a fish take hundreds of yards of line off a reel in seconds. Dream women come and go with the turn of the tide, but dream fish remain hooked in our minds forever.

*People's opinions about you don't matter.* What other people think of you is their problem, not yours. Rarely what someone says about you has anything to do with you at all. Don't absorb other people's negative energy. What someone projects on you is not reflective of who you are. It will always say more about them than you.

*Traveling.* Traveling is one of greatest things we can do with our time. It opens our horizons to new things and new possibilities. Regardless of when and where you go, however, the moment you are currently experiencing will always be the greatest place you'll ever visit. No locations are enjoyed more than the present. So try to live in the moment while on the road and when you're simply at home. Living in the past isn't living at all. Fish and life are always better fresh. Invite people over and share both. Don't freeze either for later. Later is uncertain and never as good as now!

*The one who got away.* We all have one. You will always more vividly remember the ones that got away than the ones you caught. Love the memories, and learn from your mistakes moving forward.

*Finances and happiness.* Money comes easily when you're happy. When you're unhappy, no amount of money is enough to justify what you are doing. Make sure you're doing something that makes you happy. When you do what you love, you'll attract the people and money you want. That being said, often the happiest people aren't the ones with the most possessions to appreciate but the ones who appreciate what they do have the most.

*The fastest way to help yourself is to help others.* It's unquestionable that the more you help others unselfishly the faster the universe helps you. Dream huge, however be realistic about what you want and what you are willing to do to achieve it. Setting a goal with really vague parameters can make an achievement feel meaningless and setting goals too narrowly defined can make success feel like failure. Be careful when setting goals.

*When it comes to balance.* Every dollar you make at sea costs you something on land. The opposite is also true. Every dollar made on land costs you something at sea. Balance will always be difficult to achieve, but the effort you spend on attempting to achieve balance will always be rewarded by your own smile and the smiles of others involved.

*On life in general.* Don't be so hard on yourself. We are always our hardest critics. You're probably doing way better than you realize. Practice, practice, practice!!! If you aren't good at something, keep on practicing and perfecting your craft until you are.

*On dating.* Don't fuck women who claim to be separated. A woman in a separation is less trustworthy than a shark hanging around your fish. Even if she has the best intentions not to harm you, her natural instincts will always end up biting you one way or another. She will either return to her former shark husband, leaving you to drift, or that shark husband will attack you. It's a sloppy affair either way, far more dangerous than a feeding frenzy. This is important relationship information that could save you the stress of having to get a restraining order against someone's husband.

*Stay true to who you are.* We all have our niche. Embrace it. If you're a fisherman and you love being a fisherman, stay being a fisherman. Don't change that for anyone. You're not the problem. You're beautiful just the way you are.

*Kindness.* Kindness is always the preferred option. When given the chance, always try to use it. It's true what they say about getting more bees with honey than vinegar. Kindness is free, easy to use, and highly valuable. Always treat others the way you wish to be treated and you'll be amazed how often everything works out better than expected, even in the most difficult of situations.

*The road and ocean traveled.* When you don't get what you want out of a situation, what you do get is experience. No education will ever be wasted. We will always have something to learn, even from the worst experiences. Scars can be a great motivator and reminder of what we do and do not want in our lives.

*Hurry up and wait!?* The world will not wait for you, so saddle up and ride. Before you know it, you will have missed it. Life goes by very quickly. If there is something you truly desire, then start working toward that goal today even if it's as simple as writing down a list of how you're going to get to that point to start.

*Our thought process doesn't always serve us the best.* Most things are easier to achieve once you shed other people's opinions and perceptions of what's possible and not possible. Don't let others' point of view hold you back from your dreams. Everything was impossible until someone did it. Your dreams are your dreams and your dreams alone. Don't worry about what other people think or say if what you want to do makes you happy and fulfilled. If what you want to do doesn't harm other people or cause true injustice to others, it doesn't matter what other people think. Carry on in the direction that your heart pulls you. Other people will often tell you how you're supposed to feel or tell you how they think you should feel. The truth is that only you and you alone can know how you feel about a situation. Don't let other people's perceptions of how you're supposed to feel or act become your reality. Be proud of who you are.

*Letting go.* Often what we leave behind is more important than what we keep. A life of value gives as much or gives far greater than what we receive. The irony is that the more we give without strings attached, the more our lives become balanced with gifts from other areas with also no strings attached. It's the basic law of attraction that what we put out in the universe will also be returned to us. We let giant fish go not because we believe we will ever see that exact fish again. Rather it's that we hope it will go on to spawn and continue the cycle that brings life to other fish and joy to other men.

I have never met a person unworthy of a good story or a great adventure. The common thread that most amazing stories and journeys hold is the simple act of getting started and taking the first step. The true adventure is when everything falls into place.

The endpoint is nowhere as exciting as the steps that got you there. Most every fisherman I've ever met could write an amazing book if they devoted themselves to doing so. Incredible stories are not rare upon the sea but properly documenting them is.

In fact, I would consider this book a success if it motivates even one person to write down their story; even more so if even one person is able to step out of the darkness and find the help they need because of something they read in these pages. That would make this book a home run for me. For me, writing started as homework from a therapist when I was struggling with depression following my divorce. But it ended up turning into a magnifying glass to help me put my life in perspective and navigate my feelings. Sometimes, all any of us need to do is just get the ideas outside of our minds. Sometimes, it helps us realize how ridiculous they sound, while other times it's because we need to remember what path we should be on.

I've enjoyed writing this book, although I'll be the first to admit I will always call myself a fisherman before I call myself a writer. My hope is that you found something of value in my stories that you can carry forward with you on your own personal journey, even if that was a simple laugh because of a flying fish flailing my nuts or the joy of knowing you haven't had to go down on a cop to get out of a DUI. Perhaps it's comfort in knowing you're not the only one who walks in those dark corridors that always seem like the loneliest place on Earth anytime we step in them. Maybe it's a comfort in knowing someone else has been through the living hell you're in and came out better on the other side. In any case, as Henry David Thoreau said, "Many men go fishing all of their lives without knowing that it is not fish they are after." Perhaps that is the truth on land and on sea.

Whatever it is you take away from this book, ultimately life will always be your own personal journey. Hopefully, something of value from my writing will travel with you like a lucky hat and help guide you along your path, whether that be upon the land or beloved sea.

Life is a vicious cycle. It will not stop nor would you really ever want it to. The greatest highs are only appreciated after the greatest lows. The most vibrant days only come after the darkest storms, and we only truly understand love after we have understood loss. The vicious cycle will forever carry on, and so will we. It's not that the road of life won't have obstacles, for it most certainly will. It's simply understanding that the obstacles, like pain, are temporary. Life doesn't give us obstacles to trip over but rather for us to step on and elevate us to our next level. When you remember this, you ride on the vicious cycle instead of becoming part of it.

I hope to see you at sea, just not in my fishing spot.

Forever and respectfully,

Captain Kenton Geer